NATURE WELLS GRAY

NATURE
WELLS GRAY

A VISITORS' GUIDE TO THE PARK

TREVOR GOWARD
and
CATHIE HICKSON

• LONE PINE PUBLISHING •
Edmonton, Alberta
• THE FRIENDS OF WELLS GRAY PARK •
Kamloops, British Columbia

Published by:

 Lone Pine Publishing,
206, 10426-81st Avenue
Edmonton, Alberta T6E 1X5

The Friends of Wells Gray Park
Box 1386, Kamloops
British Columbia, Canada V2C 6L7

Publisher's Acknowledgement

The publisher gratefully acknowledges financial assistance from Natural Resources Canada, Geological Survey of Canada.

Road and trail conditions in Wells Gray are subject to change; neither the authors nor the publisher can accept responsibility for any inconvenience or damages incurred through the use of this book.

Canadian Cataloguing in Publication Data

Goward, Trevor, 1952–
Nature Wells Gray

Includes bibliographical references and index.
ISBN 1-55105-065-X

1. Wells Gray Provincial Park (B.C.) – Guidebooks. 2. Natural history – British Columbia – Wells Gray Provincial Park – Guidebooks. 3. Trails – British Columbia – Wells Gray Provincial Park – Guidebooks. I. Hickson, Cathie, 1955–. II. Title.
FC3815.W44G68 1995 917.11'2 C95-910865-3 F1089.W44G68 1995

Illustrations on page 82 from W. D. Tidwell, *Common Fossil Plants of Western North America* (Brigham Young University Press, 1975). Used with permission.

Designed and typeset by The Typeworks, Vancouver, B.C.
Printed and bound by Best Book Manufacturers, Toronto
Cover Photos: Image West (BC Parks)

THE FRIENDS OF WELLS GRAY PARK
The Friends of Wells Gray Park is a registered, nonprofit society
working with B.C. Parks to inform and educate the public
about the values of British Columbia's southernmost wilderness park.
For more information, write to: The Friends of Wells Gray Park, Box 1386, Kamloops,
British Columbia, Canada V2C 6L7.

PREFACE

Wilderness, by definition, is that part of a landscape which goes unsaid. One does not set out to write a natural history of wilderness.

Wells Gray is wilderness; or better, wilderness is the essential quality which pervades Wells Gray. Every year, thousands of visitors peer inward at that wilderness; and doing so they are refreshed.

This book is written for those visitors. It is mostly a collection of glimpses, or a looking in from the edges. If it manages at the same time to be a statement about the essential wildness of Wells Gray, so much the better.

In the first edition, we restricted our glimpses to the park's "front country," lining them up along the roads and trails that run the length of the Clearwater Valley, north to Clearwater Lake.

We now extend our attention to the park's front country lakes: Clearwater, Azure, Murtle, and Mahood. Doing so has of course required a larger book, and has prompted us to modify the title to reflect what is, we hope, a more balanced portrait of the many faces of Wells Gray.

In our first dedication to this book, we celebrated those who had come before us: the "surveyors, botanists, geologists, wildlife biologists, trappers and (in the name of hydroelectric dams!) civil engineers." For it was they who initiated a tradition of research that has carried our understanding of the park forward to the late 20th century.

We hereby extend our dedication to acknowledge the founders of the recently established Wells Gray Education and Research Centre (page 61). Through their efforts a new generation of research is about to begin.

As in the first edition, so in the second: we largely overlook the human history of the park, giving pride of place to the rocks and waters, forests and wildlife that in fact comprise it. In writing this book, we have wished not so much to lead ever deeper into Wells Gray, as to provide an ever deeper appreciation of the wealth of life and geologic process the park represents.

The Clearwater Valley is a complex place. Once again we invite you to join with us in exploring its diverse natural history.

Trevor Goward   Cathie Hickson
Edgewood Blue, B.C.   Vancouver, B.C.
31 December 1995

ACKNOWLEDGEMENTS

Many people have helped make this a better book. We would especially like to thank Robert Bringhurst, Syd Cannings, Brian Chan, John Clague, Ross Cloutier, Chris Guppy, Chris Harris, Nancy Harrison, Rick Howie, Helen Knight, Bob Miller, Hettie Miller, Dave Montgomery, Bob Muckle, Harry Parsons, Doug Ray, Charlie Roots, Wilf Schofield, Gerald Straley, Richard Summerbell, Eric Tor and Frank Voysey – all of whom reviewed portions of the text for accuracy and, at times, taste. Of course we ourselves accept full responsibility for any errors (including errors of taste) that may remain.

Others have provided technical and material support of various kinds. Here we thank Paul Arduini, Lori Barron, Frank Burger, Brian Carruthers, Giggs Clarke, Monty Downs, Yorke Edwards, Ellen Ferguson, Ken Hannah, Joyce Harrington, Randy Hedlund, Clayton Hicks, Hannah Horn, Helen Knight, Eli Kohnert, Ted Lea, Bill Mathews, Bob Maxwell, Paul Metcalfe, Dave Montgomery, Don Murphy, Merton Palmer, Frank Ritcey, Pat Rogers, Bob Scheer, Jack Souther, Dirk Tempelman-Kluit, and Earl Sinclair. Mary Conibear and Susanne Gilbert, of The Typeworks, helped to bring the text to camera-ready, while Nancy Foulds, of Lone Pine, provided welcome editorial assistance. Special thanks go to Robert Bringhurst for his timely advice on design and typeface, to Shelley Higman, Paul Metcalfe, Adriana Soos and Tonia Williams for their work on the maps and figures, and to Paul Metcalfe for his generous assistance with the sections on geology.

A separate debt of gratitude is owed to Nancy Flood, John Kurta, Hettie Miller, Shelly Sim, Dave Williams and, in years gone by, Helen Knight and Gerry Warner, for doing what needed doing. Without their efforts, this book might not have happened.

The successful completion of the second edition of Nature Wells Gray has been abetted by B.C. Parks and the Royal B.C. Museum. The staff at the Cordilleran Division of the Geological Survey of Canada are also thanked for their unstinting support.

Many of the photographs and line drawings which appear in the following pages have come from the authors' own collections. The remainder have kindly been supplied by various individuals, organizations and government agencies. All are credited according to the following abbreviations: George Doerksen (GD); Trevor Goward (TG); Bess Hagensen (BH); Cathie Hickson (CH); Helen Knight (HK); B.C. Environment (BCE); members of the North Okanagan Naturalists (NONC); B.C. Parks (BCP); Harry Parsons (HP); Royal B.C. Museum (RBCM); William Tidwell (WT).

The text which follows has been enlivened by contributions from the following students of Wells Gray, past and present: Dick Cannings (owls); Rob and Syd Cannings (insects); John Clague (geology); Yorke Edwards (moose); Helen Knight (butterflies); Paul Metcalfe (geology); Harry Parsons (toads); Dale Seip (caribou); and Richard Summerbell (fungi). To one and all, our thanks.

For bringing to our attention numerous typographic and other cheek-freshening errors in the first edition, we wish to thank: Ted Antifeau, Brian Carruthers, Stephen Clayden, Bob Harris, Malcolm Martin, Dave Montgomery, Helen Knight, Bobbie Patrick, Ralph Ritcey, Pat Rogers, and Charlie Shook, and Richard Thomas.

Cathie Hickson wrote the sections on the park's geology, and arranged for the maps and illustrations. The remainder of the book was conceived and written by Trevor Goward.

CONTENTS

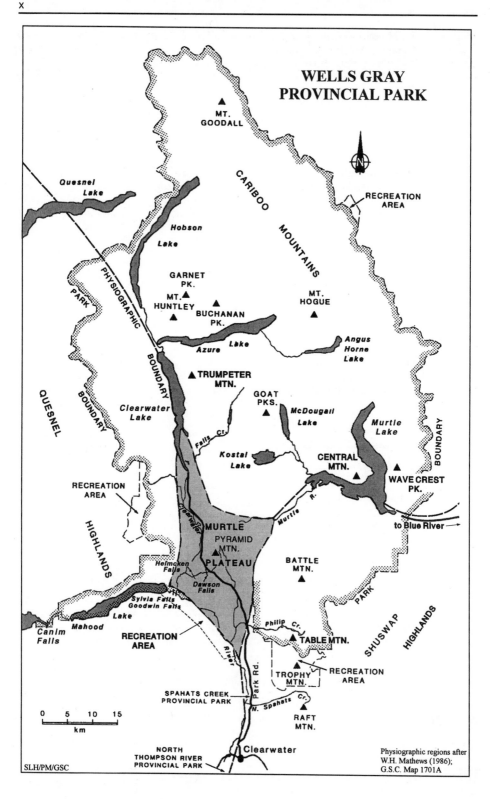

WELLS GRAY PROVINCIAL PARK

Physiographic regions after
W.H. Mathews (1986);
G.S.C. Map 1701A

SLH/PM/GSC

THE NATURE OF WELLS GRAY

THE PARK

Wells Gray Provincial Park was established in 1939, and is named after Arthur Wellesley Gray, a once prominent provincial Minister of Lands.

On the map, Wells Gray is a large green spot in east-central British Columbia. On the ground, at 515,301 ha, it is a magnificent wilderness reserve – as large as, or larger than, one in every five nations on earth!

The park's boundaries are defined primarily by the drainages of the Clearwater River and its tributaries. In freshet these rivers carry some thousand cubic metres of water out of the park every second. Having originated within Wells Gray, this water is as pure today as it was a hundred or, indeed, a thousand years ago.

East and north, Wells Gray bristles with unnamed peaks. These are the Cariboos, a subset of the Columbia Mountains. Every summer, thunder rumbles over their summits. Every winter, avalanches tumble down their slopes. And in the gaps between the mountains lie the remnants of an Ice Age past.

To the south and west, the park encompasses a very different landscape: the Shuswap Highlands. The highlands are essentially an elevated plateau which has been cut into by rivers occupying deep and narrow valleys. Where the gentle upland surface rises to subalpine elevations, look for flower-strewn meadows to take your breath away.

In the middle and lower Clearwater Valley, volcanoes have been erupting off and on over the past million years. This activity has continued almost to the present day, and has transformed this portion of the valley into a crazy quilt of lava flows, cinder cones and, in places, underglacier volcanoes. Water and ice have lately carved canyons into the lava flows, and at the heads of the canyons are the waterfalls for which Wells Gray is justly renowned.

Making Wells Gray their home is a rich variety of living things. To date, 219 species of birds and 56 species of mammals have been recorded here, not to mention 700 species of flowering plants, 275 bryophytes, 500 lichens, and 200 macrofungi. Each year our roll call of the park's residents grows a little longer.

HOW TO GET THERE AND WHERE TO STAY

At 160 km north of Kamloops, Wells Gray is only a day's drive from Vancouver, Seattle, Edmonton, Prince George and other urban centres. The main park entrance lies 40 km north of the Yellowhead Highway (Hwy 5) at Clearwater. The road is paved to a distance 6.7 km inside the park, beyond which a gravel road continues the final 23 km to Clearwater Lake.

You can also explore the park from two other points of entry. The first, 100 Mile House, on the Cariboo Highway (Highway 97), gives access to Mahood Lake (page 179) along an 88 km gravel road, open year-round. The second, Blue River, on the Yellowhead Highway, is portal to a 26 km summer-only gravel road, rough in spots, narrow in others, that terminates 2.5 km east of Murtle Lake (page 170), at the trailhead to the Murtle Lake portage.

At time of writing, a third point of entry also exists: the Clearwater River Road, which hugs the west bank of the river beginning at Clearwater Village and ending at the confluence of the Mahood and Clearwater Rivers, 39 bumpy km distant. In between lies some of British Columbia's most inspired river scenery. For an update on road conditions, call B.C. Parks at 604-587-6150.

Wells Gray is served by four government campgrounds: Spahats Creek Park (20 units); Dawson Falls (10 units); Clearwater Lake (73 units); and Mahood Lake (34 units). Water, pit toilets and firewood are provided at all of these. A fifth campground is situated outside the park at North Thompson Park (61 units), just south of Clearwater Village. Other more primitive campgrounds will be found along the shorelines of Clearwater, Azure, Murtle and Mahood Lakes. All campgrounds are closed between November and May.

Wells Gray is also served by commercial accommodations of various kinds. For standard indoor lodging in the Clearwater Valley, try Helmcken Falls Lodge (page 83), Wells Gray Guest Ranch (page 72), Nakiska Ranch (page 73), Buffalo Ranch Campground (page 60), or, in Clearwater itself, Clearwater Adventure Resort (page 32) and Wells Gray Inn (604-674-2214). Tent and RV camping are available at Clearwater Adventure Resort, Buffalo Ranch, Wells Gray Ranch and Helmcken Falls Lodge. Backcountry lodging is offered at Clearwater River Chalet (page 80) and Wells Gray Backcountry Chalets (page 186). For information on other accommodations in and near Clearwater, Blue River and 100 Mile House, write to the Wells Gray Visitor Centre, Box 1988, RR1, Clearwater, B.C. VOE 1NO (fax: 604-674-3693), or call 604-674-2646.

A Wells Gray ski marathon is held each February on the weekend nearest Valentine's Day. For more about this and other park events, write to B.C. Parks, Box 70, Clearwater, B.C. Canada VOE 1NO (fax: 604-587-6200), or call 604-587-6150.

HOW TO USE THIS BOOK

This book is divided into four parts: Part I is a series of summary statements on Wells Gray's natural history; Part II is a road log of the Clearwater Valley north to the south end of Clearwater Lake; Part III is an account of Clearwater, Azure, Murtle and Mahood Lakes; and Part IV is a portrait of the park in winter. Following this are two appendices: first a list of selected references pertaining to Wells Gray; and second a geologic time line, to help situate events from the far hazy past. The final pages of the book index what has come before.

Trail maps are included for all hikes (check the Index to Maps, page xv), but serious hikers will want to purchase one or more topographic maps. A 1:125,000 colour map of the park is available at the Wells Gray Visitor Centre, in Clearwater.

This book provides brief descriptions of scores of plants, birds and mammals, but is not primarily a field guide. To get the most from it, consult the books listed in the reference sections in Part I. Or, for a single companion reference, bring along Ben Gadd's excellent *Handbook of the Canadian Rockies* (Corax Press, Jasper, 1995).

In the following pages, the common names of most plants and many animals are accompanied by their Latin equivalents. The only exceptions are birds, mammals and trees, for which fairly standard common names are now in use.

Errors? Additions? Please let us know. Contact Trevor Goward at Edgewood Blue, Box 131, Clearwater, B.C., Canada VOE 1NO.

ATTENTION ALL DIALERS: AFTER 1 OCTOBER 1996, THE AREA CODE FOR TELEPHONE AND FAX NUMBERS LISTED IN THIS BOOK WILL CHANGE FROM 604 TO 250.

WELLS GRAY CALENDAR OF EVENTS

Month	Event	Major Entry
January		
	- early: the ski trails are now ready and waiting	187
	- mid: Moose watching begins on Green Mountain	209
	- late: watch the rivers for green bottom ice	186
February		
	- early: come view the Helmcken Ice Cone	185
	- mid: join in the Wells Gray Ski Marathon	190
	- late: owls now begin to give a hoot in the valley	212
March		
	- early: ski off-trail on firm but friendly snow	189
	- mid: listen at night for Wolf music	208
	- late: lowland skiing ends, but not mountain skiing	188
April		
	- early: hiking trails await you in the Canyonlands	74
	- mid: binocular alert: rare birds in migration	
	- late: Ruffed Grouse adrumming	78
May		
	- early: in the valley, the trees are burgeoning green	
	- mid: drive or hike wherever you like	
	- late: Black Bears nibble road edge greens	140
June		
	- early: the campgrounds officially open	
	- mid: Helmcken Falls is a thousand parachutes opening	101
	- late: Trophy Meadows: a host of golden Glacier Lilies	43
July		
	- early: the hills are still alive with the sound of bird song	78
	- mid: mosquitoes are dying off in the valleys	98
	- late: Trophy Meadows: a wildflower bouquet	44
August		
	- early: listen at night for small birds winging south	
	- mid: watch the night skies for meteor showers	
	- late: scan the mountain ridges for migrating hawks	47
September		
	- early: Bailey's Chute is jumping with Chinook Salmon	131
	- mid: camping is free, but services are limited	
	- late: Murtle Lake culminates with a festival of loons	172
October		
	- early: hike the Canyonlands for local colour	74
	- mid: hike the high points for autumn snow	
	- late: Varying Hares vary to white	
November		
	- early: Clearwater Lake Road closes north of Helmcken	
	- mid: the park is now dressed all in white	
	- late: Black Bears are sound asleep	
December		
	- early: bull Moose are losing their antlers	
	- mid: watch the Geminid Meteor Shower all night long	
	- late: join in the Wells Gray Christmas Bird Count	212

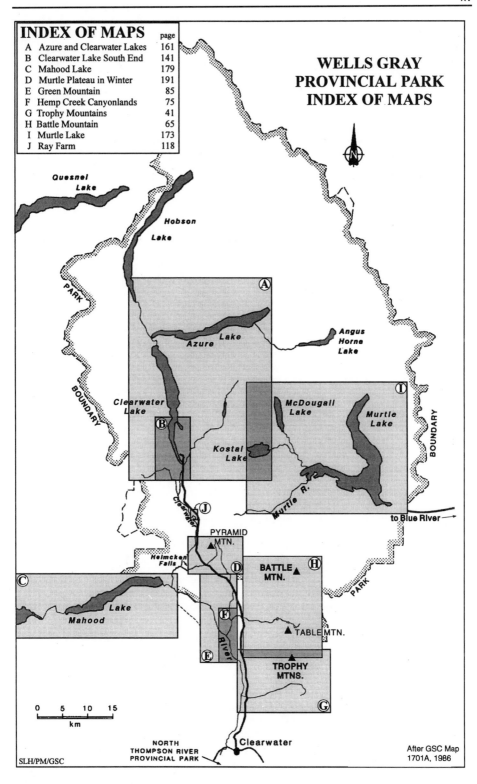

**WELLS GRAY
PROVINCIAL PARK
INDEX OF MAPS**

N

Quesnel Lake

Hobson Lake

PARK

BOUNDARY

Ⓐ

Azure Lake

Angus Horne Lake

Clearwater Lake

McDougall Lake

Murtle Lake

Ⓘ

BOUNDARY

Ⓑ

Kostal Lake

Murtle R.

Clearwater

Ⓙ

to Blue River

PYRAMID MTN.

Helmcken Falls

Ⓓ

BATTLE MTN.

Ⓗ

PARK

Ⓒ

Lake

Mahood

Ⓕ

River

TABLE MTN.

Ⓔ

TROPHY MTNS.

Ⓖ

0   5   10   15
km

NORTH
THOMPSON RIVER
PROVINCIAL PARK

Clearwater

After GSC Map
1701A, 1986

SLH/PM/GSC

PART ONE

WHO'S WHO

WEATHERING WELLS GRAY

This is the third season that I have spent on survey in [the Clearwater Valley], and I have not the slightest hesitation in saying that the climate is first-class. . . .

R.H. Lee (1913)

BROADLY speaking, Wells Gray's climate is controlled first and foremost by its geographic position relative to the Rocky and Columbia Mountains to the east, and the Coast Mountains to the west.

The former ranges tend, particularly in winter, to protect the park from outbreaks of arctic air originating in central Canada. As for the latter, they do equal service against the warm, sopping winds that blow off the Pacific, and that make such a muck of coastal British Columbia during that season.

Mild, snowy winters. Pleasant, sunny summers. About the only argument that can be brought to bear against Wells Gray's candidacy for the title of Canada's climatic Eldorado, is **June** (page 94). June is the month when the Clearwater Valley turns dark and wet. Even in the driest portions of the valley, rain can be expected on 13 days out of 30 in a typical year, and heavy cloud on perhaps 20 days.

By the second week of July (in most years), the skies have cleared, and the lakes are sparkling with reflected sunlight. Most years, too, August is even sunnier, and September sunnier still. Blessed are they who take their holidays late, rather than early.

Temperatures

Very few climatic data exist for Wells Gray. To date, only a single long-term weather station has operated here, and even that (at Hemp Creek, km 34.0: a frost pocket) has failed to record climatic patterns typical of the area as a whole. Most of the following figures are therefore based on available short-term measurements.

In July, the warmest month, daytime temperatures average a comfortable 22°C to 25°C at valley elevations, though slightly cooler on the lakes, where the evaporating surface of the water uses up a disproportionate amount of the sun's radiant energy. Moving up the mountain slopes, average temperatures decrease some 9°C for every 1000 m.

On a typical summer night, valley temperatures fall to a cool 7°C to 12°C, reflecting the relative nearness of glaciers and snowfields. Even so, summer frosts are rare, except at treeline and above, where they may occur even in mid July.

In January, daytime highs average roughly −5°C at all forested elevations, and nighttime lows about −10°C. The vertical temperature gradient in winter is much less than in summer, with a typical midday decrease of only about 1°C for each 1000 m rise. At night, temperatures are often actually warmer at treeline than in the valley, owing to the ponding of cold air.

Wells Gray's skies are frequently cloud-covered in winter. A good thing, too, as clouds block the flow of heat from the earth into space, and so help to keep air temperatures moderate. As a result, the thermometer seldom dips far below about −25°C, and when it does it seldom holds there for very long. (For more on Wells Gray's **winter climate**, turn to page 196.)

Against these averages, it is important to realize that temperatures may vary tremendously from place to place, even over short distances. A south-facing slope can be as much as 5°C warmer on a sunny afternoon than a north-facing slope only a few metres away.

Temperature differences are even more pronounced at night when, under clear skies, small topographic depressions can register 15°C colder than adjacent slopes. Pay attention to these distinctions: for the backpacker, they can mean the difference between a restful night's sleep, and eight hours of shivering. During cloudy weather, or when the wind is up, temperatures are much more likely to be uniform.

Precipitation

Generally speaking, precipitation is evenly distributed through the year, with spring, however, being somewhat the driest season, and summer (especially June) the wettest.

Amounts are lightest in the valleys of the south and west, and heaviest in the high Cariboo Mountains of the north and east. A total annual precipitation of about 450 mm at Clearwater Village increases to 550 mm at the park entrance, and then to as much as 700 mm at the south end of Clearwater Lake. Azure Lake is even wetter, possibly receiving more than 1000 mm per year. In the wettest portions of the Cariboo Mountains, precipitation probably exceeds 2000 mm. The **wet belt** (page 33) at Spahats Creek provides an interesting exception to this general pattern.

This vigorously swelling cumulus cloud promises thundershowers later in the day. Above, wispy strands of cirrus may mean wet weather over the next several days. (TG)

Afterglow

Few days are so grey that the evening sun doesn't light up the sky for at least a few moments prior to setting. Evening sun is, in fact, one of Wells Gray's meteorological specialties. This curious phenomenon has to do with the park's position relative to the Coast Mountains to the west.

The Coast Mountains are cloud makers; that is, they cause the moist Pacific air that blows against their western slopes to rise and, as it rises, to cool and so condense into cloud – often rain cloud.

Once, however, this cloud has crossed the Coast Mountains, it descends again and, as it descends, it warms and thus dissolves. The result is a window of sunshine in the lee of the Coast Range. Climatologists call that window a rain shadow. Geographers refer to the area it covers as the Chilcotin or, east of the Fraser River, the Cariboo.

Eastward of the Cariboo, the cloud cover begins to form again, banking up against the next range of cloud makers, the Cariboo Mountains. Southern Wells Gray lies just west of the Cariboos; here cloudy skies are a way of life. When, however, the evening sun finally touches down on the western skyline, its angle is such that it now shines directly through the opening provided by the Chilcotin rain shadow. Suddenly, a flash of colour lights up the sky.

Under certain circumstances, this evening performance may even cast reflections of the park's larger lakes upon the cloud bottoms overhead. If it is raining, this is the time of day to scan the skies for a rainbow.

Snow

Of the hundred thousand trillion trillion snowflakes estimated to have fallen to earth since the planet began, Wells Gray has received more than its fair share. In the northeast especially, snowpacks can be impressive. At one upper level snow station, for example, snow averages about 350 cm deep in April, with a water content of roughly 1500 mm. Using a multiplier of ten (on average one cm of water is equivalent to 10 cm of snow), this represents about 15 m of fresh-fallen snow: roughly the height of a five story building! In Canada, only B.C.'s Coast Mountains are charged with a (marginally) deeper snowpack.

Snow depth is, of course, considerably less in the valleys, with Azure Lake, for example, receiving a snowpack of approximately 150 cm. Moving south out of the Cariboo Mountains, the snows become even lighter: 110 cm at the south end of Clearwater Lake; 70 cm at the park entrance; and 50 cm at Third Canyon (km 16.2). In an average year at lower elevations, the snowpack is already at its deepest by the end of February, whereas at treeline it continues to accumulate until mid April.

For more on **snow**, turn to page 197.

Thunderstorms

Wells Gray – thunderstorm capital of Canada – throbs to the rhythm of lightning and thunder 40 to 50 days every year. June is the stormiest month, with some two or three thunderstorms per week, though of course not all affect the entire park. One study in 1980 recorded, from May through September, a total of 707 cloud-to-ground strikes in the Clearwater area, and 1697 strikes near Blue River. In another study it was observed that lightning ignites an average of 24 wildfires every summer. Bear in mind, however, that lightning touches down on earth approximately 100 times every second!

Winds

At valley elevations in Wells Gray, winds are generally light. Presumably this reflects the Clearwater Valley's north-south orientation, which thus cuts at right angles to the prevailing westerly flow.

The strongest winds tend to develop in such east-west gaps as Azure and Mahood Lakes, which thus provide major exceptions to the no-wind rule. (Tradition has it that Mahood Lake was formerly called "Windy Lake" in the tongue of the Canim Lake Indians). Another major exception will be found wherever the Clearwater Valley narrows, as it does for example near Spahats and at the north end of Clearwater Lake. Here the winds can at times be very strong. Boaters beware!

In the mountains, winds are much more prevalent, owing to a decreased drag on atmospheric circulation by irregularities in the earth's surface.

Weather watching

- *Weathering the Wilderness*, by W.E. Reifsnyder (Sierra Club Books, 1980).
- *A Field Guide to the Atmosphere*, by V.J. Schaefer & J.A. Day (Houghton Mifflin, 1981).

ROCKS OF AGES

O VER the ages, Wells Gray Park has rocked to a tumultuous geologic history. As a result the park is now host to numerous geologic processes, some ongoing, others harkening back to cataclysms that occurred hundreds of millions of years ago.

Dance of the Continents

The earth's crust – terra firma – is not as firma as it might seem. Over eons, forces within the earth have repeatedly arranged and rearranged the half-dozen-odd plates of which the earth's crust is

This rock was once marine mud. Crustal movement, combined with high temperatures and pressure, have since folded and metamorphosed it into gneiss. (TG)

composed – much as ocean currents continuously jostle ice floes in the far north. Convective cells within the upper portion of the earth's mantle (40–250 km below your feet) joggle the plates against one another, thereby wrinkling the continental margins into mountain ranges, and opening oceans half way across the world.

At present, North America is rafting northwestward toward Japan, and is moving at about 2.5 cm per year, about the same rate your fingernails grow. Over geologic time, this movement has wrought tremendous change to North America – and not least to Wells Gray. Much of this change has occurred along – and is recorded in – cracks in the earth's crust. These cracks are called **faults** (page 146).

So great has been the movement along some of the park's larger faults, including southern portions of the Clearwater Valley (page 86), that no one knows where the rocks underlying Wells Gray originated. The oldest rocks are thought to have been deposited as ocean bottom sediments near the edge of North America between 600–750 million years ago. These rocks are restricted to the northern half of the park, south to the north arm of Murtle Lake. Some of them are conglomerates, which contain even older boulders dating from 1.2 billion years ago.

Farther south the rocks are somewhat younger. Geologists hesitate to say where these rocks, called the **Kaza Group** (pages 77 and 83), and consisting of **phyllites** (page 77) and schists, may have formed. Marble pods in the mountains north of

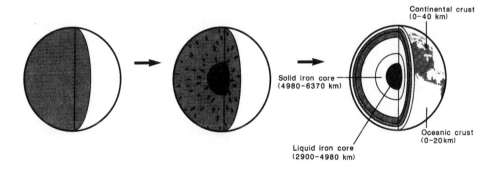

In the beginning planet earth was a rather homogeneous ball newly formed from gaseous clouds. Before long, however, the elements that comprised it began to settle out. Heavier elements, like iron and nickel, migrated toward the earth's core, while lighter elements, like silica (the stuff of quartz), buoyed to the surface, where they formed the continental crusts. This process, called differentiation, gave rise to the onion-like planet we currently inhabit. (GSC)

Azure Lake may mark prehistoric reefs. Garnet-studded gneiss on the summit of Trophy Mountain probably originated as ocean bottom muds. Possibly some of the rocks arose as oceanic islands that collided with the western edge of North America. Or again they may simply have been nearshore sediments, later buried and buckled and carried northward along faults to their present location.

By whatever means these rocks were laid down, there can be no doubt they have since undergone major transformation. As North America slid implacably westward, rocks at the continent's surface got pushed deep into the crust. Here they were subjected to increasing heat and pressure; minerals that could exist at the earth's surface were no longer stable, and were transformed (metamorphosed) into altogether different minerals.

Later, these same rocks were uplifted as mountains – only to be worn down again over countless eons. Much of the resulting sediment eventually found its way to the ocean, though some became trapped in the river valleys.

That was 45 million years ago, during what geologists call the Eocene epoch. At that time the climate was warmer than it is now, and swamps existed in the valleys; later the swamps were buried by sediments, and so transformed into coal seams. Today you can still see some of those buried sediments, now exposed along the east side of Hemp Creek, and called the **Chu Chua Formation** (page 81).

The Ages of Ice

Glaciers have come and gone in British Columbia several times during the last 2,000,000 years. The latest period of ice-sheet glaciation occurred from about 25,000 to 11,000 years ago, and is referred to as the Fraser Glaciation.

At the climax of the Fraser Glaciation, some 15,000 years ago, Wells Gray was completely covered by ice. The ice surface lay at about 2500 m, or within a few hundred m of the summit of the Trophy Mountains. The flow of ice was controlled by the lay of the land, moving from high elevations in the Cariboo Mountains, southward down the Clearwater and other valleys.

Much of the spectacular scenery of the park originated through repeated glaciation during this period. Classic alpine landforms, including **cirques** (page 53), **horns** (like Garnet Peak, page 158), and **arêtes** (page 53), have formed as a result of erosion by glaciers. Although the valleys have been initiated and, to a considerable extent, shaped by streams, they too have been extensively modified by glaciers. The park's larger lakes (for example, Clearwater and Azure) occupy elongated basins that have been overdeepened by glacial ice. Above many of the main valleys, you'll also find numerous **hanging valleys** (page 53).

Glaciation is also responsible for much of the unconsolidated sediments covering the park. The surface of the Murtle Plateau, for example, is covered by a layer of **till** (page 104) that was deposited (and at the same time compressed!) beneath the Pleistocene glaciers. Later, as the ice melted away, it deposited large quantities of sands and gravels, exemplified by **eskers** (page 135), **recessional moraines** (page 135) and **glacial outwash plains** (page 62). Most of the latter debris was laid down approximately 11,000 to 12,000 years ago, but some date to the **Little Ice Age**, roughly 300 years ago (pages 49 and 77).

Since then, the landscape has been modified by erosion and deposition. Streams have downcut through Ice Age deposits, and in places **meander** (page 118) through the unconsolidated sands and gravels. **Talus** (pages 38 and 76) has formed at the bases of steep slopes, and rockslides and slumps have occurred throughout the park. In other places, **mineral springs** (pages 122 and 129) bubble up from the underlying sediments.

John Clague

Waterfalls that form in volcanic rock tend to be precipitous, especially if the rock is basalt. The basalt erodes away like slices of bread, preserving the vertical drop. Ida Falls, Third Canyon. (TG)

Metamorphic rocks tend to erode in a more irregular manner, forming steep cataracts rather than sheer drops. Wind Falls, Grouse Creek. (TG)

Out of the Fiery Furnace

Wells Gray is justifiably famous for its volcanic features. The park contains numerous lava flows, canyons, waterfalls, basaltic columns and, not least, the volcanoes that spawned them. Scattered throughout the Clearwater Valley, these features comprise one of the most varied collections of basaltic rocks to be found anywhere.

Basalt (pages 56 and 104) is a dark volcanic rock, rich in iron and magnesium. Compared to andesite and other kinds of "lava," it is relatively low in silica (45 to 50%). The basalt found in Wells Gray originally formed at depths of between 40 and 60 km in the earth's mantle. At such depths, rocks begin to melt, and form magma.

Because magma is less dense than the rocks which surround it, it soon begins to move upward. During the magma's ascent, it picks up pieces of rock from the earth's mantle, and carries them along like pebbles in a stream. These "pebbles," or **nodules** as geologists call them, provide valuable insights into the earth's mantle. Many of Wells Gray's volcanoes have brought such nodules to the surface. Kostal Cone is one of the best places to study them.

A volcano is just a place where magma comes to the surface, fed by **dykes** (page 58). The most "volcano-like" of Wells Gray's many volcanos are the **cinder cones** (page 150) like the one at Kostal Lake. Cinder cones form when magma erupts from a vent. The magma, of course, is very hot, approximately 1200°C; when it reaches the surface, it boils and froths as dissolved gases escape.

Spurts of liquid rock are thrown in the air. The ejected blobs of magma partially harden as they rain down around the vent; when they land, they form rocks referred to as spatter and **bombs** (page 176). At the same time, the iron within the bombs is oxidized (and thereby turned a bright red colour) by oxygen in the air, and the heat of the erupting lava. Often,

Water dripping for hundreds of years on solid basaltic rock has sculpted its surface into a myriad of forms. (CH)

bubbles of gas are unable to escape before the magma "freezes," and so the resulting rock has a frothy appearance not unlike an AERO bar. This type of basaltic rock is called **scoria** (page 69), or sometimes cinder.

With each new pulse of eruption, another layer of scoria is built up around the vent, until a cone of cinder is formed, sometimes several hundreds of metres high. If enough magma comes to the surface, it may breach the cinder cone, and pour out as a **lava flow** (pages 146 and 176). The hot liquid churns and tumbles as it flows from the vent. It behaves very much like water, and will flow downhill into river valleys, ponding in depressions.

Should the eruption continue for some time, many layers of lava can build up in the valleys. In fact, there may be so much lava that it fills the valleys, and flows out over the surrounding land. This is what has happened on the Murtle Plateau. Ancient rivers were buried by lava;

modern ones are just now cutting through this modified landscape, carving new valleys.

When the basaltic lava flows harden, they are very resistant to erosion. Also, owing to a peculiarity in the way they cool, they form **columns** (pages 56 and 76). The columns are usually oriented vertically; as they erode, they tend to fall away in sections, leaving behind a sheer drop. If the erosive force involved is a river, the result is usually a canyon and, at its head, a **waterfall** (pages 34 and 111). Helmcken Falls is one of the best examples in Canada of this "lava flow" type of waterfall.

Bombs, scoria and lava flows all result from typical volcanic eruptions, referred to as subaerial eruptions. In Wells Gray, however, other very different kinds of eruptions have occurred. Geologists call these eruptions "subaqueous," because they happened under water (sometimes glacial water!).

Water can have a spectacular effect on hot magma. If cold water manages to enter the conduits (or dykes) that feed the volcanoes, huge explosions result. Such explosions blast the magma into tiny fragments that resemble grains of sand, and that later harden into a rock similar in appearance to sandstone. This kind of rock, very common at White Horse Bluff, is called **tuff breccia** (pages 9 and 89).

Should, however, the lava flow into water (rather than the other way around), there is a more peaceful marriage. The water quickly chills the surface of the lava flow, at the same time solidifying it into a thin crust. Eventually the still-molten lava breaks through this crust, and pours out as lobes into the water. In their turn, the lobes (or toes, as geologists call them) are quickly chilled, and so the process repeats itself. In this way the lava flow advances through the water, forming what is called **pillow lava** (pages 59 and 79), after its shape.

Sometimes the pillows form on the edge of an underwater slope or dropoff.

When water comes in contact with magma, the result can be a cataclysmic explosion. The shattered magma hardens into tuff breccia, a volcanic rock closely resembling sandstone. (CH)

They may break apart and tumble down the slope into deeper water. These broken bits of pillows form another type of volcanic rock called – not surprisingly – **pillow breccia** (page 57).

Much the same kinds of rock form when volcanoes erupt under glaciers, as they have done on several occasions in Wells Gray. Obviously, the heat from the eruption melts the ice; the resulting water chills the lava and thus forms pillows.

But there is a difference. Because the glacial ice acts as a barrier, it prevents the lava from flowing away. Trapped, the lava builds up, layer upon layer, into a pancake-like platform consisting of pillows and pillow breccia. As the platform builds upward, it may eventually protrude through the surface of the ice. "Normal" subaerial lava flows then erupt, and become the icing on a cake made up of pillow lava. The subaerial flows result in a flat-topped, steep-sided mound called a **tuya** (pages 69 and 109).

You can explore at least six tuyas in Wells Gray. Some date from eruptions during the Fraser Glaciation, but most are much older. Some, such as McLeod Hill, have a classic "crushed stetson" shape. Others, such as Pyramid Mountain, did not erupt for long enough, or have a sufficient amount of lava, to establish the classic tuya form (page 107).

Rock Watching:
- *A Field Guide to Rocks and Minerals*, by F.H. Pough (Houghton Mifflin, 1976).
- *Field Geology in Color*, by D.E.B. Bates & J.F. Kirkaldy (Arco Publishing, 1976).

FUNGI: UNENLICHENED

FUNGI come in many different kinds. Moulds and rusts are fungi, and so are mildews and yeasts. Of the 100,000-odd fungal species so far described (possibly another 100,000 await discovery!), most are very tiny or even microscopic. A few thousands, however, do form conspicuous fruiting bodies, and these we popularly call mushrooms.

Most mushrooms are extraordinarily widespread. Because they disperse by wind-blown spores, many species are cosmopolitan, occurring in virtually all corners of the globe. Chances are, a mushroom you find growing in the Trophy Mountains also occurs in the Alps and Himalayas.

How many species of mushrooms are known to occur in Wells Gray? About 200.

The Black Morel (Morchella elata group) appears in spring just as the Birch and Aspen leaves are burgeoning. Look for it in the Hemp Creek Canyonlands. (HK)

That figure, however, is based on very preliminary field work, and doubtless represents less than half of the actual total. The total number of other kinds of fungi probably runs into the thousands.

Mushrooms have two seasons in the Clearwater Valley: early spring and late summer. The spring fruiting commences shortly after the snows melt, and is generally over by the last week of May (but later in the mountains). It is then that the morels (e.g., *Morchella elata* and *Morchella esculenta*) and the brain mushrooms (*Gyromitra esculenta*) are most likely to be found. Near treeline, watch for the chunky Snowbank Brain Mushroom (*Gyromitra gigas*).

The late season fruiting is more variable in its timing, but normally begins in late August, continuing through early October. The best mushrooming happens after prolonged rains – the kind of weather most campers hate. In the week following, the forests may be literally strewn with mushrooms, though less so if the weather has been dry during the months preceding.

Listed below are a few of the more common and easily identified late season mushrooms in the park. Though most are fairly widespread, don't waste your time searching for them in wetlands – habitats notoriously unproductive of mushrooms. Bogs, however, can yield some interesting species, as can late-lying timberline snow patches. Check also along the rims of the canyons for some special delights, including the almond-scented *Hygrophorus monticola*.

Mushroom Watching:
- *Mushrooms of North America*, by O.K. Miller, Jr. (Dutton, 1979).
- *Mushrooms Demystified*, by D. Arora (Ten Speed Press, 1986).
- *Mushrooms of Western Canada*, by H.M.E. Schalkwijk-Barendsen (Lone Pine Publishing, 1991).

Common Fall Mushrooms of Wells Gray Park

Scientific Name	Major Entry	Common Name
Amanita muscaria	102	**Fly Agaric**
Amanita porphyria	102	**Booted Amanita**
Armillaria mellea	101	**Honey Mushroom**
Cantharellus infundibuliformis		Trumpet Chanterelle
Coprinus comatus		Shaggy Mane
Dentinum repandum		Hedgehog Mushroom
Echinodontium tinctorium	134	**Indian Paint Fungus**
Fomitopsis pinicola	134	**Red-belted Conk**
Gomphidius subroseus		Rosy Gomphidius
Herpotrichia juniperina	43	**Black-felt Snow-mould**
Hygrocybe conica		Witch's Hat
Hygrophorus eburneus		White Waxy Cap
Laccaria laccata		Common Laccaria
Lactarius deliciosus	107	**Delicious Milky**
Lactarius rufus	107	**Red Hot Milky**
Lactarius glyciosmus		Almond Milky
Laetiporus sulphureus		Chicken-of-the-Woods
Leccinum aurantiacum		Red-capped Scaber Stalk
Lycoperdon perlatum		Gemmed Puffball
Marasmius scorodonius	107	**Garlic Mushroom**
Mycena alcalina	107	**Alkaline Mushroom**
Russula brevipes		Earth Mover
Russula emetica		Emetic Russula
Suillus lakei		Lake's Suillus

FUNGI: ENLICHENED

A LICHEN is just a fungus that has discovered agriculture. Different from green, chlorophyll-producing plants, fungi are unable to produce their own sugars; to survive, they must eat. Some fungi eat plants. Others eat animals (including people!). By definition a lichen is a fungus that eats algae.

Think of a lichen as a living fungal greenhouse wherein algae – tiny photo-synthetic cells – are simultaneously being grown and harvested. Just as the farmer's greenhouse is built so as to catch the sun's rays, so the lichen hangs out in the open air. Lichens are the banners of the fungal world.

British Columbia is home to more than 1600 species of lichens. Of these, at least 500 live in Wells Gray. You'll find them growing over rock, bare earth, moss, the branches and trunks of trees, and even discarded Moose antlers.

Hair lichens (Alectoria spp. and Bryoria spp.) are an important winter food for Wells Gray's Caribou; without them there would be no Caribou in the Cariboo Mountains. (TG)

Common Lichens of Wells Gray Park		
Scientific Name	Major Entry	Common Name
TREES		
Alectoria	121	**Witch's Hair**
Bryoria fremontii	89	**Edible Horsehair**
Cetraria canadensis		Brown-eyed Sunshine
Hypogymnia occidentalis	103	**Lattice Bone**
Letharia vulpina	89	**Wolf Lichen**
Lobaria pulmonaria	128	**Lung Lichen**
Parmelia sulcata		Powdered Shield
Parmeliopsis ambigua		Green Starburst
Platismatia glauca		Rag Bag
Sticta fuliginosa	145	**Peppered Moon**
EARTH		
Cladina	121	**Reindeer Lichen**
Cladonia ecmocyna		Orange-foot Cladonia
Nephroma arcticum		Green Paw
Peltigera aphthosa	114	**Freckle Pelt**
Solorina crocea		Chocolate Chip
ROCKS		
Thamnolia vermicularis	71	**Rockworm**
Umbilicaria hyperborea	54	**Blistered Rocktripe**
Xanthoria	72	**Orange Peel**

Taking a world view, the most surprising feature of Wells Gray's lichen flora is the great number of "macrolichen" (i.e., foliose and fruticose) species it contains. Thus far, some 305 species have been reported, making this one of the richest macrolichen floras anywhere.

Particularly well represented here are the Cladonias (*Cladonia*), with 45 species, the pelt lichens (*Peltigera*), with 24 species, and the bone lichens (*Hypogymnia*), with 11 species.

Some of the better spots to look for lichens include Spahats Creek Park (km 10.3), Whitehorse Bluffs (km 36.2), the Ray Farm (km 54.5), Clearwater Lake Campground (km 65.5), and the upper forests and summits of the Trophy Mountains (km 11.4). As well, impressive stands of lung lichen (*Lobaria pulmonaria*) and reindeer lichens (*Cladina* spp.) will be found along the Ray Mineral Springs trail (km 56.1) and on the Dragon's Tongue (km 65.3), respectively.

Lichen Watching:
· *How to Know the Lichens*, by M.E. Hale, Jr. (Wm. C. Brown, 1979).
· *Mosses, Lichens & Ferns of Northwest North America*, by D.H. Vitt, J.E. Marsh and R.B. Bovey (Lone Pine Publishing, Edmonton, 1988).
· *The Lichens of British Columbia. Illustrated Keys. Part 1 – Foliose and Squamulose Species*, by T. Goward, B. McCune and D. Meidinger (B.C. Ministry of Forests, Victoria, 1994).

MOSSES AND LIVERWORTS

To many people, including many botanists, mosses and liverworts (collectively called bryophytes) are little more than green curiosities: scraps of biological chinking that fill the dead spaces in the world's vegetation. This view is unfortunate, for bryophytes are important contributors to many ecosystems. By building soil, for example, they help other plants get started. And then, by controlling the water balance of the soil, they help to maintain various plant communities.

While it is true that many bryophytes are difficult to identify, others are as easy to tell apart as birds, butterflies, wildflowers and, for that matter, people: getting to know them poses little difficulty.

About 1000 moss species have been recorded in Canada, and nearly 700 in British Columbia. No comparable figures are available for the liverworts, though the B.C. total is probably close to 225 species. By comparison, the bryophyte flora of Wells Gray – with approximately 225 mosses and 50 liverworts – could at first seem rather modest. Yet only coastal B.C. has appreciably more kinds in areas of similar size.

Primarily citizens of the wet, mosses and liverworts thrive both in the damper

Common Mosses and Liverworts of Wells Gray Park

Scientific Name	Major Entry	Common Name
MOSSES		
Antitrichia curtipendula	168	**Hanging Moss**
Cratoneuron commutatum	123	**Hooked Moss**
Hylocomium splendens	156, 168	**Stairstep Moss**
Orthotrichum obtusifolium	99	**Blunt-leaved Bristle Moss**
Pleurozium schreberi	168	Big red-stem Moss
Polytrichum juniperinum	13	**Juniper Haircap Moss**
Ptilium crista-castrensis	168	**Knight's Plume Moss**
Rhytidiadelphus triquetrus	168	**Electrified Cat's-Tail Moss**
LIVERWORTS		
Barbilophozia lycopodioides		Snow-mat Liverwort
Marchantia polymorpha		Lung Liverwort

Fruiting capsules of the Juniper Haircap Moss (Polytrichum juniperinum). *Beneath the outer "haircap"* (calyptra), *look for a tiny urn with a peaked lid* (operculum). *Herein are the spores which reproduce the moss.* (HK)

portions of the park, and in damp pockets of the drier portions. Especially productive are the spray zones of the waterfalls. Anyone who has visited Rainbow Falls at the east end of Azure Lake, for example, will not soon forget the stout, green "beards" of *Antitrichia curtipendula* that drape the branches of the trees there.

Other good places to look for mosses are in the park's fens and bogs – which are themselves composed primarily of mosses, mostly **peat mosses** (*Sphagnum* spp., page 95). Some fairly rich lowland bogs are found at Placid Lake (km 36.5) and Zeller's Lake (km 63.2); here you'll find several species of peat mosses, some confined to the wet depressions, others occurring in drier sites. Much of the bryophyte cover of Wells Gray is made up of only a few species, common over the forest floor.

Moss and Liverwort Watching:
· *How to Know the Mosses and Liverworts,* by H.S. Conard & P.L. Redfern (Wm. C. Brown, 1979).
· *Some Common Mosses of British Columbia,* by W.B. Schofield (Royal B.C. Museum, 1992).
· *Mosses, Lichens & Ferns of Northwest North America,* by D.H. Vitt, J.E. Marsh & R.B. Bovey (Lone Pine Publishing, 1988).

Look for Long Beech Fern (Phegopteris connectilis) *in cool, deep canyons throughout the park. Ferns reproduce by means of microscopic spores. Check the lower surface of the leaves* (pinnae) *for spore clusters* (sori). (TG)

FLOWERING PLANTS

DURING the last Ice Age, the Cariboo Mountains of northern Wells Gray acted as a major dividing line to the ice sheets of inland British Columbia: the glaciers to the north moved northward, and those to the south, southward.

When the glaciers later retreated, here about 11,000 years ago, they made way for advancing armies of colonizing plants. Some of the plants had waited out the Ice Age south of the ice margin, and so followed the melting ice northward. Others moved southward from glacial refugia in Alaska and the Yukon. Because the Cariboo Mountains represented a last stronghold of the Pleistocene glaciers, it was here that many of the southern and northern invaders first met.

Common Trees, Shrubs and Flowers of Wells Gray Park

LEGEND:
ABUNDANCE (in appropriate habitat):   xxx = abundant   xx = sparse   x = rare
LIFE ZONES (see pages 16 and 17):
  HB = Hemiboreal; LB = Lower Boreal; MB = Middle Boreal;
  UB = Upper Boreal; HA = Hemiarctic; LA = Lower Arctic; MA = Middle Arctic;
  UA = Upper Arctic

Common Name	Page	Abundance	Zones	Scientific Name
CONIFEROUS TREES				
Western Red-cedar	33, 94	xxx	HB - MB	*Thuja plicata*
Douglas-fir	94	xxx	HB - MB	*Pseudotsuga menziesii*
Subalpine Fir	42, 94	xxx	LB - HA	*Abies lasiocarpa*
Mountain Hemlock		x	HA (reported)	*Tsuga mertensiana*
Western Hemlock	33	xxx	LB - MB	*Tsuga heterophylla*
Lodgepole Pine	35	xxx	HB - HA	*Pinus contorta*
Western White Pine		xx	LB - MB	*Pinus monticola*
Whitebark Pine	173	x	HA	*Pinus albicaulis*
Engelmann Spruce	42	xxx	HB - LB	*Picea engelmannii*
White Spruce		xxx	HB - LB	*Picea glauca x engelmannii*
DECIDUOUS TREES				
Trembling Aspen	64	xxx	HB - MB	*Populus tremuloides*
Paper Birch	94	xxx	HB - LB	*Betula papyrifera*
Black Cottonwood	94	xxx	HB - MB	*Populus trichocarpa*
SHRUBS				
Mountain Alder	168	xxx	HB - MB	*Alnus tenuifolia*
Sitka Alder	168	xxx	LB - HA	*Alnus sinuata*
False Azalea	52	xxx	MB - UB	*Menziesia ferruginea*
Canada Blueberry	174	xx	LB - MB	*Vaccinium myrtilloides*
Oval-leaf Blueberry	137	xx	LB - HA	*Vaccinium ovalifolium*
Redsteam Ceanothus	92	x	HB - LB	*Ceanothus sanguineus*
Devil's Club	78	xxx	HB - MB	*Oplopanax horridus*
Dwarf Cranberry	168	xx	LB - MB	*Vaccinium oxycoccus*
Falsebox	101	xxx	HB - MB	*Paxistima myrsinites*
Hardhack	125	xxx	HB - MB	*Spiraea douglasii*
Hazelnut	120	xxx	HB - LB	*Corylus cornuta*
White Moss Heather	48	xxx	HA - LA	*Cassiope mertensiana*
Pink Mountain Heather	48	xxx	UB - LA	*Phyllodoce empetriformis*
White Mountain Heather	48	xxx	HA - MA	*Cassiope tetragona*
Yellow Mountain Heather	48	xxx	LA - MA	*Phyllodoce glanduliflora*

Many plant species remain at or near the edge of their ranges in the Wells Gray area. Yellow Anemone (*Anemone richardsonii*), Alpine Sweet Grass (*Hierochloë alpina*) and **Wild Lily-of-the-Valley** (*Maianthemum canadense*: page 133) all have their southern limits here, whereas **Poison Ivy** (*Toxicodendron rydbergii*: pages 78 and 89), **Glacier Lily** (*Erythronium grandiflorum*: page 43), Western White Pine (*Pinus monticola*), and **Cascade Willow** (*Salix cascadensis*: page 51) are all near their northern or northeastern limits.

This mix of northern and southern elements has endowed the Clearwater Valley with an unusually rich vascular flora. To date, more than 700 species of trees, shrubs and herbs have been recorded, and there is no reason to suppose that another 100 species might not eventually be added to this total. Species "new" to the park are being discovered every year.

One group of plants not particularly well represented in Wells Gray is the rare and/or endangered element. Because glacial ice covered the park until rela-

Tall Mountain Huckleberry	137	xx	LB - MA	*Vaccinium membranaceum*
Rocky Mountain Juniper	89	x	HB	*Juniperus scopulorum*
Shrubby Penstemon	59	x	HB	*Penstemon fruticosus*
Mountain Rhododendron	52	xxx	MB - UB	*Rhododendron albiflorum*
Snowbrush	92	xx	HB - LB	*Ceanothus velutinus*
Soopolallie	99	xxx	HB - LB	*Shepherdia canadensis*
Bebb's Willow	108	xxx	HB - LB	*Salix bebbiana*
Western Yew	155	x	LB	*Taxus brevifolia*

FLOWERS AND HERBS (more on page 46)

Moss Campion	70	xx	HB - MA	*Silene acaulis*
Skunk Cabbage	132	xx	HB - MB	*Lysichiton americanum*
Queen's Cup		xxx	HB - MB	*Clintonia uniflora*
Spreading Dogbane	72	xx	HB - LB	*Apocynum androsaemifolium*
Dwarf Dogwood		xxx	HB - MB	*Cornus canadensis*
Long Beech Fern	167	xx	HB - LB	*Phegopteris connectilis*
Anderson's Holly Fern	167	x	HB - LB	*Polystichum andersonii*
Maidenhair Fern	167	x	HB - LB	*Adiantum pedatum*
Fireweed	40	xxx	HB - HA	*Epilobium angustifolium*
Foamflower		xxx	LB - UB	*Tiarella unifoliata*
Indian Rice Grass	**182**	xx	HB - LB	*Oryzopsis asperifolia*
Columbia Lily	131	xxx	HB - LB	*Lilium columbianum*
Corn Lily	52	xx	UB - HA	*Veratrum viride*
Glacier Lily	42	xxx	HA	*Erythronium grandiflorum*
Wild Lily-of-the-Valley	133	x	LB	*Maianthemum canadense*
Arctic Lupine	133	xxx	LB - HA	*Lupinus arcticus*
Dwarf Mistletoe	35	x	LB	*Arceuthobium americanum*
White-rein Orchid	93	xx	LB -HA	*Platanthera dilatata*
Indian Pipe	143	x	HB - LB	*Monotropa uniflora*
Rattlesnake Plantain	103	xxx	HB - MB	*Goodyera oblongifolia*
Woolly Pussytoes	69	xx	HA	*Antennaria lanata*
Prince's Pine	158	xxx	HB - MB	*Chimaphila umbellata*
Trailing Rubus	52	xxx	LB - UB	*Rubus pedatus*
Wild Sarsaparilla	78	xxx	HB - LB	*Aralia nudicaulis*
False Solomon's Seal	145	xxx	HB - MB	*Smilacina racemosa*
Meadow Spiraea	54	xx	HA	*Luetkea pectinata*
Round-leaved Sundew	96	xx	LB - MB	*Drosera rotundifolia*
Touch-me-not	131	x	LB	*Impatiens capensis*
Twinflower	147	xxx	HB - MB	*Linnaea borealis*
Rosy Twistedstalk	52	xxx	LB - UB	*Streptopus roseus*
Yellow Waterlily	135	xx	HB - MB	*Nuphar polysepalum*

tively recently, very few plants occur here that do not also occur – often abundantly – elsewhere in the province.

Still, a few rarities do occur, including the Adders' Tongue Fern (*Ophioglossum pusillum*), Mosquito Fern (*Azolla mexicana*), Crested Shield Fern (*Dryopteris cristata*), Wind-river Whitlow-grass (*Draba ruaxes*), and Oregon Willowherb (*Epilobium oregonense*).

The Zones

Among the most important factors controlling the distribution of plants is climate. Climate is just long-term weather.

In Wells Gray, climatic conditions at valley bottom are very different from those in the mountains, so perhaps it is not surprising that the plants are different too.

As you go up a mountainside, the overall climate takes a turn for the colder – just as it does when you go north. On the mountain, however, climatic change is much more abrupt, so that for every 110 m you climb, you are, in a sense, moving northward 1° of latitude.

At 2000 m (the elevation of the Trophy Meadows), the climate has cooled to the latitudinal equivalent of about 70° north

---

Life Zone Watching

As you explore the park, pay attention to its life zones; doing so will help you become more sensitive both to the ecology of individual plants, and to the complex relationship between climate on the one hand, and the distributions of birds, mammals, insects, on the other. The following descriptions of the subzones should help you get started.

In the bottom-most of the subzones – called the **Hemiboreal Subzone** (hemi, Greek for "half") – deciduous trees such as Trembling Aspen and Paper Birch are very common. By contrast, Spruce is sparse (restricted to moist sites), and Subalpine Fir is essentially absent. The Wells Gray road passes a representative section of Hemiboreal between km 11.5 and km 20. Likewise, most of the Hemp Creek Canyonlands (km 29.9) belong to this subzone.

Above about 550 m, the Hemiboreal gives way to the **Lower Boreal Subzone**. Here Spruce becomes more common, and Subalpine Fir turns up, though only in moister sites. It is here too that blueberries and huckleberries first begin to appear. From km 20 to Clearwater Lake, the terrain adjacent to the park road should give you a good feeling for this subzone.

Upward again, at about 1000 m, the **Middle Boreal Subzone** cuts in. Here Engelmann Spruce and Subalpine Fir

are again more common, whereas other tree species are dropping out. First to go are the deciduous trees, next the Douglas-fir, and then the Western Redcedar and the Western Hemlock. At the top of this subzone, the Spruce and Subalpine Fir are the only trees left, at least in mature forest types. A good place to explore the Middle Boreal forest is along the upper reaches of the road to the 88 Ridge trailhead (page 53).

Above 1450 m, an obvious thinning of the forest begins, and the understory gradually becomes dominated by dense thickets of Mountain Rhododendron (*Rhododendron albiflorum*) and False Azalea (*Menziesia ferruginea*). This is the **Upper Boreal Subzone**; of all the forested subzones, here plant diversity is lowest. The lower several hundred metres of the Trophy Meadows trail belong to this subzone, but much of it has recently been clearcut.

It is in the **Hemiarctic Subzone**, above 1800 m, that the thickets finally give out, and the arctic element first appears. As you continue up the Trophy Meadows trail, for instance, note how the forests become interspersed with ever-larger subalpine meadows. Eventually the **Hemiarctic Subzone** opens up completely, and the forests are replaced by extensive **flower meadows** (page 42) in which, however, clumps of (the northern Yukon). Both in the north, and in Wells Gray's mountains, this is treeline, and the average daily temperature in July is a cool 10°C.

Many of the plants that cling to the barren summits above treeline are essentially plants of the arctic. They survive at this latitude only because mountains rise high enough to approximate an arctic climate. At treeline and below, temperatures are more moderate, and the climate more resembles a boreal climate. Boreal, too, is the vegetation – which here consists primarily of conifer forests and, in the understory, copious mosses.

Virtually all of Wells Gray's plants can be described as belonging to either the arctic zone or the boreal zone. The only exceptions are those species which are restricted to the warmest valley bottoms; these, however, are perhaps best thought of as outliers from the temperate zone farther south.

The broad life zones just described can be divided into subzones, each characterized by its own assemblage of plants. In all, there are eight subzones in Wells Gray. With practice, you'll soon learn to recognize them using various indicator plants, including trees and shrubs. And while

---

trees may still persist. Whether on the Trophies or on Battle Mountain, the Hemiarctic is everybody's favourite subzone.

At about 2100 m, the flower meadows uniformly give way to heaths comprised of various low heathers, willows and sedges. This is the **Lower Arctic Subzone**. Recognize it also by the trees, which are now suddenly, and quite conspicuously, dwarfed. Two indicator species to look for are the White Mountain Heather (*Cassiope mertensiana*) and Yellow Mountain Heather (*Phyllodoce glanduliflora*). The highest of Wells Gray's lakes and tarns are located in this subzone, though none contain fish.

The peaks of the Trophies, above 2400 m, rise into the **Middle Arctic Subzone**. This is a cold, windy world, in which snow drifts persist through the summer in the lees of the ridges. No trees at all exist in this subzone – dwarfed or otherwise. As for the heaths, they are now represented only by scattered turfs that manage to eke out a spartan existence in shallow depressions. The plants that grow here may be small, but their flowers are often large and colourful. A land of vistas and broken rock.

Finally, the **Upper Arctic Subzone**. Only about eight peaks in the park extend upward past its lower limits at 2700 m; of these the most accessible

is Garnet Peak. Here no vascular plants occur at all, and snow regularly falls even in July. The only plants left are a few mosses and lichens which on favourable exposures somehow maintain a meagre photosynthesis.

The above zonation is known as the Bioclimatic Zone System. In middle latitude mountains, many authors prefer to add the prefix "oro-" (*Oros*, Greek for mountain), as a way of emphasizing that they are not talking about the "true" arctic and boreal zones, but about their mountain equivalents. Thus Hemiboreal becomes Orohemiboreal, Lower Boreal becomes Lower Oroboreal, Middle Boreal becomes Middle Oroboreal, and so on.

The Bioclimatic Zone System was developed in northern Europe, and was first applied in North America to Wells Gray by Leena Hämet-Ahti. It is, however, only one of many different systems which have been developed to describe the patterning of vegetation over space. In British Columbia, many foresters prefer to use the Biogeoclimatic Zone System, in which the zones are named according to the dominant climax tree species. Translated to this system, the zones represented in Wells Gray would be called the **Interior Cedar-Hemlock Zone** (page 143), the **Engelmann Spruce–Subalpine Fir Zone** (page 144) and the **Alpine Tundra Zone**.

SOME ZONALLY REPRESENTATIVE
LAKES AND MOUNTAINS
IN WELLS GRAY PARK

ZONE	PLANTS (TREES)	LAKES	MOUNTAINS
UPPER ARCTIC 2700m	No flowering plants at all, only mosses and lichens		GARNET PEAK
MIDDLE ARCTIC 2400m	No trees at all, heaths scattered		TROPHY MTN.
	(UPPER LIMIT OF FRASER GLACIATION)		
LOWER ARCTIC 2100m	Trees dwarf, understory of heaths	BLUE ICE TARN	BATTLE MTN. 88 RIDGE
HEMIARCTIC 1800m	Trees clump, understory of meadow herbs	FIGHT LAKE	52 RIDGE TROPHY MEADOWS
UPPER BOREAL 1450m	Forests begin to open, Rhododendron thickets form in understory	PHILIP LAKE STEVENS LAKE	SUMMITS UNNAMED
MIDDLE BOREAL 1000m	Few deciduous trees, forests dominated by conifers	KOSTAL LAKE MURTLE LAKE	McLEOD HILL
LOWER BOREAL 550m	Mix of decid-uous trees and conifers includ-ing Spruce and (in moist sites) Subalpine Fir	CLEARWATER LAKE ALICE LAKE PLACID LAKE	GREEN MTN. PYRAMID MTN. OSPREY LOOKOUT
HEMIBOREAL	No Subalpine Fir, Spruce in wet sites only.	MAHOOD LAKE	WHITEHORSE BLUFF

you're at it, you might also like to explore some of the park's more unusual **plant communities** (pages 69 and 104) [see: LIFE ZONE WATCHING].

The Trees

In the lowlands of the southern Clearwater Valley (south of Azure Lake), most forests are fairly young, dating to forest fires (pages 60 and 142) that swept the area early this century. Oldgrowth forests do occur, however (pages 155 and 167), and in the wetter northern half of the park, these are the rule, not the exception.

Owing to the moister, cooler weather at higher elevations, oldgrowth forests are a common feature of timberline throughout the park, even in the south. The oldest timberline trees in the Trophy Mountains, for example, are approximately 250 years in age, though it is likely that the forests containing them are much older. When fire (or logging, page 40) does extend to timberline, the forest may take many decades to regenerate, in the mean time creating temporary subalpine meadows (page 64).

Plant Watching:

· *Wild Flowers of the Pacific Northwest*, by L.J. Clark (J.G. Trelawny, ed.) (Gray's Publishing Ltd., 1976).
· *Flora of the Pacific Northwest*, by C.L. Hitchcock & A. Cronquist (University of Washington Press, 1973).
· *Trees, Shrubs and Flowers to Know in British Columbia and Washington*, by C.P. Lyons & W. Merilees (Lone Pine, 1995).

INSECTS

I F there is strength in numbers, then surely insects are the strongest of all creatures. More kinds of insects exist than all earth's other life forms put together. Estimates of their total numbers vary widely, from 2,000,000 to 12,000,000 species. To date, about 1,000,000 have been described. Of these, about 100,000 inhabit North America.

Wells Gray's insect fauna doubtless numbers in the several thousands, though virtually nothing is known about the status of any except the most conspicuous groups.

One group that has received some attention is the dragonflies (page 96), order Odonata. Thus far, 27 species have been found, though another 20 species are expected to occur. In 1984, *Aeshna tuberculifera* (a species very rare in western Canada) turned up in a bog just north of Shadow Lake. For other records, check the distribution maps in Rob Cannings' excellent *The Dragonflies of British Columbia* (see below).

No less eye-catching are the butterflies and moths, order Lepidoptera. At least 30 butterfly species are known to occur in the Clearwater Valley, the most conspicuous being the **Comma Tortoiseshell** (*Nymphalis vau-album*: page 117), the **Eastern Swallowtail** (*Papilio glaucus*: page 152) and the Green Anglewing (*Polygonia faunus*). Some good places to watch for butterflies are the Ray Farm, Clearwater Lake Campground, and along lakes and streams.

The butterfly calendar which follows is based on observations along the park road; it was provided by Helen Knight.

Many times more diverse than butterflies are the moths. Most moths are night-flyers, unlikely to be noticed. The presence of one moth, however, is patently obvious in some years, and may cause undue concern. The caterpillar of the Spruce Budworm (*Choristoneura occidentalis*) feeds on young needles of Douglas-fir and Subalpine Fir (rarely Spruce!), causing the trees to turn reddish brown, but seldom killing them. Later the brown, nondescript moth may be seen in great numbers. Another common insect larva that attacks trees is the **Spruce Bark Beetle** (*Dendroctonus rufipennis*: page 40).

Also hard to overlook are certain members of the insect order Diptera, the "true flies." Although most flies are harmless, some have evolved the annoying habit of drinking our blood. Most troublesome in Wells Gray are the **mosquitoes** (*Culicidae*: page 98), Black Flies (*Simuliidae*), Biting Midges or No-see-ums (*Ceratopogonidae*), and **horse** and **deer flies** (*Tabanidae*: page 110).

As you explore the park, keep an eye out also for "hatches" of flying ants, fir sawyer beetles (remarkably long antennae!), cicadas (loud, shrill buzzes in the trees), **hover flies** (page 45), lady bird beetles (orange-and-polka-dotted, common on mountain tops), mayflies (look for the long upward-pointing "tails") and **stoneflies** (page 154). Winter insects (page 209) are also worth watching for.

Insect & Spider Watching:
· *How to Know the Insects*, by R.G. Bland (Wm. C. Brown, 1974).
· *The Dragonflies of British Columbia*, by R.A. Cannings & K.M. Stuart (B.C. Provincial Museum, 1977).
· *How to Know the Spiders*, by B.J. Kaston (Wm. C. Brown, 1978).
· *Audubon Society Field Guide to Butterflies*, by R.M. Pyle (Knopf, 1986).

FISH

I N the beginning were the glaciers: rivers of ice 1000 m deep that surged southward out of the Cariboo Mountains, gouging deep depressions in the valley floor. Today the glaciers have retreated to the highest mountains, but the depressions remain. We call them lakes.

Within Wells Gray there are five large lakes, a dozen medium-sized lakes, and scores of smaller ponds, tarns and puddles. In total these water bodies contain roughly 20 billion cubic m of water – enough to submerge the entire surface of the park four m deep.

Notwithstanding all this water, and Mahood Lake excluded, Wells Gray supports relatively few species of fish. Why? In the first place, most of the park's lakes are cold, austere environments essentially lacking in nutrients. And in the second place, virtually all of them are inaccessible to migrating fish owing to downstream waterfalls. It is in fact a minor miracle that fish occupy any of the park's lakes at all.

Wells Gray Park Butterfly Calendar								
Species/Groups	March	April	May	June	July	Aug	Sept	Oct
Admirals				+	+	+		
Anglewings		+	+	+	+	+	+	+
Blues	+	+	+	+	+	+		
Mourning Cloak		+	+	+		+	+	+
Coppers					+	+		
Crescents				+	+	+		
Fritallaries		+	+	+	+	+	+	
Painted Lady		+	+	+	+	+		
Wood Nymphs				+	+	+		
Skippers		+	+	+	+	+	+	
Sulfurs		+	+	+	+	+	+	
Swallowtails		+	+	+	+			
Comma Tortoiseshell	+	+	+	+	+	+	+	
Fire-rim Tortoiseshell	+	+	+	+	+	+	+	
Whites		+	+	+	+	+	+	
Hairstreaks		+	+	+				

And yet they do. Rainbow Trout, Redside Shiners and Coarsescale Suckers all inhabit Clearwater and Azure lakes, and have apparently done so time out of mind. How did these species manage to overcome the triple barrier of Bailey's Chute, Marcus Falls and Myanth Falls? Three explanations seem plausible: 1) they were air-lifted by fish-hungry Osprey that inadvertently dropped their prey; 2) they were transplanted by native peoples wishing to enhance food supplies at their lakeside summer camps; and 3) they swam there on their own at a time when water levels downstream were raised by temporary ice dams.

Even so, most of the park's lakes contained no fish at all until stocking pro-grammes were instituted by various gov-ernment agencies beginning in the 1920s. Murtle Lake, for example, entertained its first fish in 1928 and 1929, when the Canadian Department of Fisheries planted some 40,000 Rainbow Trout (page 172). Steven's Lakes, near Battle Mountain, were "accidentally" stocked with Trout at about the same time.

Virtually all of the smaller lowland lakes (Placid Lake, Smith Lake, Pyramid Lakes, etc.) are also now stocked – again with Rainbow Trout. It is worth noting that Kostal Lake remained "barren" until September of 1987, when the B.C. Ministry of Environment dumped 30,000 Rainbow Trout into it. Will any of the park's water bodies be allowed to persist in their original, wild, fish-free condition? It seems unlikely. For a brief discussion of some above-water ecological changes triggered by stocking programmes, see FESTIVAL OF LOONS, page 172.

But surely Wells Gray's biggest fish story involves the thousands of Chinook Salmon (page 131) that enter the Clearwater River in late summer, having wrestled their way 550 km upstream from the Pacific Ocean. In due course, most of them find their way to the Horseshoe (km 54.0); here they dig their gravelly nests, spawn, and then die.

A few of the salmon continue upriver until their passage is blocked by the churning waters of Bailey's Chute (km 57.0). In late August and September, these enormous fish – averaging 85 cm in length – can be seen leaping out of the river in valiant and (presumably) vain attempts to overshoot the Chute.

Some 200 Sockeye Salmon and 500 Coho also spawn in the Clearwater River,

Fishes of Wells Gray Park

LEGEND: 1 = Mahood Lake; 2 = Clearwater Lake and Azure Lakes; 3 = Clearwater River; 4 = Murtle Lake; 5 = Hobson Lake

Species	Location: 1	2	3	4	5	Scientific Name
Burbot	+					*Lota lota*
Kokanee	+		+	+		*Oncorhynchus nerka*
Chinook Salmon			+			*Oncorhynchus tshawytscha*
Coho Salmon			+			*Oncorhynchus kisutch*
Sockeye Salmon			+			*Oncorhynchus nerka*
Redside Shiner	+?	+			+	*Richardsonius balteatus*
Northern Squawfish	+?		+			*Ptychocheilus oregonense*
Largescale Sucker	+?	+	+		+	*Catastomus macrocheilus*
Longnose Sucker	+					*Catastomus catastomus*
Peamouth	+?					*Mylocheilus caurinus*
Lake Trout	+					*Salvelinus namaycush*
Rainbow Trout	+	+	+	+		*Salmo gairdneri*
Dolly Varden		+?	+			*Salvelinus malma*
Mountain White Fish	+	+	+			*Prosopium williamsoni*

Any Rainbow Trout this fisherman nets below Dawson Falls will have ultimately been washed downstream from Murtle Lake over five tall waterfalls. Downstream again is the waterfall-of-no-return. (TG)

their numbers peaking in August and late October, respectively. A few spawning grounds have already been identified in the lower portions of the river, and doubtless others will eventually be discovered upstream. The base of Whitehorse Bluff is one likely location.

During the rest of the year, the easiest way to see fish is, of course, to go fishing. Failing that, the best places to fish-watch are in sheltered bays, particularly when the sun is behind you; at Clearwater Lake, try the wharf at the end of the park road. And then, to identify what you've seen, check the identification tables in your copy of B.C.'s Freshwater Fishing Regulations (available at the Wells Gray Visitor Centre, km 0.0).

Fish Watching:
· *Freshwater Fishes of Canada*, by W.B. Scott & E.J. Crossman (Fisheries Research Board of Canada, 1985).

REPTILES AND AMPHIBIANS

WELLS Gray is not big on reptiles and amphibians. Of snakes and lizards, the park has a meagre three species (or possibly now only two), and of frogs, toads and salamanders, the totals are three, one, and one, respectively. These figures translate to about 0.05% of the world's reptiles, and 0.2% of its amphibians.

Reptiles and amphibians are ectotherms, that is, they are unable (different from birds and mammals) to produce their own body heat, and must make do with whatever warmth they can soak up from their immediate environment. When outside temperatures are cool, they become sluggish. When the thermometer drops to freezing, they must either escape to a warmer place underground, or else die.

The herptile's answer to winter is hibernation. Even so, there are limits to how long a body can stay curled up underground. Even in the valley, snow persists for about five months of every year, whereas at treeline it may linger some four months longer.

When a herptile finally rouses from its winter sleep, it needs heat and suitable habitat in order to perform the vital functions of feeding, reproducing, and avoiding being eaten. Wells Gray is simply not hot enough for most amphibians and reptiles to cram all that living into the short space between spring and autumn.

Most reptiles and amphibians keep to the lowlands. The snakes primarily inhabit warm, south- or southwest-facing sites below about 1000 m. Here they can be found basking in the sun as early as April and as late as October. Look for the Common Garter Snake in open meadows and forest edges. The Ray Farm (km 54.5) and the Dragon's Tongue (km 65.3) are good places to see them. The Terrestrial Garter Snake, by contrast, is more common near water.

Neither of Wells Gray's snakes makes a living eating people. Nor are they in the least venomous. Their prey consists of earthworms, insects, rodents, small fish, frogs and toads. Enjoy.

Only the amphibians make it to treeline. One of these, the Spotted Frog, can be found in small lakes to about 2000 m, whereas another, the Western Toad (see page 126), occurs virtually throughout the park – even sometimes on the summits of the mountains.

The Pacific Treefrog and the Northern Alligator Lizard are both near the northern edge of their range here. The former species is most easily seen among the broken rocks of the Dragon's Tongue (km 65.3). The latter may no longer occur in the area.

Reptile & Amphibian Watching:
- *The Amphibians of British Columbia,* by D.M. Green & R.W. Campbell (B.C. Provincial Museum, 1985).
- *The Reptiles of British Columbia,* by P.T. Gregory & R.W. Campbell (B.C. Provincial Museum, 1984).

Common Garter Snake (RBCM)

Reptiles and Amphibians of Wells Gray

VIEWING STATUS: (in appropriate habitat):

*** = regularly seen	* = occasionally seen
** = often seen	? = possibly no longer present

Common Name	Major Entry	Status	Scientific Name
Northern Alligator Lizard	106	?	*Elgeria coerulea*
Common Garter Snake	148	**	*Thamnophis sirtalis*
Western Terrestrial Garter Snake		*	*Thamnophis elegans*
Western Spotted Frog	92	**	*Rana pretiosa*
Wood Frog		*	*Rana sylvatica*
Long Toed Salamander		*	*Ambystoma macrodactylum*
Western Toad	126	***	*Bufo boreas*
Pacific Treefrog	148	**	*Hyla regilla*

BIRDS

Two hundred and nineteen different kinds of birds have been recorded in or near Wells Gray. This represents approximately half of all the bird species ever recorded in British Columbia, and roughly 30% of the birds of North America – but only 2.5% of the world total!

Much of what has been learned about Wells Gray's birdlife is summarized in two publications. The first, *The Birds of Wells Gray Park – An Annotated List*, by Yorke Edwards and Ralph Ritcey, appeared in 1967. The second publication is *Checklist of the Birds of Wells Gray Provincial Park*, issued by B.C. Parks in 1984, and most recently revised in 1993. The latter is available free of charge: write Zone Supervisor, Wells Gray Zone, Box 70, Clearwater, B.C., Canada VOE 1NO. Or pick one up at the Wells Gray Visitor Centre.

Birds of the northern forest spend a lot of time sunning, and the Merlin is no exception. (TG)

Approximately 23 of the birds included in the checklist can be considered casual or accidental, that is, they apparently do not occur every year. In fact some, like the Black-crowned Night-heron and Northern Mockingbird, may not soon turn up again. Especially noteworthy is the Black-throated Sparrow sighted by Hettie Miller at Murtle Lake on 8 June 1959: for more than two decades this remained the only Canadian record.

Another 78 species are rare or very rare – at least in the sense that they are not often observed. Many of Wells Gray's owls belong here, as do several of the ducks and sandpipers that pass through during migration. Locating such as these can pose a real challenge.

Approximately 117 bird species can be classified as reasonably common. At the height of breeding season (May through June), you might well check off as many as 70 of these during a two-day visit. To do so, divide your time between the Horseshoe – Ray Farm – Alice Lake

area on the one hand, and the Trophy Mountains (upward to the peaks) on the other.

After about the beginning of July, most species stop singing, and thus take a sudden turn for the inconspicuous. Now the question of the day becomes "Why are there so few birds here?" In a sense this question is ironic, for with the recent recruitment of newly hatched nestlings, birds are actually now at their most abundant in the park. Yet there is no denying they are hard to see. Only in August, with the increasing restlessness that precedes migration, will they again come into public view.

Very few of Wells Gray's birds can be called resident in the sense that they live here year-round. For most, home is in the tropics and temperate zones; they come to Canada only to raise their young on the abundant and otherwise unexploited food resources of mid summer. By early August, many of them are beginning to retreat south again. About 110 bird

Birds of Wells Gray Park: the Lister's Checklist

LEGEND:

c = Common (more than 10/day)

u = Uncommon (at least 1/day)

r = Rare (not seen every day)

n, s, e, w = of interest to northerners, southerners, etc.

a = of general interest (especially owing to ease of viewing)

p; s; t = Permanent resident; Summer visitor; Transient

| The Birds | Status | Who's Looking? | | | | | Where to Find |
		n	s	e	w	a	(in summer)
Cinnamon Teal	T(C)/U	+					-small lakes
Barrow's Goldeneye	S/U		+				-small lakes
Golden Eagle	P/U				+		-above treeline
Spruce Grouse	P/U				+		-upper forests
White-tailed Ptarmigan	P/U				+		-above treeline
Greater Yellowlegs	S/U		+				-upper lakes
Solitary Sandpiper	S(T)/U		+				-lake & river shores
California Gull	P/U			+			-large lakes
Barred Owl	P/U		+				-forests throughout
Vaux's Swift	S/U		+				-forests throughout
White-throated Swift	S/U				+		-canyons
Rufous Hummingbird	S/U		+				-forest edges
Three-toed Woodpecker	P/R				+		-old spruce forests
Willow Flycatcher	S/U	+					-dry thickets
Alder Flycatcher	S/C		+				-wet thickets
Hammond's Flycatcher	S/C			+			-conifer forests
Dusky Flycatcher	S/C			+			-mixed forests
Northern Rough-winged Swallow	S/U	+					-lowland forests
Gray Jay	P/C				+		-upland forests
Steller's Jay	P/U		+				-lowland & mid forests
Mountain Chickadee	P/C		+				-upper forests
Boreal Chickadee	P/C				+		-upper forests
Chestnut-backed Chickadee	P/U		+				-low conifer forests
American Dipper	P/U		+				-rushing streams
Townsend Solitaire	S/U		+				-dry conifer woodlands
Veery	S/U	+		+			-wet lowland thickets
Varied Thrush	T(S)/U		+				-conifer forests
Gray Catbird	S/U	+					-wet thickets
Magnolia Warbler	T(S)/R		+	+			-deciduous forests
Townsend's Warbler	T(S)/U			+			-open conifer forests
Blackpoll Warbler	S/U		+				-upper conifer forests
Northern Waterthrush	S/U			+			-stream-edge thickets
MacGillivray's Warbler	S/U		+				-mixed forests
Golden-crowned Sparrow	S/C		+			+	-subalpine meadows
Rusty Blackbird	T(S)/R		+				-wet thickets
Rosy Finch	S/C			+		+	-above treeline

species belong in this category, including warblers, thrushes, flycatchers, vireos and swallows.

Roughly 50 species are migrants, passing through the park en route to and from their nesting grounds farther north. Additionally, a very few species range here on a kind of post-breeding holiday. The former category includes many of the sandpipers and most of the ducks, whereas in the latter belong the gulls. Because the migrants are most in evidence during May and September – October, it is then that the lakes and ponds take on special interest.

Four bird species occur primarily in winter, namely the Northern Shrike, Common Redpoll, Bohemian Waxwing and, rarely, Black-billed Magpie. All arrive with the onset of the cold season, and all disappear again once the weather starts to warm.

The rest of Wells Gray's birds – some 30 species in all – might be called its resident species: they can be found during any month of the year. This is not to say that the individual birds necessarily stay put. Indeed, without recruits from elsewhere, the park might well lose a goodly number of its so-called resident species every autumn. Yet resident individuals do occur among such groups as the owls, the woodpeckers, and especially the grouse.

The Clearwater Valley is at something of a geographic crossroads between the Columbia Mountains and the Interior Plateau. Because it contains elements of both the wet Interior Cedar – Hemlock Zone and the drier Interior Douglas-fir Zone, many birds are at or near the edge of their range. The Alder Flycatcher breeds at its southern limits here, whereas its look-alike, the Willow Flycatcher, is at its northern limits. Here the two species can sometimes be found singing almost on the same bush.

This edge-of-range effect adds a certain zest to birdwatching in Wells Gray. Watch especially for the following species, all at their northern limits: the Calliope Hummingbird, Gray Catbird, Nashville Warbler, Lazuli Bunting, Rufous-sided Towhee, American Goldfinch, and, surprisingly, the White-throated Swift.

Just which birds are likely to interest which birdwatchers depends very much on where they (the birdwatchers) are coming from. A birder from eastern Canada, for example, will doubtless want to concentrate on Wells Gray's western birds, whereas a lifetime resident of Vancouver would presumably focus on the boreal species. You'll find a list of the park's more sought-after species on page 25.

Birds feature prominently in the following pages. Some of the major entries are the **American Dipper** (page 139), **Common Loon** (page 172), **Merlin** (page 139), **Osprey** (page 151), **Owls** (page 73), **Barn Swallows** (page 124), **Hermit Thrush** (page 42), **Warbler songs** (page 78), **Winter Wren** (page 156) and **winter birds** (page 211).

Much remains to be learned about Wells Gray's birdlife. You can help either by entering your sightings in the "Wells Gray Wildlife Register" (ask at the desk at the Wells Gray Visitor Centre), or, in the case of any new or otherwise unusual records, by writing to Trevor Goward, Edgewood Blue, Box 131, Clearwater, B.C. Canada VOE 1NO. You might also want to consider the final paragraph on page 212.

Birdwatching:

- *The Birders Handbook*, by P.R. Ehrlich, D.S. Dobkin and D. Wheye (Simon & Schuster, 1988).
- *A Field Guide to Western Birds*, by R.T. Peterson (Houghton Mifflin, 1990).
- *Birds of North America*, by C. Robbins, B. Bruun and H. Zim (Golden Press, 1983).
- *Field Guide to the Birds of North America*, edited by S.L. Scott (National Geographic Society, 1983).

MAMMALS

After spending a summer engaged in a survey of Wells Gray's wildlife, I left with a conviction that here is an outdoor laboratory par excellence. Within the park we now have populations of wolverine and fisher as dense as any on the North American continent. There is almost as great a variety and abundance of game and predatory animals as can be found in any other comparable area within the province.

summarized from P. W. Martin (1950)

WELLS Gray is inhabited by 56 species of native mammals – a figure representing some 33% of all the land mammals known to occur in Canada. Such diversity reflects the many habitats encompassed by the park's boundaries.

None of Wells Gray's mammals ranges throughout the park. Whereas the Mountain Goat clings to rocky mountainsides, enduring snowstorms in mid July, the **Grizzly Bear** roams the upper forests and meadows, digging for Glacier Lily bulbs and Columbian Ground Squirrels.

The greatest variety of mammals doubtless occurs in the vicinity of the Ray Farm, where a conservative estimate might run as high as 35 species. Keep in mind, however, that most mammals are shy, retiring creatures; you'll be lucky if you observe more than ten species during your stay.

Possibly the most common and widespread mammal is the **Deer Mouse**, found from valley bottom to the low alpine tundra. Occurring sparsely throughout much the same range are the Ermine and the Long-tailed Weasel – two of the Mouse's fiercest predators.

A few of the larger mammals also tend to have broad distributions, though they seldom occupy their total range at any one time. Here belong the **Gray Wolf**, the Coyote, the **Black Bear** and the **Mule**

These poopsicles were almost certainly deposited by a she-Moose. (TG)

Mammals of Wells Gray Park

VIEWING STATUS: (in appropriate habitat):
   *** = regularly seen   • = rarely seen
   ** = often seen   ? = possibly no longer present
   * = occasionally seen   ! = further study required

Common Name	Major Entry	Summer Status	Winter Status	Scientific Name
Common Shrew		!		*Sorex cinereus*
Dusky Shrew		*	*	*Sorex monticolus*
Pygmy Shrew		•		*Sorex hoyi*
Vagrant Shrew		!		*Sorex vagrans*
Water Shrew		*		*Sorex palustris*
Big Brown Bat		**		*Eptesicus fuscus*
Little Brown Bat	125	***		***Myotis lucifugus***
California Bat		!		*Myotis californicus*
Hoary Bat		!		*Lasiurus cinereus*
Long-eared Bat		!		*Myotis evotis*
Long-legged Bat		!		*Myotis volans*
Silver-haired Bat		*		*Lasionycteris noctivagans*
Varying Hare	205	*	*	***Lepus americanus***
Common Pika	51	**		***Ochotona princeps***
Beaver	111	*		***Castor canadensis***
Yellow Pine Chipmunk	175	**		***Eutamias amoenus***
Columbian Ground Squirrel	124	***		*Spermophilus columbianus*
Golden-mantled Gr. Squirrel	175	•		***Spermophilus lateralis***
Northern Bog Lemming		•		*Synaptomys borealis*
Hoary Marmot	51	**		***Marmota caligata***
Deer Mouse	205	**	*	***Peromyscus maniculatus***
Western Jumping Mouse		*		*Zapus princeps*
Muskrat		*		*Ondatra zibethicus*
American Porcupine		*	*	*Erethizon dorsatum*
Bushy-tailed Woodrat		•	•	*Neotoma cinera*
Northern Flying Squirrel		•	•	*Glaucomys sabrinus*
American Red Squirrel	204	***	***	***Tamiasciurus hudsonicus***
Heather Vole		!		*Phenacomys intermedius*
Meadow Vole		•	•	*Microtus pennsylvanicus*
Long-tailed Vole		!		*Microtus longicaudus*
Southern Red-backed Vole	205	*	*	*Clethrionomys gapperi*
Water Vole		!		*Microtus richardsoni*
Woodchuck		*		*Marmota monax*
Coyote	207	*	**	***Canis latrans***
Red Fox	207	•	•	***Vulpes vulpes***
Gray Wolf	165, 207	*	*	***Canis lupis***

Black Bear	30, 140	**		*Ursus americanus*
Grizzly Bear	43, 169	•		*Ursus arctos*
Badger	93	•		*Taxidea taxus*
Ermine	206	•	•	*Mustela erminea*
Fisher	206	•	•	*Martes pennanti*
Marten	206	**	**	*Martes americana*
Mink	206	*	*	*Mustela vison*
River Otter		*	*	*Lontra canadensis*
Striped Skunk		*		*Mephitis mephitis*
Least Weasel	206	•	•	*Mustela nivalis*
Long-tailed Weasel	206	**	*	*Mustela frenata*
Wolverine		•	•	*Gulo gulo*
Bobcat	207	*	•	*Lynx rufus*
Cougar	207	*	•	*Felis concolor*
Lynx	207	•	•	*Lynx canadensis*
Caribou	64, 202	*	*	*Rangifer tarandus*
Mule Deer	208	***	**	*Odocoileus hemionus*
Moose	86, 208	**	***	*Alces alces*
White-tailed Deer		?		*Odocoileus virginianus*
Mountain Goat		*		*Oreamnos americanus*

Deer, all of which occur, in summer, from valley bottom to treeline, and sometimes above. In autumn deepening snows force them to retreat to the southern lowlands.

Some mammals are at or near the edge of their range in Wells Gray. The northernmost records of the Wandering Shrew and the California Bat, for example, have come from Hemp Creek. By contrast, the Pygmy Shrew and the Least Weasel are very close to their southern limits in the same area.

Wells Gray's fauna has changed dramatically over the past 50 or 60 years, largely in response to fire. Some species have prospered, while others have gone into relative decline. Especially momentous was the great fire of 1926, which blackened 520 square km of bottomland and, in so doing, temporarily introduced an open "parkland" element to the Clearwater Valley.

Under these more open conditions, shrubs and herbaceous plants began to dominate. To the animals that eat shrubs and herbs, this meant food in abundance.

Mule Deer were plentiful in those early years (declining only during winters of heavy snowpack), and so were Moose and Varying Hares. **Columbian Ground Squirrels** and Yellow Pine Chipmunks also thrived in the open burns, and later, as Trembling Aspen began to colonize, the **American Beaver** prospered in the wetter places.

Hunting these tasty morsels were healthy populations of Gray Wolves, Cougar, Coyote, and, among the small-time predators, Ermine and Fisher. Clearly the period from the 1930s to the early 1950s was one of prosperity for them.

Possibly it was during this period, too, that **White-tailed Deer** and **American Badger** first entered the valley. Both these animals are here very close to the northern edge of their range.

All this prosperity was to be short-lived. By the 1950s, the conifer forests had begun to close in again, and browse plants to disappear. As a result, many of the above animals went into relative decline. **Moose** populations decreased from about 2000 animals in 1952, to probably fewer than 1000 by 1965. In an attempt to rejuvenate some of Wells Gray's most productive winter Moose ranges, a burning programme was initiated in the late 1960s.

Even so, Wells Gray's wildlife is clearly not all it used to be. Nowadays, the Chipmunk is confined largely to the man-made burns, while the Beaver has in many areas run out of Aspen to gnaw. As for the Columbian Ground Squirrel, its lowland range is now mostly restricted to road edges and meadows. Meanwhile, the White-tailed Deer may have disappeared altogether.

Yet a number of species do remain common, and some – for example, the Woodchuck, the Varying Hare and the **Caribou** – are probably more abundant now than they were 20 years ago.

Above is a list of the park's mammals; winter mammals are discussed in detail beginning on page 203.

A Word on Black Bears

Bears are killed not only by people with guns, but also by people with handouts. Having once learned to associate people with food, bears can become aggressive. Eventually they may even chase picnickers from their picnic tables, and break into tents in the dead of night. In the end there is nothing for the park staff to do but destroy the offending bear.

Please. Resist the urge to feed the bears. Just as important, keep a clean camp – and never more so than when you leave it.

Mammal Watching:

· *A Field Guide to Mammal Tracking in North America*, by J. Halfpenny (Johnson Books, 1986).
· *The Audubon Society Field Guide to North American Mammals*, by J.O. Whitaker, Jr. (Knopf, 1980).

FIRST PEOPLES

WELLS Gray may be wilderness, but it is certainly not without human tradition. Long before Europeans arrived on scene, these rivers and mountains were part-time home to untold generations of native peoples.

Most of what is now Wells Gray Park lies within the traditional territory of the Shuswap (or Secwepemc) Indians, a subgroup of the Interior Salish. Archaeologists detect native use of the park at some 50 sites. Apparently these peoples arrived not long after the post-glacial return of Chinook and other Pacific salmon, roughly 5,000 years ago.

The Shuswaps were hunters and gatherers. In summer they inhabited small temporary camps, which they relocated according to the availability of fish, deer, caribou, roots and berries. In winter they congregated in permanent villages outside the park, for example at the junction of the Clearwater and North Thompson Rivers. This settlement was abandoned after an outbreak of smallpox in the early 1860s, and was set aside about a century later as North Thompson River Provincial Park. The half-dozen-odd depressions in the ground near the picnic site mark winter pithouses, or "kekuli," of not-so-long ago.

Apart from these and other archaeological sites, little remains to remind that native peoples once called this valley home. Three poignant mementos, however, are carried in the names Battle Mountain, Caribou Meadows, and Fight Lake – all alluding to a skirmish now lost in time.

Nowadays most of us are reluctant to wander very far off the beaten trail. The native peoples would have been less constrained. Ironically, though the park now entertains nearly 100,000 visitors every year, many corners of it are doubtless less peopled today than they were a thousand years ago.

PART TWO

THE CLEARWATER VALLEY

0.0 km

WELLS GRAY PARK VISITOR CENTRE

START your visit to the Clearwater Valley with a stop at the Wells Gray Visitor Centre, with its interpretive displays, gift shop, topographic maps and, not least, friendly staff. Pick up your copy of the Wells Gray Bird Checklist and Wildlife Viewing Guide. For an up-to-date record of bird and mammal sightings, browse the Wildlife Register. Contact the Visitor Centre by fax at 604-674-3693 or by phone at 604-674-2646.

> THERE ARE NO GAS STATIONS BEYOND THIS POINT. CHECK YOUR GASTANK AND SUPPLIES BEFORE PROCEEDING.

0.2 km
(0.1 mile)

CLEARWATER ADVENTURE RESORT

OVER the next 65 km, the road threads past nine private and public campgrounds. The largest and most elaborate is Clearwater Adventure Resort, offering chalets, tent pads, RV sites, electrical hookup, sani-station, showers, coin laundry, playground, golf course, museum and licensed solarium-style restaurant and guided tours. Open from March through October. For more information, call 604-674-3909 (fax: 604-674-1916), or write Box 1831, 643 Kennedy Road, Clearwater, B.C. VOE 1NO.

3.2 km
(2.0 miles)

SPAHATS PLATEAU

SINCE leaving the Yellowhead Highway, the park road has climbed steeply. Here it finally levels onto the upper surface of Spahats Plateau: a lava remnant more than 100 m thick. The lava was erupted from volcanoes beginning about a half million years ago. Since then the Clearwater River has carved a spectacular canyon just west of here. Explore part of that canyon at Spahats Creek Provincial Park (km 10.3).

TURNOFF TO YELLOWHEAD MUSEUM

5.5 km
(3.4 miles)

L OCATED approximately one km east of here at the end of a dirt road, the Yellowhead Museum is a colourful point of entry into the human and natural history of the Clearwater Valley.

The Museum was founded in 1975 by Ida DeKelver and her family. Today it houses everything from bear skulls to Indian spearpoints.

Visitors are welcome at any time, but from early September through June it's a good idea to call ahead (604-674-3660). Admission is by donation.

SPAHATS CREEK

10.2 km
(6.3 miles)

T HE lush, dark forests identify this part of the Clearwater as a "wet belt," in which rain, snow, thunderstorm activity and general cloudiness are all more frequent than at points farther north or south.

All this wet is related to the relative narrowness of the valley; where the valley walls lie farther apart the clouds tend to keep to the ridges, dissolving over the valley in response to the subsiding air; here the valley is simply too narrow to allow much subsidence, and so the wetter "mountaintop weather" extends off the peaks and right across the valley.

Reflecting the wetter climate is a widespread occurrence of Western Red-cedar and Western Hemlock in the forests here. These trees can easily be recognized from your vehicle at 80 kmph by their broad sprays of featherlike branches – silky in the Red-cedar versus furry in the Hemlock. Both require considerable moisture during the growing season. Farther down valley, in Clearwater, Hemlock is essentially absent altogether.

For a look at some notable old trees, turn in at Spahats Creek Park, and take a stroll along the Forest Loop Walk.

If the Vaux's Swift is flying low overhead, can rain be far behind? Probably not.
(RBCM)

10.3 km
(6.4 miles)

- SWALLOWING
- LICHEN
  LOOKING
- MISTLETOEING
- WATERFALLING
- CANYONING

SPAHATS CREEK PROVINCIAL PARK

AT Spahats Creek Park, you'll find a 20-unit campground, complete with good drinking water, firewood, outhouses and a short, self-guiding nature trail (alias the Forest Loop Walk). You'll also find one of British Columbia's better-kept secrets: Spahats Falls. To view the falls, bear left off the Clearwater Valley Road to the viewpoint parking lot, then stroll ten minutes along the canyon edge.

The Spahats viewing platform is a good place to linger awhile. Seventy-five m Spahats Falls pours off the edge of the same volcanic bench over which the park road has passed since leaving the North Thompson Valley. The lava flows here were erupted about 600,000 years ago; more recently, Spahats Creek has sculpted this 120 m canyon.

Spahats Creek Canyon dates from the end of the last Ice Age, about 11,000 years ago. As the Ice Age glaciers melted, they released enormous quantities of silt-laden water into Spahats Creek. This water poured off the edge of the plateau into the already-existing canyon of the Clearwater River. The falling water began to erode backward into the unconsolidated gravels that underlie the lava. Because the lava itself is composed of vertical columns, it soon began breaking off and falling inward in large slabs – like slices of bread. Spahats Canyon is the end result of this process.

Once the glaciers had melted, Spahats Creek shrank to a mere whisper of its former power and fury. Today the creek continues to down-cut a mini-canyon into the headwalls of the older canyon: a canyon within a canyon within the Clearwater Valley.

Revealed in the canyon walls opposite are about a dozen layers of lava. These probably built up quickly, as pulse after pulse of lava issued from the parent volcano. Beneath the bottom layer, notice a deposit of sand and gravel; this marks the place of a prehistoric

The Spahats Falls viewing platform is perched atop multiple layers of basaltic lava flows. (TG)

Clearwater River. Where did the lavas come from? No one knows. Erosion has removed any sign of a volcano.

From the colour of the canyon walls, it would be easy to suppose that the rock here is orange. Actually what you are looking at is the colour of three species of orange peel lichens (*Xanthoria* spp.) which colonize the rock surface. These lichens are literally the "patina of age"; much of the recent history of Spahats Canyon can be read in their patterning over the canyon walls. Because the orange peels require several decades to establish once an cliff face has fallen away, the youngest (uncolonized) surfaces typically have a grey, rather than orange, appearance. Once established, they still require scores, if not hundreds, of years to form the continuous colonies now covering parts of the canyon.

Near the viewing platform, check the branches of Lodgepole Pine for Dwarf Mistletoe (*Arceuthobium americanum*). Mistletoe is a diminutive, leafless parasite which derives its nutrients from the living wood of the host tree. In late summer, watch for its fruits; when ripe, these explode, scattering the tiny seeds. The presence of Mistletoe here has spurred more than one visiting couple on to shameless acts of public romance – blissfully unaware that *that* tradition celebrates the European Mistletoe (*Viscum album*), a species not even remotely related to the species here.

From the viewing platform, you may wish to follow the trail that loops north to the Clearwater Valley Lookout. If so, set aside about 90 minutes for a pleasant, canyon-edge ramble through middle-aged conifer forests. Here listen for Townsend Warblers sweetly singing "Siddle-siddle-siddle-see" or "Great big bumblebee."

Lodgepole Pine has needles in bundles of two. (RBCM)

The Clearwater River once occupied the centre of this valley, but was later pinned against the western wall by lava flows pouring down off the Trophy Mountains, to the right of the photo. Now the river has carved a canyon into the lava. (CH)

SPAHATS PLUNGE POOL TRAIL
2.5 hours (2 km) return.
Elevation change: 250 m.

EYE-OF-THE-NEEDLE TRAIL
5 hours (6 km) return.
Elevation change: 300 m.

- RIVER BEDDING
- ROCK BREAKING
- WATER FALLING

- RIDGE WALKING
- WILD GINGERING
- DRY GULCHING
- NATURAL BRIDGING

Both these trails are canyon-threaders: Arizona, Wells Gray style. Explore them at your own risk.

The Spahats viewing platform provides a convenient starting point for both hikes. From the platform, follow the canyon rim downstream past the safety fence to a fork in the trail. Here turn left onto a foot-worn path that descends steeply over a mossy basalt escarpment, and then over a grassy talus cone. Descending, watch for numerous "swayback" trees: testament to instability.

Having dropped 150 m, the path intercepts a more heavily used trail running left and right. If the Spahats Plunge Pool is your destination, turn left here. Otherwise turn right and continue downhill: the next left fork leads south to Eye-of-the-Needle (described on page 37), whereas the next right-hand fork – at river level – leads north to First Canyon (not described, but indicated on the accompanying map).

Spahats Plunge Pool Trail

First stop en route to the plunge pool is an outcropping of granitic Raft Batholith: an enormous protrusion of intrusive rock (rock formed deep within the earth's crust), hereabouts mostly buried by lava. Notice the consolidated sands and gravels sandwiched between granitic rock below and the basaltic rock above. These are the remains of an ancient riverbed.

As you continue uptrail, you can hardly fail to be impressed by this bottoms-up view of Spahats Canyon. Layered vertical walls tower above you. The sky is a narrow slit. And at your feet, a thousand broken boulders remind you that your life, cosmically speaking, is of tenuous purchase at the moment.

Check among the rubble for various crannied flowers, including Spotted Saxifrage (*Saxifraga bronchialis*), with its low, prickly mats of tiny, overlapping leaves,

Spotted Saxifrage demands a second look. (NONC)

and its delicately spotted white petals. Bend low to observe how the spots of each petal grade outward from paler to darker. Saxifrage is from Latin, meaning "rock breaker."

As you negotiate the talus en route to the base of the falls, take care not to slip on the blue-green algae (mostly *Nostoc*) covering the rocks. This is raincoat country: notice how the force of the spray organizes algae, mosses, grasses, shrubs and trees in more or less concentric bands outward from the falls. Trail end is a narrow ledge just beyond the falls, fronted quite literally by a tower of water falling from the sky. Assuming you live to remember it, this is a prospect you are unlikely soon to forget.

Eye-of-the-Needle Trail

This hike forms part of a more extensive trail system constructed by the B.C. Ministry of Forests along the east bank of the Clearwater River, south from Camp Creek (km 17.8) to the village of Clearwater. Contact the local Forest Service office at 604-587-6700 for more information.

At the Eye-of-the-Needle, the Clearwater Valley is a constricted gap 500 m wide. The canyon here is defined east and west by basalt and granite. To the east, an unbroken basalt wall towers 175 m above you. To the west the valley walls consist of steep granitic slopes rising nearly 700 m.

Occupying the north end of the canyon is a narrow ridge along which the trail passes. Today this ridge rises to the east of the river. A half million years ago it would have stood to the west. How is this? In the beginning, the Clearwater used to flow down the centre of the Clearwater Valley, somewhat east of its present position. An outpouring of lava later pinned it tight against the valley's west wall. The cleft the river has cut since then now defines the western flank of the ridge.

South of the ridge, the trail enters a small valley occupied by a small creek and, beyond the creek, a sizable patch of Wild Ginger (*Asarum caudatum*), with its hairy, valentine's-shaped leaves and unforgettable aftertaste. A short distance beyond, the trail passes close to the east wall of the valley, and here gives curious glimpses of former waterfalls now gone dry. Growing from cracks in the canyon walls, watch for Pellitory (*Parietaria pensylvanica*): a delicate, petal-less member of the Stinging

Pellitory (TG)

Nettle Family, but without the sting.

Ninety minutes south of Spahats Creek, and having reached the lower end of the Canyon, the trail veers eastward, and climbs steeply to the upper surface of the Spahats Plateau. Be prepared to negotiate both an unsteady talus slope and, above it, an unsteadying basalt outcrop. Some distance past the talus, watch (where eagles dare) for a natural rock bridge ten m below the trail. This was once the lip of one of the dry waterfalls earlier seen from below. The "bridge" is what remained when the creek that used to waterfall here was diverted through a crack just upstream of the lip. Erosion took care of the rest.

Back on level ground again, the trail forks. Here take the left fork back to the park road, ten minutes distant, then walk two km north to Spahats Creek Park and your waiting vehicle.

CLEARWATER VALLEY LOOKOUT

The Clearwater Valley Lookout offers a first impression of southern Wells Gray, and is well worth the ten minute stopover.

Reach the Lookout by vehicle from the turnoff to Spahats Creek Park. To do so, simply follow the road marked "Picnicking" to a parking area two minutes ahead. (The Lookout road rejoins the Wells Gray Road at km 11.5.) Here you'll find picnic tables and outhouses, but no water.

Dominating the distant skyline to the north is 2900 m Garnet Peak – one of the tallest of Wells Gray's mountains. Garnet's Matterhorn-like profile will turn up again and again, each time a little nearer, as you approach the park.

From this vantage, it is easy to get a sense that lava flows once filled this valley. The lava benches along the valley walls are the last remnants of these flows. At the base of the benches are heaps of broken rock called "talus slopes," indicating that the cliffs continue to break away at intervals. The same, of course, is happening in Spahats Canyon, but there you'll see little talus because the water continually washes it away.

The dark recess in the canyon walls just north of here is called the Shadden. A trail to this enormous grotto leaves the park road at km 12.7.

The road on the far side of the river leaves from Clearwater Village.

TROPHY MOUNTAINS ROAD

11.4 km
(7.1 miles)

Visible from the Yellowhead Highway south of Clearwater, and again from several places along the Wells Gray road, the Trophy Mountains form an impressive crown of nine peaks, the highest of which, at 2577 m, rises far above treeline. Below the peaks themselves stretches a three km lap of rolling plateau – the upper surface of the Shuswap Highlands.

As long as the sun shines, the cicada sings its shrill song in the tops of trees. (BCP)

It is here that the famed Trophy Meadows open for inspection every summer, to the delight of thousands. In 1987 these mountains – Wells Gray's answer to Julie Andrews – were added to the park as the Trophy Mountain Recreation Area.

The Trophies offer unlimited opportunities for day hiking and overnight backpacking. Most of the best hiking is accessed by two separate trailheads, both of which can be reached via the gravel road which branches east (uphill) off the Wells Gray Road at this point. The road is clearly signposted, and is generally passable even to low clearance vehicles; motorhomes, however, should proceed with caution, owing to the steep grades. But do check with B.C. Parks for current road conditions.

At km 4.0 the Trophy Mountain road divides: here veer left if you wish to explore the western Trophies (i.e., the Trophy Meadows and Trophy Mountain Skyline); if your destination is Silvertip Falls or 88 Ridge, continue straight ahead.

Trophy Mountains: Wells Gray's southern skyline. (BCP)

- CLEARCUTTING
- FLOWER
  LOOKING
- TREE PROBING
- SNOW MOULDING
- HOVER FLYING
- BIRD SINGING

TROPHY MEADOWS TRAIL
3 hr (6 km) return.
Elevation change: 200 m.

Every summer, millions of flowers open in the Trophy Meadows. Their blossoms cover whole square kilometres of rolling subalpine: a flower festival unsurpassed in British Columbia. And beyond the Meadows rises the Trophy Skyline, offering the finest possible view of Wells Gray Park.

The 13.3 km drive to the trailhead involves an elevation gain of 1000 m. For every 100 m gained, the temperature drops (on average) 0.5°C. As you climb, the growing season becomes shorter and the winter snows more lasting; forest species drop out one by one.

By km 7.0, at 1400 m, most of the deciduous species have disappeared. The only ones left are a few scraggly Trembling Aspen and Black Cottonwood. Even the conifers are now less diverse.

Eventually the road levels off onto a narrow lava plateau called "Sheep Track Bench." The lava here is much younger than in the valley bottom; it was erupted about 300,000 years ago, at a time when glacial ice filled the Clearwater Valley. The ice hemmed in the

---

Clearing in the Forest

The enormous clearcut through which the road passes en route to the trailhead was formerly a virgin stand of Subalpine Fir and Engelmann Spruce.

The first trees to be cut were felled in 1978, though at that time the logging was confined to several small cut blocks, with "leave strips" between them. Soon, however, the strong winds at this elevation began to topple the standing trees at the edges of the leave strips.

The fallen logs provided excellent habitat for the Spruce Bark Beetle (*Dendroctonus rufipennis*), and before long these wood-hungry insects were spreading into the adjacent forest, where they caused considerable damage to the standing trees. For this reason, the leave strips were eventually also cut, and the 550 ha cutblock you see before you is the result.

The clearcut is now growing up to Fireweed (*Epilobium angustifolium*) and various shrubs. These are the vanguard of natural forest regeneration; their ecological function is to prepare the soil for the eventual establishment of the forest trees.

But modern silvicultural practices dictate that conifers should appear sooner rather than later, and already thousands of young spruce seedlings have been planted on this site. Unfortunately, the seedlings are now being shaded out by the natural regeneration. To save the seedlings, chances are good that this cut block may in time be sprayed with heribicides, thus continuing the chain of ecological disruption that began more than a decade earlier. So much for high elevation logging.

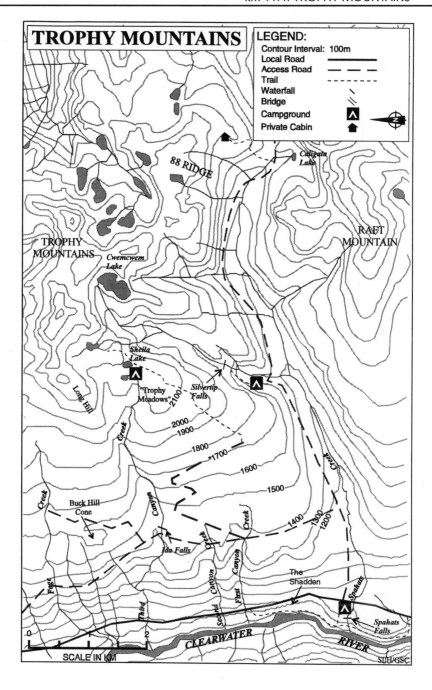

TROPHY MOUNTAINS

LEGEND:
Contour Interval: 100m
Local Road
Access Road
Trail
Waterfall
Bridge
Campground
Private Cabin

Contrast the clean, spire-like outline of the Subalpine Fir (left) with the branchy profile of the Engelmann Spruce. (TG)

The Black-felt Snow-mould (Herpotrichia juniperi) *feeds not only parasitically on tree needles, but also on algae – somewhat in the manner of a lichen.* (TG)

lava flows against the valley wall, thus forming a vertical pie-shaped wedge composed of pillow lava and pillow breccia. The upper surface of that wedge is Sheep Track Bench.

To reach the Trophy Meadows trail, turn right off Sheep Track Bench at km 7.8, and continue another 5.5 km through a clearcut to the posted trailhead [see: CLEARING IN THE FOREST, page 40].

From the trailhead, the trail passes through the top end of the clearcut, and then into the forest. The grades are relatively easy throughout, and should be manageable to stout hearts of all ages. Water is available in several places along the trail.

As you climb through the subalpine forest to the meadows, listen for the Hermit Thrush – the finest of a family of fine singers. Its song is unmistakable: a series of delicious phrases, each introduced by a single flute-like note, and each separated by a deliberate pause. The first phrase is low in pitch, the second a little higher, and the third so thin and ethereal that you may not even hear it unless the bird is close at hand. A more moving song could hardly be imagined. One naturalist has rendered it thus: "Oh, holy, holy. Ah, purity, purity. Eeh, sweetly, sweetly." Enjoy.

Other common birds of the subalpine forests are the Mountain and Boreal Chickadees, Red Crossbill, Pine and Evening Grosbeaks, Blue and Spruce Grouse, Gray Jay, Dark-eyed Junco, Golden-crowned Kinglet, and Red-breasted Nuthatch.

You are now climbing through a climax forest of Subalpine Fir and Engelmann Spruce. These are the only trees left at this elevation. They are easily told apart both by the needles and by the bark. The needles are soft and "furry" in the Fir, and sharp in the Spruce ("When you get all spruced up, you look pretty sharp!"). As to the bark, it is smooth in the former, and flaky in the latter. With practice you can also learn to recognize these (and all of Wells Gray's other conifer species) by the smell of the crushed needles. Go ahead. No one's watching.

As you climb, the forest becomes less dense. Yet to judge from the size of the trees, it would appear they grow well once established; apparently the trick is to get established in the first place. Conditions must be just right. Timberline trees put on good cone crops only once in several years, and only then are seeds available. Also, any seeds that do exist must find suit-

able growing places – something not easy to do in herb-dominated forests and meadows. And even if they do manage to germinate, the young seedlings are unlikely to survive the summer frosts and drought characteristic of this elevation.

Along the edge of the meadows, the young trees face another challenge: the Black-felt Snow-mould (*Herpotrichia juniperi*). This remarkable fungus grows in snow at temperatures near freezing. Sending out its hyphae, it sucks the life juices from buried tree branches. Later, after the snow has melted, the dead and dying branches look as though they are covered in black tar. In winters of prolonged snow lie, entire trees may be killed by this fungus.

About an hour from the trailhead, the forest gives way to the Trophy Meadows. Flower meadows are by no means a universal feature of treeline. Even in British Columbia, subalpine flower meadows are essentially restricted to mountains south of about Prince George. Nowhere are they more spectacular than here.

Two waves of flowers occur on these meadows every summer. The first, in late June, is dominated by Glacier Lilies (*Erythronium grandiflorum*), which often begin to push up even before the snow has melted. Imagine millions of clear yellow blossoms crowding the slopes as far as the eye can see. The best of the display lasts only a few days, but because the lower meadows (at 1900 m) bloom up to three weeks earlier than the upper (at 2050 m), you can usually find at least a few Glacier Lilies still flowering in late July.

Glacier Lilies are enjoyed not only by hikers, but also by Grizzly Bears. Early in the season the Grizzly may visit the Trophy Meadows, digging up the lily

(Left) In the Glacier Lily (Erythronium grandiflorum), the tassel-like anthers (pollen-bearing organs) are yellow in some plants, but purple in others. (TG)

(Right) Look long enough among the millions of Glacier Lilies that deck the Trophy Meadows each spring, and eventually you'll find a pale-flowered "albino" form. (TG)

The Grizzly usually overwinters in dens above 1000 m, and emerges from hibernation in early or mid May. Food is scarce at this season, so the bear resorts to eating carrion. In its search for food, it may invade the low country. By early summer, it is back at treeline, where Glacier Lily bulbs are its main food. Glacier Lilies appear to be the key to Grizzly distribution during July and August.

　　summarized from R.W. Ritcey (1955)

THE TROPHY MEADOWS ARE AMONG THE FEATURE ATTRACTIONS OF WELLS GRAY; PLEASE KEEP TO THE TRAIL AT ALL TIMES – EXCEPT, PERHAPS, TO LUNCH AT THE "SOFT ROCK CAFE": A BOULDERY AREA LOCATED NEAR THE LOWER END OF THE MEADOWS.

bulbs which provide a much needed source of carbohydrates. Though you're unlikely to see a Grizzly, it isn't hard to find evidence of their diggings: just look for abrupt depressions in the ground.

The second wave of flowers is at its best during the last weeks of July and the first weeks of August. Then the meadows are a rising crescendo of colour: Arnica yellows, Daisy mauves, Lupine blues, Monkeyflower reds and Valerian whites.

Specialties of the season include, for the nose, some impressively large clove-and-cinnamon-scented colonies of White-rein Orchid (*Platanthera dilatata*) and, for the eyes, the multicoloured blossoms of Indian Paintbrush (*Castilleja occidentalis* and others). These range in hue from rich, creamy white, through yellow and orange, to the deepest possible crimson. Worthy of mention, too, are the brightly coloured flowers of Orange Agoseris (*Agoseris aurantiaca*) which come in two distinct colour phases, one orange, and the other a deep pink. The latter was recently named *A. lackschewitzii*.

With all this mass of blossoming flowers, you may wonder where the butterflies are. The answer is: they

In August, the Trophy Meadows are carpeted with the blossoms of more than two dozen kinds of wildflowers. (TG)

are in the valley. Here, at nearly 2000 m, the weather is simply too unpredictable, and cool, for butterflies to really thrive. So their place as pollinators is largely taken over by several species of flies. Especially common are the hover flies [see: MELLOW YELLOW].

With the arrival of the first heavy frosts, generally around the middle of August, the summer flowers have crested, and soon subside. Now in the place of flowers there rises a sweet, melancholy fragrance of decay. Particularly dismal-looking are the great corn-like leaves of the Corn Lily (*Veratrum viride*): green and luscious only days before, now brown and tattered.

On dry, sunny afternoons toward the end of the month, you may be startled by the sudden snap, crackle and pop sounds of exploding Lupine seed pods. By September, the meadows are ready for winter. And a good thing, too, for now the first snow flurries of the season begin.

Birds are also common, though not particularly diverse. Listen especially for the songs of sparrows: the Fox Sparrow ("Oh dear me-oh, mimimimi"), the Chipping Sparrow (a dry, continuous trill); the Savannah Sparrow (an absent-minded "Tsit-tsit-tsit, tseeee-tsaaay"); the Lincoln's Sparrow (a sweet operatic gurgle: "her her her he he he, mimimimi"); and the Golden-crowned Sparrow (a mournful, descending "Oh dear me").

After mid July, the sparrows are joined by the Rufous Hummingbird. Though this species nests pri-

Hover flies come in many shapes and sizes. Most, however, resemble wasps and bees, but none are harmful. (BCP)

Mellow Yellow

Visiting the flowers at this season are various species of hover flies (syrphid flies): wasp-like creatures whose bodies are cross-banded with an ominous patterning of yellow and black. Because these harmless flies so closely resemble wasps, most predators are content to leave them alone. And so do most people, the power of mimicry being what it is.

Wells Gray is home to dozens of species of hover flies, though not all resemble wasps. Some, like the drone fly (*Eristalis tenax*), resemble Honeybees, and others, including species of *Criorhina*, are Bumblebee mimics. All these insects feed on flower nectar and pollen.

Telling hover flies from wasps is usually easy. Wasps have narrow waists and long, thread-like antennae. In hover flies, by contrast, the waists are broad, and the antennae very short, almost horn-like.

Once you've learned to recognize hover flies with certainty, you might like to "befriend" one. Do so by slowly placing your hand close to a flower where a hover fly is feeding. After a time, the fly should lose interest in the flower, and begin to fix its attention on you. Once it lands, you may gently stroke it without it flying away.

Syd Cannings and Rob Cannings

Subalpine tree islands are reflected in the still waters of a mountain tarn, here wrong way up. (TG)

marily in the lowlands, later it removes to treeline to sip nectar from the flowers now in bloom. Tiniest of all birds, hummingbirds are unmistakable. They show a distinct preference for red flowers, and will often "buzz" you if you're wearing clothing of that colour.

After mid August, hawks begin to migrate out of the

Trophy Meadows Flower Calender

LEGEND: xxxx = flowering; . . . . = seed dispersal
Note: Flowering times may vary as much as two weeks, depending on weather.

Common Narme	Scientific Name	June	July	August
Western Anemone	*Pulsatilla occidentalis*	xxx		. . . .
Marsh Marigold	*Caltha biflora*	xxxxxxxx		. . . .
Spring Beauty	*Claytonia lanceolata*	xxxxxx		
Glacier Lily	*Erythronium grandiflorum*	xxxxxx		. . .
Snow Buttercup	*Ranunculus eschscholtzii*	xxxxxx		. . . .
Globeflower	*Trollius laxus*	xxxxxx		. . .
Indian Paintbrush	*Castilleja occidentalis*		xxxxxxxxxx	
Arctic Lupine	*Lupinus arcticus*		xxxxxxxxxx	. .
Alpine Veronica	*Veronica wormskjoldii*		xxxxxxx	
Meadow Rue	*Thalictrum occidentalis*		xxxxxxx	. . .
Broad-leaved Arnica	*Arnica latifolia*		xxxxxxxxxx . . .	
Hairy Arnica	*Arnica mollis*		xxxxxxxxxx . .	
White-rein Orchid	*Platanthera dilatata*		xxxxxxxx	
Slender Bog Orchid	*Habenaria saccata*		xxxxxxxx	
Wood Betony	*Pedicularis bracteosa*		xxxxxx . . .	
Mountain Valerian	*Valeriana sitchensis*		xxxxxxxx . .	
Mountain Daisy	*Erigeron peregrinus*		xxxxxxxx .	
Triangle-leaved Ragwort	*Senecio triangularis*		xxxxx . . .	
Corn Lily	*Veratrum viride*		xxxxxxxx	
Mountain Sage	*Artemisia norvegica*		xxxxxx	
Cow Parsnip	*Heracleum lanatum*		xxxxxxx	
Pink Monkeyflower	*Mimulus lewisii*		xxxxxx	
Orange Agoseris	*Agoseris aurantiaca*		xxxxx	
Showy Aster	*Aster foliaceus*			xxxxxxxx

north country. Flying southward, they keep to the high open ridges and meadows. In the Trophy Meadows, it is then easy to see as many as a dozen raptors in an afternoon, and sometimes many more. The most common are the Red-tailed Hawk, the Cooper's Hawk, the American Kestrel and the Northern Harrier. Later in the season, after the first snows, watch also for the Rough-legged Hawk, en route from the arctic to its wintering grounds in the Okanagan and points south.

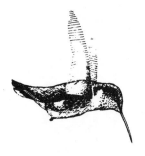

The Rufous Hummingbird (RBCM)

TROPHY SKYLINE TRAIL
7 hr (12 km) return.
Elevation change: 600 m.

- TREE CLUMPING
- HEATHER PROBING
- GLACIER GAZING
- WILLOW WATCHING
- PIKA BOOING

The nine peaks of the Trophy Mountains are really just more resistant points in a long, forking ridge which has been dissected by erosion. The ridge, however, is still easy to make out and, seen from above, resembles the letter "Y." It is to the stem of the Y that the following account will lead you. Be ready for a most impressive view over southern Wells Gray.

To reach the Skyline, continue north along the Trophy Meadows trail, passing en route an old, dilapidated shepherd's cabin. Beyond the cabin the trail becomes a narrow footpath which soon forks; here keep left.

Not far north of the cabin, the trees begin to dwarf. Probably you'll have noticed that conifers at this elevation tend to be clustered as smallish "tree islands." The clustering increases the trees' chances of survival by providing better shelter from the wind, mutual mechanical support, warmer temperatures (the clumped trees absorb the sun's warmth), and a longer growing season. Apparently the operating principle is "United we stand. . . ."

Because tree growth is favoured at the perimeter of the tree islands, young trees readily become established here, and the islands continue to enlarge. In time, the parent trees in the centre succumb to old age, and the tree island develops a hollow centre; it is now called a "tree atoll." Tree atolls are fine places to wait out a summer rainstorm.

Freeze, thaw, crack and crumble: so the process of erosion works on solid rock, producing boulders, then cobbles and ultimately soil. (HK)

The nodding, urn-shaped flowers of White Moss Heather (Cassiope mertensiana) *are characteristic of the Heather Family* (Ericaceae). *Look for similar flowers among the blueberries.* (TG)

At length the trail descends to the shores of Sheila Lake where you'll find the only designated camping area on the mountain. If that's your destination, fine; otherwise make your way onto the crest of the ridge rising east above the lake. The Skyline is now in full view; no trail is needed. Simply continue north to the low saddle directly ahead.

Among the mountains of Wells Gray, the Trophies are distinctive for their many lakes and tarns – at a conservative estimate, more than 50. Most owe their existence to mountain glaciers which once clung to the faces of these slopes. Blue Ice Tarn, at 2100 m, is the highest body of water in Wells Gray. On average, its surface remains ice-covered until about the second week of July. Watch for it along the route to the Skyline.

As you climb, watch for permanent snowfields with a strangely pink hue. The colouring agent is a tiny green alga sometimes called the Watermelon Alga (*Chlamydomonas nivalis*). This is actually a tiny, single-celled organism which, perhaps surprisingly, contains green chlorophyll, just as other plants do. Here, however, the green is masked by a red pigment that probably helps to preserve the alga from the harmful effects of intense ultraviolet radiation. And, to help it continue photosynthesizing at temperatures below freezing, each algal cell contains a small shot of mineral "antifreeze." What does it feed on? Sunlight and dust.

Heather Weather

Above treeline, the herb meadows give way to shrubby heaths. Here grow White Moss Heather (*Cassiope mertensiana*), White Mountain Heather (*Cassiope tetragona*), Pink Mountain Heather (*Phyllodoce empetriformis*) and Yellow Mountain Heather (*Phyllodoce glanduliflora*). To tell these shrubs apart, pay attention to the flower colour. Pink and yellow ones are no problem, but if the flower is white, you'll have to pay attention to the backs of the needly leaves: if each of them bears a fine, narrow groove, you are looking at a White Mountain Heather; if not, it is the White Moss Heather that has caught your eye.

All the heathers have evergreen leaves, for deciduous leaves are at a disadvantage here. In the first place, summer is brief in the alpine, and most plants simply have not enough time to put on a new set of leaves each year. It is much better, if you can manage it, to use the same leaves year after year.

In the second place, deciduous leaves are poor water-retainers. Strange as it may seem, drought is a real threat to plants of the high country – both in summer and in winter, but especially in winter. Because these ridges often blow clear of snow, the shrubs are exposed to extreme drying by the wind. The needles have evolved as moisture-preservers in which the breathing pores (or stomata) are recessed in the lower surface of the needle, thus creating a dead air space which reduces evaporation. Also, the outer surface of the needles is covered in a thick, waxy coating not unlike that of a desert cactus.

The view from the Trophy Skyline (at 2350 m) is breathtaking. In good weather, you can look 75 km north to the Matterhorn-like profile of Garnet Peak; everything you see in that direction lies within Wells Gray. On rare occasions it is possible to see even farther – to the summit of 3954 m Mount Robson, grandest of the Canadian Rockies, towering like a cumulus cloud above the northeast horizon.

Below the summit of Trophy Peak clings the southernmost glacier in Wells Gray. The crevasses at its head (the bergschrund) mark the point at which the ice begins to flow. (TG)

The Little Ice Age

Glaciers in the high mountains of Wells Gray have fluctuated during the Holocene (the past 11,000 years) in response to climatic changes. Shortly after the close of the Fraser Glaciation (the last Ice Age), the climate was warmer than it is today, and the glaciers probably were smaller.

This warmer period lasted until about 5000 to 6000 years ago, and was followed by a period of cooling and glacier expansion. The first well documented Neoglacial advance in the park is called the Battle Mountain advance; it culminated between 3400 and 2400 years ago.

Even more dramatic was the cooling of the past several centuries, which is known locally as the Mammoth Creek advance, and worldwide as the Little Ice Age. At that time, most glaciers were larger than at any other time since the Fraser Glaciation. The fresh, sparsely vegetated morainal ridges adjacent to most existing glaciers were produced at this time.

Glaciers began to recede from their maximum Little Ice Age positions at various times during the 18th, 19th and 20th centuries. Since then they have undergone sporadic retreat interrupted by standstills and readvances.

John Clague

The Northwest Territories?
No, the Trophy Mountain
Skyline. Where frost comes
early and snow lies late,
ice-shattered rocks form
boulder fields as far as the
eye can see. (TG)

Clinging to the north face of the Trophies are snow-fields and, farther east, the only glacier in southern Wells Gray. The latter is a left-over from cooler times.

In the high mountains, temperatures are close to freezing for much of the year, and the climate is said to be periglacial. Not surprisingly, the freezing and thawing of water plays an important role in geological

Rocks in Turmoil

The rocks that form the Trophies are quite unlike the volcanic rocks in the valley. They form part of what geologists call the Shuswap Metamorphic Complex which is, in turn, part of a much larger zone of rock known as the Omineca Crystalline Terrane. This terrane runs the length of British Columbia, and actually records a collision that occurred between the former North American continent to the east, and several smaller land masses to the west. The collision lasted about 40 million years, starting some 200 million years ago when the dinosaurs were just entering their heyday.

In the contact, or suture, zone right here, the movements of the earth were particularly powerful. Rock layers were folded as you might fold pieces of paper, and then folded again in different directions. At the same time crystalline minerals in the rocks were reoriented so that they ran parallel to one another, thus imparting cleavage to the rocks.

All this geologic commotion generated intense pressure and heat. As a result, minerals contained within the original sedimentary and volcanic rocks began to react with one another, and to metamorphose into entirely new minerals. Clay minerals, for example, turned into garnet. So much have these rocks changed, that geologists have a very difficult time deciphering their origins. This is metamorphism at its most extreme.

Paul Metcalfe

processes. When water freezes in the cracks of rocks, it expands, and so gradually wedges the rocks apart. This wedging eventually shatters the rocks to a jumble of small boulders. Such boulderfields are common in the Trophies, and are called felsenmeers (rock seas).

Check the crannies between the rocks for as many as 20 different species of flowering plants, some of them more delicate in appearance than would seem possible on this windswept summit. The Alpine Harebell (*Campanula lasiocarpa*) is one of these, with its seven cm stalks, and disproportionately huge sky-blue bells.

Also growing here are the tiniest trees in the world – willows that stand scarcely two cm tall. Watch for two of these: the Snow Willow (*Salix nivalis*) and the Cascade Willow (*Salix cascadensis*). Tell them apart by the leaves, which are blunt-tipped in the first, and pointed-tipped in the second. Though not evergreen, like the heathers, they survive even more drastic conditions. Their trick is simply to lie flat against the ground, where the sun's warmth is greatest, and the wind's purchase weakest.

Fewer plants to eat means fewer animals. This is especially true of plant-eating mammals, which are represented here by only two species. These, the Hoary Marmot and the Pika, find shelter among the tumbled boulders, and have actually made the alpine tundra their home. Recognize them at a distance by their calls: a shrill whistle in the Beaver-sized Marmot, and a nasal, ventriloquial "Eeep!" in the Guinea-Pig-sized Pika.

Here the big challenge, besides finding food, is to simply stay warm. This the Marmot and Pika accomplish by having thick fur, by spending much of their time sunning, and by having body shapes that minimize heat loss. The most heat-retentive shape of all is a sphere, so it is not surprising that both resemble furry balls with short ears and limbs.

Finally, the birds. Species to watch for include the White-tailed Ptarmigan, the Golden Eagle, the Water Pipit and the Rosy Finch.

The Snow Willow (Salix nivalis) comes in two sexes. Pictured here is a female shrub with fruiting capsules. Notice the bright, shiny Canadian penny. (TG)

When you cross a mountain boulderbed, watch for the Pika's little "haystacks," left out to dry in the sun. (BCP)

• WATERFALL
   WOWING
• CIRQUE LURKING
• ROADSIDE
   GRASSING

SILVERTIP FALLS TRAIL
1 hr (2 km) return.
Elevation change: 75 m.

Silvertip Creek rises in Cwem Cwem Lake, at the foot of Trophy Peak. At Silvertip Falls, five km southwest, the creek cataracts over the headwall of the second of two "glacial armchairs," or cirques, that punctuate its course [see: ICE SCULPTURES, page 53]. At 175 m, the falls are taller even than Helmcken. In freshet they are fulsome indeed, though by mid July they have usually dwindled to a mere silver thread whispering.

Silvertip Falls is now the focus of a Forest Service "Rec Site," offering primitive camping places for about eight tents. To reach the Falls drive east up the Trophy Mountain road to the junction at km 4.0, then continue right for another 2.5 km to the bridge at Silvertip Creek.

Notice how the road verges here have been seeded to grass species alien to the region. Timothy (*Phleum pratense*), with its compact, bottle-brush seed heads, is the most familiar of these, but other genera include Ryegrass (*Lolium*) and Fescue (*Festuca*). If the trail is overgrown, or the campsite strewn with litter, direct your comments to the B.C. Ministry of Forests (604-587-6700).

With a base elevation of only 1400 m, the Silvertip cirque is among the lowest in the southern Clearwater Valley. It is also both a cool place on a hot day and, for campers, a cold place on a warm night, owing to downdrafts from the high Trophies directly above. The cold nights partly explain the presence here of several plant species more typical of subalpine forests: False Azalea (*Menziesia ferruginea*), Mountain Rhododendron (*Rhododendron albiflorum*), Broad-leaved Arnica (*Arnica latifolia*), Lesser Twisted-stalk (*Streptopus roseus*), and Corn Lily (*Veratrum viride*).

The trail to the base of the falls is uphill all the way. The forests are old and sprucy, and the understory lush. After mid August, watch here for the raspberry-like fruits of Trailing Rubus (*Rubus pedatus*). The fruits are tangy, but edible.

The Mountain Rhododendron (Rhododendron albiflorum) *may not be showy, but it's tough. Look for it near treeline.* (RBCM)

88 RIDGE TRAIL
4 hr (8 km) return.
Elevation change: 650 m.

- BIRD WATCHING
- PLANT LOOKING
- ICE SCULPTING
- LICHEN PROBING

88 Ridge is gateway to the southeast corner of the Trophy Mountains. It is also Wells Gray's most direct route into the alpine-tundra. Be ready for steep.

The trailhead is signposted, and will be found at 1600 m at km 12.5 on the Trophy Mountain Road; keep right at km 4.0.

From the trailhead, a 15 minute hike leads you through logging slash to the edge of a virgin forest of Engelmann Spruce and Subalpine Fir. The trail climbs steeply, levelling only some 30 minutes later near the first of several small subalpine glades. En route it penetrates a fairly well-delimited band of False Azalea (*Menziesia ferruginea*) and Mountain Rhododendron (*Rhododendron albiflorum*) thickets.

Thirty minutes farther, and having left the glades behind for a drier understory of heaths and sedges, the trail rounds onto a prominent ridge. A remarkable feature of this ridge is the profusion of Meadow Spiraea

Ice Sculptures

Glaciers have shaped all the mountains of Wells Gray, and in places continue to do so. The views from 88 Ridge are an object lesson in glacial landforms. Much of what you see has resulted from a scouring of the bedrock by loose rocks caught in the undersurface of glaciers.

The scouring is greatest near the head of the glacier, where in time it carves out a deep bowl called a cirque. Several cirques are obvious on the north face of Raft Peak, just across the valley. After the ice melts away, the bottom of the cirque often contains a small lake known as a tarn. The ponds just west and north of 88 Ridge are tarns. That the Trophy Mountains are dotted with more than 50 such tarns testifies to the many glaciers which once clung to these peaks.

When glaciers form on opposite slopes of a mountain, as they they have done here, the cirques erode backward, forming sharp, razorback ridges between them, called arêtes. With just a little more carving, 88 Ridge could be called an arête.

The glacier that once occupied Spahats Valley has deepened the valley and broadened it, carving it to a somewhat U-shaped cross-section. Interestingly, the Spahats glacier was fed by a tributary glacier that filled the small valley immediately west of here. Today, the tributary valley is left hanging above the larger Spahats Valley, and so is known by just that name: a hanging valley. Not far from here, another hanging valley is marked by Silvertip Falls.

Paul Metcalfe

Meadow Spiraea
(RBCM)

(*Luetkea pectinata*) which grows here. You'll recognize this small, but attractive, rock plant by its cluster of tiny, cream-coloured flowers and finely dissected leaves. The Meadow Spiraea, a member of the Rose Family, occurs only in the mountains of western North America.

Another 15 minutes brings you to the summit of the ridge, beyond which the trail passes the Trophy Mountain Chalet: a year-round alpine shelter erected in 1988. (Make reservations by calling 604-587-6444.) Nearby, a small stream may provide a welcome lunch stop.

The chalet stands at treeline; above, the mountain slopes are open and offer easy access. Strike upward to the prominent ridge that rises to the northwest, then keep to the height of land around the head of a small valley. About an hour from the chalet, you should be standing on the summit of 88 Ridge. To the west and north, near-vertical dropoffs separate this height of land from the rest of the Trophy Mountains.

The vista from 88 Ridge is stunning: southward looms the face of Raft Mountain, a great rising wall of rock and snow; eastward lie the rolling Shuswap Highlands and, beyond them, the sawtooth profile of the Monashee Mountains; to the distant north the low summits of Battle Mountain can be discerned; and bunching together in the northwest, like so many storm-tossed waves, are the 2400 m summits of the Trophy Mountains themselves. If the day is young, these latter are invitations to further exploration.

No less spectacular than the scenery is the lichen flora of these wind-ravaged ridges. Curiously, many species are actually favoured by the strong winds here. In winter, the wind blows the ridge crests bare of snow, and so provides excellent growing conditions for many lichens rare or absent in less exposed sites. Particularly favoured are certain dark-coloured species, which absorb the sun's warmth more efficiently than lichens of paler hue.

Among the best represented lichens are the rocktripes (*Umbilicaria* spp.): small, black, papery lichens that generally grow attached to the rock by a central holdfast. About a dozen species of rocktripe can be found on 88 Ridge. If you have some water to spare, sprinkle a little of it over them, and watch (and listen to) what happens!

One of many species of rocktripe to look for on mountain summits is Umbilicaria hyperborea. (TG)

THE SHADDEN TRAIL
1.5 hr (2.5 km) return.
Elevation change: 60 m.

12.7 km
(7.9 miles)

- LAVA PROBING
- PLANT LOOKING
- SWIFTING

THE Shadden (= "Den of Shade") is an enormous grotto which has formed in the basalt cliffs below the road. It provides an excellent introduction to the volcanic history of the Clearwater Valley. The trail is steep in places, and will require some sureness of foot.

The trailhead is unmarked, but finding it should present little difficulty: from the Trophy Mountain

The horizontal bands in these basalt columns are called chisel marks; they represent short spurts of cracking as the lava cooled and contracted. (CH)

Lava pillows like these abound in Wells Gray, testifying to the existence of ancient rivers, lakes and glaciers. (CH)

(Left) Look carefully at the spaces between these rounded lava pillows, and you'll see lake-bottom mud that was long ago fired to pottery by erupting lava. (CH)

(Right) The head wall of the Shadden is stained white by mineral salts. (TG)

road, continue 1.3 km north along the park road, stopping where a guywire crosses to a single anchor pole on the downhill side. Park here, well off the road, or at the parking area just ahead on the left side.

For the first five minutes, the trail descends steeply (but not precipitously!) over the edge of the lava bench you've been driving on. Continuing, you'll soon find yourself passing beneath some impressive basalt colonnades.

Here look closely for horizontal marks running across the face of the columns. Geologists call these chisel marks. Chisel marks form when the lava cools. Because the cooling lava contracts by about 7%, it gradually splits into vertical columns. The splitting process does not happen all at once, but proceeds in small spurts, each of which is recorded as a chisel mark.

As you continue along the trail, the cliff above becomes higher and more overpowering. At the same time, the columns are replaced by lava "pillows." These pillows would be rather uncomfortable to sleep on; they are so named because that is what they look like. They form when molten lava flows into cold water.

Some of the pillows are interspersed with lumps of fired clay. Apparently the lava flowed into a temporary lake, the bottom of which was composed of mud. The pillows pressed into the mud and, in so doing, caused it to ooze upward between them. Though by now solid, the pillows were still hot enough to fire the clay, as in a kiln.

Still the trail descends, and the cliffs grow taller. Now you are walking through river and glacial deposits laid down as the lavas began to cover this valley more than half a million years ago. The lavas, in fact,

have helped to preserve evidence of a glacial period prior to the latest (Fraser) Ice Age.

The trail crosses below the Shadden, then climbs to a switchback at the base of the cliffs. Here turn left and watch the crevices for various cliff-hugging plants, supported by the same groundseeps that are undermining the Shadden to this day: Swamp Gooseberry (*Ribes lacustre*), Woodsia Fern (*Woodsia scopulina*), Smooth Cliff Brake (*Pellaea glabella*), and the tiny, delicate, yellow-flowered Chickweed Monkeyflower (*Mimulus alsinoides*).

The Shadden itself is 25 m deep and 45 m high. The trail runs along the back wall, offering picturesque views of the Clearwater Valley, framed by the sides of the grotto. The crusty white material you'll notice on the columns, and along the base of the ceiling, are mineral salts which have evaporated from seeping water.

Pillow breccia forms when underwater lava pillows break apart and tumble downslope. (CH)

Perhaps not surprisingly, birdlife along this dry hillside is in some ways more typical of the interior drybelt farther south. In season, listen for the liquid enthusiasms of the Townsend's Solitaire – a song sometimes difficult to distinguish from that of another common species here, the Western Tanager. Western Flycatchers have also been noted nesting in the walls of the Shadden, whereas a colony of White-throated Swifts – far north of their main range – nowadays lodges in the crevices of the ceiling, high out of harm's way. Listen for their excited, but descending "jejejejejeje."

FIRST CANYON CREEK

13.5 km
(8.4 miles)

OVER the next three km you will cross as many creeks, each entrenched in a narrow gorge. The bedrock is again of volcanic origin, though here it erupted along the edge of a valley-filling glacier. If you have visited the Trophy Mountains, you will have driven over the upper surface of this wedge-shaped deposit of pillow breccia.

The winds along this section of road blow hard, owing to a venturi effect created by the constricted valley walls. Because they thus dry out the soil, the winds give these slopes an uncharacteristic arid appearance. They also lead to early snowmelt. In the 1940s and 1950s, when the winter mail in Upper Clearwater used to be delivered by sleigh, the postman would often change over to wagon at this point, reverting again to sleigh north of Camp Creek at km 17.8.

**14.2 km
(8.8 miles)**

SECOND CANYON CREEK

THE narrow gorge of Second Canyon Creek is called the "Wind Tunnel." Though not very impressive from the road, it is well worth a brief stop. Be careful as you clamber down the steep embankment on the uphill side of the road. Also watch your step as you thread your way 20 m along the creek to the hidden chamber just around the corner, where the canyon walls are a castle corridor 35 m tall. On a hot afternoon, there can be few places more refreshing.

The story behind the Wind Tunnel began about 300,000 years ago with the eruption of a volcano on the mountain side above. The Clearwater Valley was at that time filled with glacial ice to a depth of about 1000 m. (You are here at 700 m). As the lava melted the ice, a slurry of freshly hardened volcanic bits and pieces flowed down the slope. Along the way, granitic boulders that had been carried in the glacier were incorporated in the slurry. When the whole mess finally hardened, it formed what geologists call pillow breccia: a sort of volcanic Christmas cake. Second Canyon Creek has since carved a small, deep gorge into the breccia, exposing the consolidated slurry.

Visible in the cliff above the road, a few metres south of the creek, is what is descriptively called "The Garter," but what is more technically called a dyke. Dykes are cracks or conduits through which magma flows upward to the earth's surface (see page 89). Here, however, the magma actually began high on the slopes above. Then, hemmed in by the valley-filling glacier, it flowed downhill through a cooling mass of pillow breccia.

If you examine the Garter closely, you'll notice its edges are black and shiny. The glassy texture reveals that the dyke flowed through the pillow breccia while the breccia was cold enough to cause rapid cooling of the dyke, but not yet hard enough to prevent the dyke from invading it. The cold pillow breccia prevented the usual crystal formation in the dyke, and resulted in glassy sideromelane (volcanic glass) instead.

The Garter is a basalt dyke fed by eruptions above and later exposed by erosion. (CH)

Notice also the miniature columns that radiate outward from the centre of the dyke. Basalt columns always form at right angles to the cooling surface; their alignment here therefore serves to re-emphasize that the dyke was enveloped in cooler rock.

THIRD CANYON CREEK

THE rocky slopes above the road are softened in early summer by the lavender, foxglove-like blossoms of Shrubby Penstemon (*Penstemon fruticosus*). Seemingly out of place on these barren outcrops, the Penstemon would soon perish if obliged to compete with other plants under less arid conditions. Though here a conspicuous ornament, it is rare farther north in Wells Gray.

Exposed in the small road cut at the south end of the bridge, watch for a grouping of perfectly preserved basalt pillows. Pillows are rounded lumps of lava that form under water. Looking closely, you'll notice that they have an outer skin made up of shiny black glass. Geologists call this substance sideromelane; it develops when water cools the lava quickly enough to prevent the formation of crystals. Other pillows, less eroded, are exposed in the canyon walls below the bridge.

A towering storehouse of seeds for winter finches, Mullein (Verbascum thapsus) is among the most tenacious of Wells Gray's introduced plants. (TG)

As you continue north along the park road, watch for tall snags rising above the trees. These are remnants of old Cedar forests; though fire-killed, they have remained standing since 1926 [see: FIRE! p 60]. Such snags are the favourite nesting places of the park's largest woodpeckers, especially the Pileated Woodpecker and the Northern Flicker.

Mule Deer tend to be common near the canyon, and particularly so in winter, when they find shelter from the deeper snows elsewhere. Watch for them along the road side.

CAMP (FAGE) CREEK

NORTH of Camp Creek stretches the Hemp Plateau: second of four volcanic plateaux and benches traversed by the Wells Gray Road en route to Clearwater Lake. Though basaltic rock underlies the road from here to Hemp Creek at km 32.8, the only sign of volcanism you're likely to notice over the next eight km are lava boulders left in the till by receding glaciers. This is this same glacial debris which obscures the volcanic origins of so much of the park.

20.2 km (12.5 miles)

BUFFALO RANCH CAMPGROUND

WHILE Bison are hardly a common sight in the Clearwater Valley, one place they can be seen – and eaten! – is Buffalo Ranch Campground. Other conveniences include cabins, tenting pads, RV sites, group campsite, electrical hookups, water, showers and, not least, Upper Clearwater's only convenience grocery store. For equine tastes, guided trail rides are also available. Open from June through October. For further information, call 604-674-3095 (fax: 604-674-3131), or write Box 1768, RR 1, Clearwater, B.C. VOE 1NO.

Fire is no stranger to Wells Gray. Here the Murtle River Valley recovers from the fire of 1926. (BCP)

Fire!

Forest fires have loomed large in the history of the Clearwater Valley, and have shaped its destiny in various ways.

The most catastrophic fire occurred on July 16, 1926, when a smouldering lightning strike on the west bank of the Clearwater River just south of here was fanned by strong south winds. Jumping the river, the fire raced upvalley and soon engulfed the entire Hemp Plateau, Green Mountain, and much of the Murtle Plateau. Another tongue continued up the Murtle River, burning almost to the subalpine in the vicinity of Stevens Lakes.

By the time the holocaust burned itself out, 540 square km later, most of the valley residents had lost their homes. They had also lost contact with the outside world, the Canyon Creek bridges having been destroyed. As to the valley itself, it was now transformed into a blackened wasteland. Everything before you was burned.

The Clearwater Valley was indeed a valley of totem poles, a valley of grey ghosts when the winds howled and moaned through the burned snags, the loose bark torn and tattered, flapping and rattling against the tree skeletons. How well I remember coming home at night as the wind howled through the trees and the rain poured down.

C. Shook (1972)

MOUL FALLS TRAIL
1.5 hr (4 km) return.
Elevation change: 100 m.

**22.2 km
(13.8 miles)**

• WATERFALLING

T HE main entrance to Wells Gray still lies some 13 km distant, at the northern end of a long, narrow corridor of private land which interrupts the general outline of the park at this point. Between here and there, however, are three other designated points of entry, including the trail which begins at this mileage.

The Moul Falls trailhead is unmarked. As a landmark, use the large garage which closely fronts the road at this mileage; the trail turns west off the road immediately south of this.

Moul Falls is an attractive Helmcken-style cascade pouring off the edge of the Hemp Plateau in a single, unbroken 35 m leap; it more than makes up for the clouds of mosquitoes that sometimes lurk along the trail. The trail, moreover, doubles as an alternative access to the Hemp Creek Canyonlands: some of the most mellow hiking in the park. More on this at km 29.9.

WELLS GRAY EDUCATION & RESEARCH CENTRE

**25.8 km
(16.3 miles)**

• LEARNING

T HE red one-room schoolhouse to the right of the road is both a thing of the past and a promise for the future. For 17 years, beginning in 1950, it served as a place of learning for the children of Upper Clearwater. Forty-two years later, in 1992, it opened its doors to a different kind of learning: outdoor education and research.

Though the schoolhouse – now called the Wells Gray Education and Research Centre (there's got to be a better name!) – is owned by the University College of the Cariboo, in Kamloops, its day-to-day operation is managed by an independent community group. The objectives of the Centre are twofold: to promote study of the park's natural history; and to help develop, especially in young people, a deeper appreciation for wild places.

Rustic accommodations are available here to groups or individuals dedicated to these objectives. The centre is open year-round. For more information, call 604-828-5467, or write Box 3010, Kamloops, B.C. v2c 5n3.

Education Wells Gray style (TG)

26.2 km
(16.3 miles)

PHILIP CREEK

O N the Hemp Plateau, the land is bony and boulder-covered. Most of the boulders you see are not volcanic in origin; they have been carried here by glaciers from the granitic and meta-morphic peaks to the east and north.

Notice how rounded the boulders are: not just in the creek, but also in the fields. The rounding tells of a time when these rocks were embedded in a glacier. The advancing ice dragged them along the ground, thus smoothing off their rough edges. Later, meltwaters running through the ice tumbled the rocks, rounding them further. When the meltwaters finally escaped the confines of the glacier and washed downstream, they deposited a vast apron of boulders which geologists call a glacial outwash plain.

Rising to the north as a low dome in the middle distance is McLeod Hill, the oldest of Wells Gray's many volcanoes. In the geologist's lingo, McLeod Hill is a tuya, that is, a volcano that erupted under a glacier. The mountains on the far northern skyline are the Goat Peaks – front-runners of the Cariboo Mountains.

The fields here, though privately owned (please observe the NO TRESPASSING signs), offer one of the most productive spots in the Clearwater Valley for hawk and owl watching. (The Ray Farm, at km 54.5, offers another). Some of the more common species include the American Kestrel, the Cooper's Hawk, the Red-tailed Hawk, the Northern Saw-whet Owl, the Great Horned Owl and the Barred Owl [see: NIGHT FLYERS, page 73].

In 1960 the Ox-eye Daisy (Leucanthemum vulgare) *was sparse in the Clearwater valley. Today this hardy Eurasion invader covers entire fields with its white ray flowers.* (TG)

BATTLE MOUNTAIN ROAD

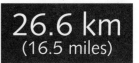

26.6 km
(16.5 miles)

THE double peaks of Battle Mountain dominate a broad expanse of upland plateaux and ridges stretching away to the south. The name Battle Mountain will be used here to include the entire landmass lying between Philip Creek to the south and the upper reaches of Hemp Creek to the north. As thus defined, Battle Mountain comprises an enormous alpine and subalpine area, quite large enough to absorb a backpacking trip of several days.

The Hoary Marmot, alias the Whistler. Listen for it in the high mountains. (BCP)

South of Philip Creek runs the long green ridge known as Table Mountain. This is the only alpine area in the park open to horse use: but do use the (unsigned) trail beginning in the vicinity of the Upper Clearwater Community Hall. For more information, call B.C. Parks (604-587-6150).

All the hikes described below – the short one to Philip Lake, the longer ones to Table Mountain and Fight Lake Meadows, and the longest one to Battle Mountain summit – begin at the end of the 7.1 km access road which turns east off pavement at this mileage.

The double summit of Battle Mountain rises from the rolling Shuswap Highlands. Pictured here is Branta Lake, just northeast of Fight Lake. (CH)

- FISHING
- PHOTOGRAPHING
- MEADOW
  RAMBLING
- LICHEN LOOKING

PHILIP LAKE TRAIL
3 hr (4 km) return.
Elevation change: 250 m.

The road to the trailhead is steep and, in places, bouldery, though manageable to most medium clearance vehicles. This is no place for motorhomes, however; if you're driving one, park it at the information kiosk at km 2.4, and add two and one-half hours to the hiking time, return.

From the trailhead, the trail ascends steeply, switchbacking some 250 m to the rim of a hanging valley, at 1600 m. The forests here date from the great fire of 1926. As you climb, notice how the Trembling Aspen and other deciduous trees gradually become smaller and sparser – an indication of the shorter growing season at this elevation. A similar gradient is also apparent on the north-facing slope across the valley, where the trees – Engelmann Spruce and Subalpine Fir – are much denser and larger below than above. There, however, the upward thinning has to do with competition from ever denser thickets of Mountain Rhododendron (*Rhododendron albiflorum*) and False Azalia (*Menziesia ferruginea*): eloquent testimony to the folly of high elevation logging.

Once at the rim of the headwall, the trail levels. Here you'll enter a virgin forest festooned with green and black hair lichens. In winter, these lichens provide food for Woodland Caribou; without them, Caribou could not survive in this portion of British Columbia. As it is, Wells Gray contains the southernmost large Caribou herd in western North America.

Lying to the west of Philip Lake are some attractive flower meadows which provide an interesting mix of subalpine and lowland species. Look for the Pink Mountain Heather (*Phyllodoce empetriformis*) blooming side by side with the Fireweed (*Epilobium angustifolium*), and the Mountain Daisy (*Erigeron peregrinus*) growing next to the Dandelion (*Taraxacum officinale*).

Why do meadows occur here, when the adjacent slopes are so heavily forested? To judge from the abundance of fire-scarred snags, part of the answer has to do with the great fire of 1926, which initially opened the meadows. The rest of the answer has to do with frost. Because the meadows are located in a shallow depression – a frost pocket – trees are able to establish only in exceptional years. And so the meadows persist.

Hair lichens come in many kinds. Learn to distinguish among them by their colours, and by the fact that some have "dandruff" (soredia), and others don't. Pictured here are Bryoria fuscescens *(left) and* Alectoria sarmentosa. (TG)

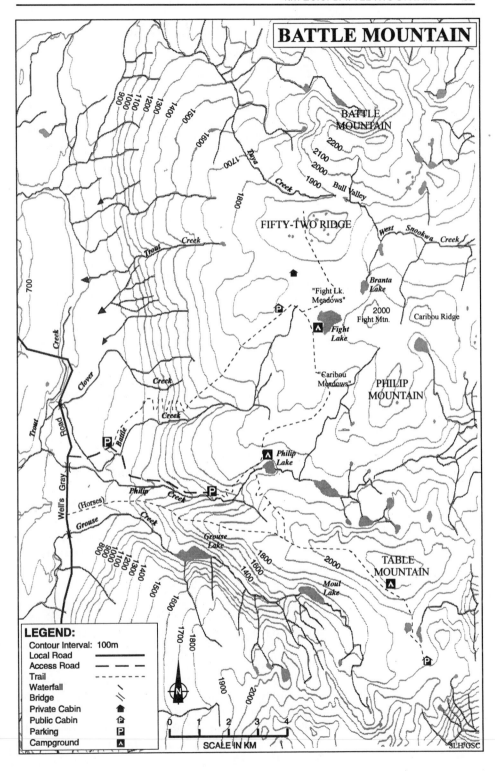

BATTLE MOUNTAIN

BATTLE
MOUNTAIN

Bull Valley

FIFTY-TWO RIDGE

West Snookwa Creek

Branta Lake

"Fight Lk. Meadows"

2000 Fight Mtn.

Caribou Ridge

Fight Lake

"Caribou Meadows"

PHILIP MOUNTAIN

Philip Lake

Philip Creek

(Horses)

Grouse Creek

Grouse Lake

Moul Lake

TABLE MOUNTAIN

Trout Creek

Clover Creek

Trout Creek

Well's Gray Road

Beate

Tuya Creek

LEGEND:
Contour Interval: 100m
Local Road
Access Road
Trail
Waterfall
Bridge
Private Cabin
Public Cabin
Parking
Campground

0 1 2 3 4

SCALE IN KM

SLH/GSC

TABLE MOUNTAIN TRAIL
9 hours (16 km) return.
Elevation change: 850 m.

Pink Mountain Heather. Heathers are at home in acid soils; fertilize them, and they die. (RBCM)

Table Mountain affords splendid views of Wells Gray's more mountainous mountains north and south.

From the west end of the meadows at Philip Lake, the Table Mountain Trail crosses Philip Creek (fill water bottles here), then roller coasters through second growth forest dating from 1926. The dips in the trail are meltwater channels left behind at the close of the last Ice Age. Mushrooms are plentiful here in early September. After 15 minutes, the trail enters oldgrowth Spruce and Fir forest and begins to climb steeply. Some minutes later, a short spur trail to the right gives a commanding view down Philip Creek Valley.

Back on the main trail again, the thickets eventually thin to small herb openings in which nodding grass-like panicles of Woodrush (*Luzula* spp.) are at home. Watch here also for Pink Mountain Heather (*Phyllodoce empetriformis*), with its diminutive "fir bough" branches.

Stay left at the next fork in the trail (the right fork leads to km 25.2 on the park road, 1500 m below), and continue upward through occasional wet meadows ditched for benefit of horses. Near treeline, 90 minutes from Philip Creek, the trail crosses to the north side of Table Mountain for views of Battle Mountain. Occupying the cirques (glacial scourings) directly below are various unnamed Philip lakes.

Some minutes later, the "distant" summit of Table Mountain comes into view. Actually the peak is much closer than it appears: the trees are dwarfed in the direction of the peak, and give a false sense of great distance. To reach the peak, leave the trail at this point, and stump 40 minutes across bouldery tundra, at the same time watching for Water Pipits and White-tailed Ptarmigan. (The trail itself crosses the ridge southward to a primitive campground 15 minutes away, and then descends through flower meadows to the damp headwaters of Grouse Creek, 200 m below).

Having once signed in at the 2200 m summit (you'll find a hikers' register in the rock cairn here), check the snowfields to the north for tracks, fur or other sign of Caribou. In summer, Caribou spend a lot of time in places like this, apparently in an effort to avoid the flies that bite them – and you.

FIGHT LAKE MEADOWS TRAIL

7 hr (18 km) return.
Elevation change: 500 m.

BATTLE MOUNTAIN SUMMIT TRAIL

2 days (30 km) return.
Elevation change: 1000 m.

- FISHING
- FLOWER
  STALKING
- BIRD WATCHING
- VOLCANO
  PROBING
- LICHEN LOOKING

To explore the subalpine meadows of Fight Lake from the end of the Battle Mountain road is the matter of a day, though admittedly a long one. To explore the double summit of Battle Mountain can also be done in a day, but better to budget for at least two days, or better still three.

These destinations can be reached by two different trails, the more strenuous of which begins at the information kiosk at km 2.4 on the Battle Mountain road. The second (recommended) trail is a continuation of the Philip Lake trail, already described.

From the meadows at Philip Lake, the trail veers northeast and enters an ancient fir-scented forest. The going, unfortunately, is very muddy in places, owing to overuse by horses, now banned from the area.

About an hour later, the trail emerges into another, larger opening, the Caribou Meadows. From here it is still another hour to Fight Lake through a series of pleasant subalpine glades. Here you are walking through what is called "inverted timberline." As at Philip Lake, the forest trees are slow to establish in the colder draws. This phenomenon intensifies as you continue upward.

Finally, round a rise, and there it is: Fight Lake and its attendant meadows. Fight Lake was stocked during the 1950s, and is (at 1800 m) the most elevated body of water in Wells Gray to contain fish. The lake is very shallow, and would presumably freeze to the bottom

Trophy Mountain summit from Table Mountain summit (TG)

except for the deep snow which settles over the ice in early winter.

This area is rich in birdlife. Among the more common summer waterfowl are the Canada Goose, Mallard, White-winged Scoter, and Barrow's Goldeneye. Hunting them are the Red-tailed Hawk and Golden Eagle, among others. The open spaces make birdwatching easy.

Consider setting up base camp here. In addition to some good tenting areas, you'll find two cabins: one a tiny hut, maintained by B.C. Parks, and available on a first-come-first-served basis; and the other a more spacious, privately operated chalet, available for booking throughout the year (call 604-587-6444). Both are sign-posted.

Fight Lake Meadows, alias "The Moors," show all the earmarks of having once been underlain by permafrost (possibly during the Little Ice Age of about 150 years ago). The shallow, angular pools near the outlet of the lake recall the polygons of high arctic landscapes. Interspersed with these are patches of what might be described as "earthen goosebumps" – unless, that is, you're a geomorphologist, in which case you'll recognize them as examples of "patterned ground," another remnant from a colder time.

From Fight Lake, allow three hours to the summit of Battle Mountain, and possibly two hours for the return. The hike there and back is 11 km, and the total elevation gain, 500 m.

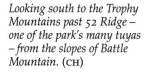

Looking south to the Trophy Mountains past 52 Ridge – one of the park's many tuyas – from the slopes of Battle Mountain. (CH)

Rising like a garden trellis between Fight Lake and the main peaks of Battle Mountain is 52 Ridge. Though the slopes of 52 Ridge are today accented by a complex

brocade of forest and meadow, its summit reveals a very different past.

52 Ridge is yet another tuya – a volcano that erupted under glacial ice. Only 125 m tall, it has the distinction of being one of the smallest tuyas in Wells Gray. It is also the only tuya whose upper surface has been more or less preserved. The deep, conical pits that pockmark its summit are craters, and the frothy, reddish coloured rocks that line the craters are called scoria.

The scoria was formed when gas-charged magma rose to the surface and fire-fountained into the air. Its existence here suggests that the ice through which the eruption occurred was thick enough to confine the

Flower Stalking

Several plant communities have been identified around Fight Lake, and these make an interesting study. In the wettest areas, you'll find fens and shallow marshes. The former are more or less permanently water-covered, whereas the latter tend to dry out by mid summer. Two species common in these wetlands are Russet Sedge (*Carex saxatilis*) and Cottongrass (*Eriophorum angustifolium*: look for snow-white cottony plumes). In the drier marshes, look also for Bluejoint Reedgrass (*Calamagrostis canadensis*) and Haircap Moss (*Polytrichum commune*: the largest upright moss in western Canada).

Lying above the marshes in level areas, are wet meadows. Here the Russet Sedge gives way to the Showy Sedge (*Carex spectabilis*: check the uppermost flowering spike, which rises above the terminal leaf on the flowering stalk), and the Small-headed Sedge (*Carex illota*: look for heads of clustered spikes). Who said sedges are hard to identify?

Slightly higher again, but still on wet ground, you'll find numerous moist, nutrient-poor meadows. Here only one plant is common: another sedge! Black Alpine Sedge (*Carex nigricans*) is easily recognized by the single, blackish flowering spike. It seems to be favoured by seasonal flooding.

Another step up (extending from Fight Lake to the summit of 52 Ridge!) brings you to the mesic meadows. These are Wells Gray's wildflower showcases, and here plant diversity is considerable. Common species include the Mountain Daisy (*Erigeron peregrinus*), Arctic Lupine (*Lupinus arcticus*), Triangle-leaved Ragwort (*Senecio triangularis*), Mountain Valerian (*Valeriana sitchensis*), and many others. In wetter spots that have been enriched by seepage, look also for Marsh Marigold (*Caltha biflora*) and Globeflower (*Trollius laxus*).

Next are the heaths, which can be found both over the summit of 52 Ridge, and (lower down) along the forest edges, usually on gentle southern exposures. Heaths mean low shrubs, and the shrubs you'll find most common here are Pink Mountain Heather (*Phyllodoce empetriformis*) and White Moss Heather (*Cassiope mertensiana*).

Finally there are the dry meadows. These occur on low ridges and dry gentle slopes, usually at some distance from the trees. Here Woolly Pussytoes (*Antennaria lanata*) are common, and give a distinct greyish cast, easily recognized. Other colonizers include the Dwarf Blueberry (*Vaccinium caespitosum*) and, among the nonflowering plants, various haircap mosses (*Polytrichum* spp.) and club lichens (e.g., *Cladonia* spp.).

(Left) 52 Ridge in an off year (TG)

(Right) The volcanic craters of 52 Ridge contain temporary ponds in early summer. Note the hikers (circle) for scale. (TG)

The White-tailed Ptarmigan has evolved to blend in with the lichen-covered rocks that are its home. (CH)

flows, yet too thin to cap them. Still, there must have been plenty of water around, for it was this which, upon coming into contact with the hot magma, caused the vents to explode, thus forming the craters.

Today you can explore nearly two dozen craters on 52 Ridge. In early summer, some are partly filled with water. Close examination soon reveals that some of the eroded scoria which lines the bottoms of the craters actually floats like pumice.

Eastward, the ridge culminates in the "Snow Leopard," a high tower of lava colonnades, so called because chemical weathering of the surface of the basalt has created numerous white splotches.

At 2300 m, the double peaks of Battle Mountain rise out of the forests into a tundra-like landscape where winter conditions are never very far away. If you're a newcomer to the mountains, it may be tempting to assume that the only things that really thrive here are the likes of snowfields and boulderbeds.

A closer look, however, will quickly reverse this impression. Even well beyond the upper limits of the Mountain Heathers (*Phyllodoce* and *Cassiope*), many flowers are still quite at home, including the magenta-covered cushions of Moss Campion (*Silene acaulis*), the reddish tassels of Mountain Sorrel (*Oxyria digyna*), and the blue thimbles of Alpine Harebell (*Campanula lasiocarpa*).

The summit of Battle Mountain is really just a high point along a long horseshoe-shaped ridge which doubles as the headwalls of a deep, narrow valley that was carved by a glacier. To the north rise the Cariboo Mountains of central Wells Gray, while to the south

loom the Trophy Mountains, poking up out of the Shuswap Highlands.

Mountain peaks are good places for perspective. Particularly sobering is the small, white lichen (resembling little scraps of shoelace) which you'll find growing among the highest windswept boulders. This is *Thamnolia vermicularis* – a species that is apparently more of a monument than the mountains it crowns.

Thamnolia is a bit of an enigma. Though it lacks reproductive organs of any kind, it occurs on the mountains of every continent on earth, save Africa. How has it managed to become so widespread? The answer seems to be that the species is very old; possibly it predates not only these mountains, but North America itself. Some lichenologists suspect that it had already evolved to its present form prior to the breakup of Pangaea, about 150,000,000 years ago. Since then it has continued to trace North America's slow incarnations without change.

The summit of Battle Mountain. Cornices can give way without warning. (TG)

Above treeline, recognize the Mountain Sorrel (Oxyria digyna) *by its reddish "tassels."* (RBCM)

Moss Campion (Silene acaulis) *survives in its mountaintop location by keeping a low profile, and out of the wind.* (TG)

27.0 km
(16.8 miles)

WELLS GRAY GUEST RANCH

O FFERED here is everything from afternoon trail rides through the Hemp Creek Canyonlands, to week-long pack trips into the subalpine of Table Mountain. Overnight guests can choose among log cabins, camping cabins, RV sites and tent pads. The Black Horse Saloon is a popular recent addition to the Ranch. For more information, call 604-674-2792 (fax: 604-674-2197), or write Kanata Wilderness Adventures, Box 1766, Clearwater, B.C. VOE 1NO.

Outside the ranch house, Cottonwoods line the park road; notice how orange their trunks are. What you're looking at is an abnormally heavy incrustation of orange peel lichens (*Xanthoria* spp.). The orange peels are apparently nitrogen-lovers; here they are colonizing in response to nitrogen (and probably calcium) from the droppings and urine of the horses in the adjacent fields.

28.2 km
(17.5 miles)

BATTLE CREEK

Spreading Dogbane (Apocynum androsaemifolium), alias Indian Hemp, grows along the cutbank at this mileage, and may have provided Battle Creek with its earlier name. (TG)

I N this part of the valley the last receding ice of the most recent Ice Age made a last stand. As evidence, notice the small tree-covered hummocks rising along the road. These are recessional moraines. They were created during periods of temporary, but significant pause in the final retreat of the glaciers. As the glaciers paused, rocks and boulders melted out to form piles of debris along the leading edge of the ice.

In the Clearwater Valley, water is never very far away. Between Battle Creek and Clearwater Village the park road passes no fewer than 20 mapped water courses – 18 of which occur within the last 12 km.

Given such a confusion of waterways, it is not surprising that many of the valley's streams have carried different names at different times. Battle Creek, for example, appeared on the first map of the valley in 1912 as Hemp Creek – presumably in recognition of the "Indian Hemp" which still thrives on the nearby hillsides. Since then, however, that name has migrated westward to a somewhat larger stream (see km 32.8), formerly known as the Little Clearwater River.

NAKISKA RANCH

NAKISKA Ranch, one km north of here on Trout Creek Road, is a 300 ha working cattle ranch. The owners offer well-appointed rooms and log cabins set amidst some of the most arresting scenery in the valley. Scan the meadows here for hawks and owls [see: NIGHT FLYERS]. For more information, phone 604-674-3655, or write Box 1763, Clearwater, B.C. V0E 1N0.

At Trout Creek, 0.5 km north of this junction, the Wells Gray Road leaves the Hemp Plateau to climb to the top of Mailbox Ridge – a southward arm of the volcanic Murtle Plateau (km 37.7). Over the next three km, especially in spring, scan the road edges for Mule Deer and Black Bear. In winter, watch here also for Moose.

Night Flyers

When the sun sets behind the western mountains, a whole new cast of woodland creatures emerges for the nightshift, including, in summer, Deer Mice, Flying Squirrels, bats, moths and, above all, owls.

Wells Gray is home to at least eight kinds of owls, from the tiny Northern Pygmy-owl, no bigger than a large sparrow, to the great Great Horned Owl, with a wingspan of almost 1.5 m.

Owls are superbly adapted to life in the dark. Their eyes, of course, are huge, and specially shaped to be sensitive in very dim light. Most owls, furthermore, are able to capture their prey using only sound clues. In Northern Saw-whets, the right ear is larger and placed higher on the head then the left ear; this enables them to pinpoint the source of sound with deadly accuracy. And, because loudly flapping wings might drown the sound of a distant mouse stepping on dried leaves, the wing feathers have a comb-like leading edge and a soft pile surface to ensure a silent flight.

The owl you are most likely to see by day is the Northern Pygmy-owl. Because of its habit of eating small birds, the "Pygmy" is often mobbed by flocks of chickadees, nuthatches and kinglets, which are intent on keeping the enemy in their sights, and on pestering it until it decides to move on. This phenomenon is useful in calling small birds out of the forest: simply imitate the owl's call, a whistled "kook" repeated once every five seconds or so. With luck, a Pygmy-owl will show up as well.

The best time to see an owl, however, is at night. All that's required is a flashlight and a little knowledge of owl calls. Happily, owl calls are easily imitated and, if done convincingly, can serve to bring the owl into view.

The Saw-whet utters a simple, whistled song (about two short whistles per second), which is usually only heard during the breeding season from March through June. More long-winded is the Barred Owl, whose call can be heard at intervals throughout the summer. Listen for a low-pitched, nasal "Who-cooks-for-you; who-cooks-for-YOU-awll."

Dick Cannings

29.9 km
(18.6 miles)

- FISHING
- CANYON
  PROBING
- CREEK FORDING
- HOODOOING
- WARBLING

HEMP CREEK CANYONLANDS TRAIL
2.5 – 8 hr (8 to 13 km) return.
Elevation change: 20 to 275 m.

A N inauspicious pulloff near the top of Mailbox Ridge marks the trailhead to Hemp Creek Canyonlands. From here, it would be hard to guess that only a few kilometres distant are waterfalls, hoodoos, mesas, precipices, hogback ridges, and narrow defiles – some of the most engaging hiking terrain in Wells Gray Park.

This is a land of Paper Birch and Trembling Aspen. Treat yourself to a hike here in early October, when the leaves are hanging apricot.

You can reach the Canyonlands from three places along the park road: at km 22.2; at km 27.0; and here. The km 27.0 access is through the Wells Gray Ranch. At time of writing, the Ranch managers encourage visitors to explore the Canyonlands by this route – an offer which enormously enhances the accessibility of this area to the average hiker. They request, however, that hikers check in at the office.

The Canyonlands trail system is intricate. You will probably prefer to select your own route from among the many possible hiking circuits. Here are some pointers:

Autumn in Hemp Creek Canyonlands (TG)

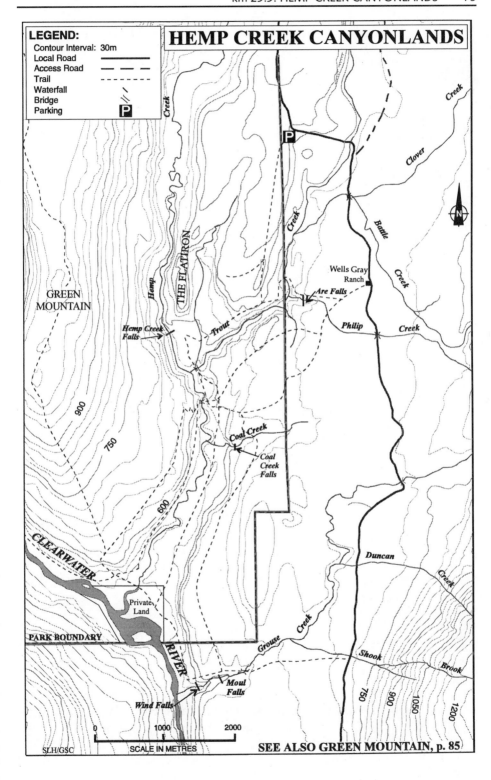

LEGEND:
Contour Interval: 30m
Local Road
Access Road
Trail
Waterfall
Bridge
Parking

HEMP CREEK CANYONLANDS

Creek

Clover Creek

Creek

Battle Creek

Wells Gray Ranch

Are Falls

GREEN MOUNTAIN

THE FLATIRON

Hemp

Trout

Philip Creek

Hemp Creek Falls

900

750

Coal Creek

Coal Creek Falls

600

Duncan Creek

CLEARWATER

Private Land

PARK BOUNDARY

RIVER

Grouse Creek

Shook

Brook

Moul Falls

750 900 1050 1200

Wind Falls

0   1000   2000

SLH/GSC   SCALE IN METRES

SEE ALSO GREEN MOUNTAIN, p. 85

The Flatiron is an outcropping lava flow distinctive for its long, symmetrical columns. (CH)

The walls of Trout Creek Canyon are composed of a soft metamorphic rock called phyllite. In some places phyllite is blue in colour, and in others pink. (TG)

- From the Canyonlands trailhead to the Moul Creek trailhead (km 22.2), allow approximately six hours; to this add another 90 minutes for the 5.6 km road walk back to Mailbox Ridge.
- The hike from the Canyonlands trailhead to the Wells Gray Ranch can easily be completed in under three hours; to this, however, add another 30 minutes if you intend to walk the road back to the trailhead.
- Not all creek crossings are bridged (see map). Ask about stream conditions at the Wells Gray Ranch.
- Unmarked trails make it is easier to come out at the Wells Gray Ranch than to go in that way.

After an hour's walk through Lodgepole Pine and Douglas-fir, a view of the Clearwater Valley opens to the south, with the dome-like summit of 2600 m Dunn Peak occupying centre stage on the horizon.

Here take the short spur trail to the right for a first view of the Flatiron. The Flatiron is a remnant of an ancient lava flow that once filled an earlier version of Hemp Creek Valley. One million, four hundred thousand years in age, this flow is roughly three times older than most of the park's other lava flows. Hemp Creek has cut deeply into the flow to the west of the Flatiron, whereas to the east the lava was similarly eroded away by an earlier version of Trout Creek. The Flatiron is what remains in between. Most of the downcutting occurred as receding Pleistocene glaciers were unleashing huge quantities of meltwater. Since then, Trout Creek has removed to the next valley east of here, leaving its original valley high and dry.

The intricate pattern of columns in the massive flow that forms the Flatiron suggests that the lava here cooled very slowly. These columns are among the most slender and best developed in the park. Some of them are 20 m tall, though only 10 to 15 cm in diameter. They have been peeling off the cliffs ever since they were exposed, thus building up an apron of talus at the base.

As you gaze across the valley at the Flatiron, you may notice that the talus at its base is distinctly lobed – as though it had once actually flowed. And so perhaps it did.

Only in the lowlands do deciduous trees really thrive, and nowhere more so than in the Hemp Creek Canyonlands. Listen here for warblers and vireos of many kinds. (TG)

Talus made up of broken basalt columns tends to be very open. In winter, the interspaces become filled with cold air which, because it is relatively heavy, is not soon displaced by the warmer, lighter air of summer; this is called Balsh ventilation. During the Little Ice Age of 150 years ago, the air in the talus slope may never have warmed at all. Any ground water trickling through the rocks would have frozen, filling in the cracks with ice. When enough ice had built up within, the talus would have begun to flow: a rock glacier!

As you hike the Canyonlands, watch for four different kinds of club moss, each with its spore-filled clubs (strobili). Pictured here is Ground-cedar (Lycopodium complanatum). (RBCM)

Head back now to the main trail, and follow it off the south end of Mailbox Ridge until it branches. Here a left turn leads, in succession, to Trout Creek Canyon (breathtaking views), to Trout Creek crossing (no bridge), to Philip Creek Canyon (more fine vistas), to Are Falls (a miniature Helmcken), and finally to the park road at the Wells Gray Ranch. If you have only three hours to spend exploring the Canyonlands, spend them here.

A right turn at the fork leads you deeper into the Canyonlands. Notice that the rocks along the canyon rim are foliated, like the pages of a book. These are a kind of metamorphic rock called phyllite (after the Greek "phyllos"– leaf); they belong to the Kaza Group.

The Kaza Group phyllites began perhaps 750 million years ago as mud at the bottom of an ocean. Later the mud was buried, and changed into rock called mudstone. The mudstone, in turn, was subjected to tremendous heat and pressure which, over time, transformed the grains within it into leaf-like minerals such as mica. It's the mica that imparts the layered look to the rock.

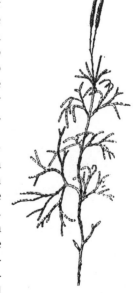

Wild Sarsaparilla (Aralia nudicaulis) *is widespread in mixed forests throughout the park. Though somewhat resembling Poison Ivy, it is entirely harmless.* (NONC)

These slopes are a favourite wintering grounds for some of the park's 820 Moose and 650 Mule Deer. Here the snows come late, usually not until the latter part of November, and disappear early, often in March.

Also at home is the Ruffed Grouse, a chicken-like bird favoured by the relatively warmer (and drier) climate of the Canyonlands. The precocial young leave the nest within a few hours of hatching, and so are especially vulnerable to cold and wet. They remain with the mother until autumn; watch for family groups.

Descending farther, the trail passes close by the south end of the Flatiron, providing a convenient point from which to explore its basalt columns. Should you decide to proceed cross-country, beware! Poison Ivy (*Toxicodendron rydbergii*) lurks among the talus boulders here – one of only two localities in the park. You'll easily recognize this low, semi-shrubby, rash-producing plant by committing to memory the old adage: LEAVES IN THREE; LEAVE IT BE!

Now about 90 minutes from the park road, and having descended into a narrow gulch, the trail finally crosses Trout Creek on a sturdy footbridge. Below the bridge a rough sidetrail leads to Trout Creek's confluence with Hemp Creek, only a few metres downstream.

The ground here is wet in places, and supports lush colonies of two wetland species more common farther north in the park: Skunk Cabbage (*Lysichiton americanum*), recognized by the tropical-rain-forest proportions of its leaves; and Devil's Club (*Oplopanax horridus*), whose spine-covered stems and leaves will surely need no introduction.

Words to Warble by

In these woodlands, dominated by Paper Birch, warblers find insect pablum aplenty with which to feed their young. From late May through mid July, the woods ring with their singing. Listen for:

- the Orange-crowned Warbler: a descending trill, often rising at the end.
- the MacGillivray's Warbler: a methodical "Sweet-sweet-sugar-sugar," or the reverse.
- the Nashville Warbler: "SibibiSibi-titititi."

- the Yellow-rumped Warbler: "Chory-chory-chory-chory-chee-chee," and other operatic warbles.
- the American Redstart: "One-two-three-four-*five*-six" or "See-be-See-be-See-be" or other similar songs.
- the Magnolia Warbler: "One-two. One-two-three."
- the Northern Waterthrush: "Wheat-Wheat-Wheat-Sweet-Sweet-Sweet-chew-chew-chew." (The breakfast cereal song.)
- the Yellow Warbler: a bright, sunlit "Tsee-tsee-tsee-tsee-Titi-wee," or other similar songs.

South of Trout Creek bridge, the trail becomes a maze of intersecting pathways (see map). To get to Moul Falls, choose here among four possible routes: two lower, and two upper. The two lower trails roughly parallel the east and west banks of Hemp Creek. The latter is more scenic. Having briefly hugged the east bank of the creek (dramatic country, this), the trail crosses on a bridge to the other side, then continues down creek for another hour, past talus slopes, pillow breccia pillars, and open Douglas-fir woodlands unique in the park. Watch for Mule Deer, or possibly even White-tailed Deer.

More scenic still are the Coal Creek and Hoodoo Rim Trails, which climb, respectively, to the east and west volcanic rims overlooking the valley. At any of several lookouts along both these trails, you are standing on 150 m of pillow lava: evidence that the lake that once occupied this valley was briefly transformed into a steaming cauldron. At Coal Creek Falls, the lava is much older than elsewhere in the Clearwater Valley, perhaps dating from the Eocene, roughly 45 to 50 million years ago. This was a period of widespread volcanic eruption in western North America.

If it's a Warbler with a "window" on its tail, it's either an American Redstart or, as above, a Yellow-rumped. (TG)

Both the West Hemp and the Hoodoo Rim Trails intercept the Green Mountain River Trail (see page 90) at the south end of Green Mountain; here turn south (left), and continue downhill to the mouth of Hemp Creek. En route the trail passes through a riverine forest of enormous Black Cottonwoods. Excellent habitat, this, for Black Bear: watch for their telltale claw marks on the trunks of the trees, not to mention in the sandy beach at riverside.

The dipping beds of pillow lava pictured here tell of a lake which once filled Hemp Creek Valley. (CH)

Strange to relate, the cabin at the mouth of Hemp Creek now belongs to the Catholic Church of Canada. (TG)

Moul Falls offers abundant opportunity for getting abundantly soaked. (TG)

You'll find no bridge at Hemp Creek: to continue south, either ford the creek (which can be tricky) or cross on a log – assuming you can find one. Again, check with B.C. Parks or the Wells Gray Ranch for an update of conditions.

South of Hemp Creek, the West Hemp Trail joins the East Hemp Trail at an old fisherman's cabin, once owned by H.R. MacMillan (now of Vancouver Planetarium fame). Here you may wish to loop north either back to the Hemp Creek Canyonlands trailhead at km 29.9, or to the Wells Gray Ranch: should you decide in favour of the latter route, be prepared to ford Philip Creek. In either event, allow at least three hours for the return.

The trail to Grouse Creek (and km 22.2 of the park road) turns east from the cabin toward an impressive line of basalt cliffs. Turn right at the next intersection, and follow the trail south along the base of the cliffs. You are now crossing private land; please obey the signs. The owners particularly ask that hikers not approach the Clearwater River Chalet, located below the trail, and overlooking the river. For more information, call 1-800-667-9552, or else write to Clearwater River Chalet, 250 Lansdowne Street, Kamloops, B.C. v2c 1x7.

Now begins the long, steady ascent to the Hemp Plateau, some 250 m above; follow the signs to Moul Falls. To help make the climb less arduous, listen for Townsend's Solitaires, holding forth in long, warbled soliloquy.

Should the day be young, consider making a half-hour side trip to the base of an oh-so-refreshing waterfall. To do so, turn right (downstream) on the south (far) side of the Grouse Creek bridge, then follow the trail five minutes to the brink of Moul Falls. There are no safety fences here, so take care. Another ten minutes later, and you're standing at the base of a 35 m column of falling water – with the heady option of proceeding *behind* the falls to a grotto on the far side, plush-carpeted in leafy liverworts.

Back at the brink of Moul Falls, budget about 45 gradual uphill minutes to the park road. Keep to the south of the creek.

CORRAL ROAD

32.0 km
(19.9 miles)

T HE turnoff to Corral Road marks the upper end of a sequence of buried sands and gravels that culminates, near the bottom of the hill, in a blackish fossil-bearing outcrop [see: BURIED ALIVE]. Northward, it commands a first clear view of the Murtle Plateau

Pyramid Mountain as seen from Hemp Creek. What seems to be a smaller cone on the right flank of this volcano is really a landslide. (TG)

Buried Alive

The sediments preserved in the cutbank between Corral Road and Hemp Creek bridge belong to the Chu Chua Formation, and date from a warmer time 45 to 50 million years ago.

Imagine a tepid, muggy swamp occupying a hummocky valley floor. Through the middle of the swamp, and shaded by the branches of Walnut trees, Beech, Ginkgo, Sequoia and Bald Cypress, runs a stream. Most of each year this stream is much like the Hemp Creek of today: a brisk, meandering brook narrowly contained between steep banks. During the wet season, however, its swollen waters pour out across the swamp, depositing a heavy sediment of silts, sands and gravels.

First to settle out are the gravels, which are confined mostly to the streambed itself. In the adjacent swamp, the receding floodwaters leave behind a much finer sediment of silt. The silt buries grass, leaves, twigs, logs and other organic debris that has accumulated over the previous year. Eventually a particularly vigorous flood flushes a layer of coarser material into the swamp, so covering the finer sediments already laid down.

As the layers of sediment deepen, their accumulating weight eventually transforms the grasses, leaves, and logs into coal. At the same time the silt is compacted into siltstone, the sand into sandstone, and the gravel into conglomerate. The greenish quartz-veined rock near the top of the hill records a knob of greenstone around which the stream once meandered. Much later, this complex history of flooding is exposed by the downcutting of Hemp Creek.

Near the bottom of the hill, watch for a bulging outcrop of blackish siltstone. The dark coloration reflects the presence of organic material. Recorded here are the imprints of leaves of trees whose descendants now grow thousands of km farther south. All this, and more, is revealed to the discerning eye in the cutbank below Corral Road.

and, rising out of it, Pyramid Mountain. Both plateau and mountain will be described in detail at km 41.2 and km 42.0, respectively.

The "corral" in Corral Road harkens to a time, during the 1950s, when the park's wildlife biologists built a corral near here for tagging and studying Moose. Strange to relate, Jerry the Moose, B.C. Park's mascot, lived for time in a Moose corral not far from here.

*The original
Jerry the Moose
(BH)*

*Some exotic fossils to
watch for in the road cut
below Corral Road. The
fossils are of low quality,
but nevertheless provide
invaluable insight into the
Hemp Creek of 50 million
years ago. Be gentle. (WT)*

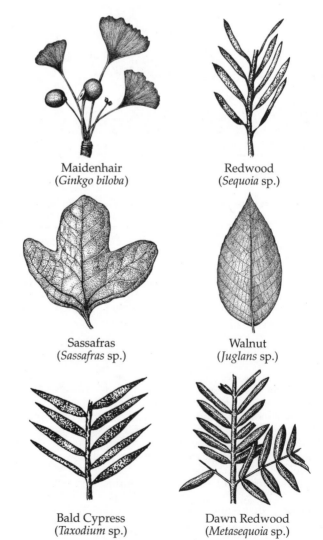

Maidenhair
(*Ginkgo biloba*)

Redwood
(*Sequoia* sp.)

Sassafras
(*Sassafras* sp.)

Walnut
(*Juglans* sp.)

Bald Cypress
(*Taxodium* sp.)

Dawn Redwood
(*Metasequoia* sp.)

HEMP CREEK

32.8 km
(20.4 miles)

A T Hemp Creek, the sedimentary rocks of the Chu Chua Formation of Corral Road (page 81) give way to the very different rocks of the Kaza Group. In the roadcut here you'll see foliated rock similar in appearance to the phyllites already discussed in connection with Trout Creek Canyon (km 29.9). These rocks, however, owe their leaf-like structure to a very different geologic process: grinding.

To understand what happened here, it helps to know that a large fault trends along the Clearwater Valley. Movement along the fault has milled the adjacent rocks over a long period, in some cases causing new minerals to form parallel to the plane of motion. When the minerals involved are micas, the rock acquires a platy structure, and may resemble phyllite, but is called phyllonite.

HELMCKEN FALLS LODGE

34.6 km
(21.5 miles)

H ELMCKEN Falls Lodge is arguably the most established of Wells Gray's satellite tourist accommodations. Built in 1948, only nine years after the park was created, this rustic log building has had a long tradition of catering to the needs of Wells Gray's visitors. The lodge is renowned as much for its fine views and warm hospitality as for its verandas abuzz with Rufous and Calliope Hummingbirds.

Guided hiking, canoeing, whitewater rafting, skiing, snowshoeing and dogsledding: these are only a few of the activities available at (and from) the lodge. Also offered – both at the lodge and across the road, at Stillwater Horseback Adventures – are guided horseback rides of differing endurance.

Overnight guests can choose from a wide assortment of rooms, or may prefer to camp out in the tent and RV spaces provided. The lodge has a licensed dining room, lounge and gift shop, while the campground is equipped with water and electrical hookup, as well as showers. For more information, phone or fax 604-674-3657, or write: Box 239, Clearwater, B.C. V0E 1N0.

You are now approaching the entrance to Wells Gray. Standing outside the Lodge, and seeming rather out of place beside the road, is a solitary pay phone. Henceforward this will provide your closest 24 hour link with the outside world.

35.8 km
(22.2 miles)

WELLS GRAY PARK ENTRANCE

A LEVEL spot in the road, a pull-off, and an information kiosk – these constitute the main portal to one of Canada's grandest wilderness parks. Here you might wish to sign in at the register board, pick up a park brochure, find out about the naturalist programmes, or put the finishing touches on your itinerary for exploring the park.

In that itinerary, be sure to incorporate the next side trip covered at km 36.2.

36.2 km
(22.5 miles)

GREEN MOUNTAIN ROAD

- OVERVIEWING
- FAULT FINDING
- MOOSE MANAGING

T HE side road which begins at the foot of the first hill past the park entrance leads to the Green Mountain viewing tower, some 3.5 km distant, and 250 m above. En route, at km 2.6, it also passes the White Horse Bluff trailhead, doubling as the trailhead to the Green Mountain River Trail.

The viewing tower is a sturdy 10 m-tall gazebo commanding a superb panorama of southern Wells Gray. On display are several panels depicting and naming the park's major valleys, lakes, volcanoes and mountains. Nearby are four picnic tables and outhouses, but no water.

Though steep in sections, the Green Mountain road is passable to most vehicles, including motorhomes. In winter, the road is effectively closed owing to deep snow, and most years it remains so until the second week of May.

Green Mountain Viewing Tower: don't miss it. (TG)

The view from the tower reveals that Green Mountain rises near the south end of a broadening in the Clearwater Valley, here nearly 20 km across. This broadening is the Murtle Plateau. Southward, by contrast, the valley narrows to a mere gap, less than 500 m from wall to wall. The varying width is controlled by two geological faults which together run the length of the valley.

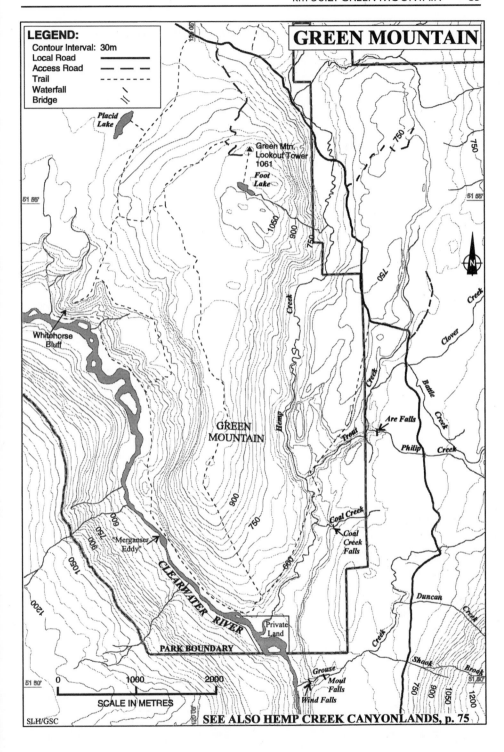

LEGEND:

Contour Interval: 30m	
Local Road	
Access Road	
Trail	
Waterfall	
Bridge	

GREEN MOUNTAIN

Placid Lake

Green Mtn. Lookout Tower 1061

Foot Lake

Whitehorse Bluff

GREEN MOUNTAIN

Creek

Hemp

Trout

Are Falls

Philip Creek

Battle Creek

Clover Creek

"Merganser Eddy"

CLEARWATER RIVER

Coal Creek

Coal Creek Falls

Duncan Creek

Shook Brook

PARK BOUNDARY

Private Land

Grouse

Moul Falls

Wind Falls

0   1000   2000

SCALE IN METRES

SLH/GSC

SEE ALSO HEMP CREEK CANYONLANDS, p. 75

The faults are offset such that the more southerly one parallels the park road along the east side of the valley, and ends just north of McLeod Hill. The north fault begins west of Green Mountain, and runs northward along the west side of the valley, passing the east end of Mahood Lake. In the overlapping region between the two faults, the land appears to have dropped by as much as 1000 m, forming the widening in the valley, and hence the Murtle Plateau. By contrast, the more narrow Clearwater Valley south of here (and north of Clearwater Lake) represents a single fault. Weakened by movement along this fault, the rocks have been worn away by water and ice to form a narrow gap.

From near the base of the tower, a trail leads to Foot Lake. This walk can be completed in under an hour and features Beaver lodges, Yellow Pond-lilies (*Nuphar polysepalum*), Labrador Tea (*Ledum groenlandicum*) and a finely framed vista of the Trophy Mountains. Standing along the lake shore, notice how soft and muddy the lake bottom is – and how devoid of green plants. This is an artifact of many decades of unvarying water levels.

They Came With Fire

The Moose is a relatively recent arrival into southern British Columbia. Joseph Hunter, a surveyor, and apparently the first non-native to visit the Clearwater Valley, in 1877, comments on its bountiful Caribou, Deer and Bear, but makes no mention of Moose. It wasn't, in fact, until half a century later that the first Moose turned up. The year was 1923.

Three years later, fire swept up the Clearwater Valley from Spahats, destroying 540 square km of lowland forests. The destruction, though catastrophic, was good news for the valley's newest (and brawniest) resident. By 1930, in response to the fire, dense thickets of Falsebox, Red Osier Dogwood, Thimbleberry, Soopalallie and, especially, Willow were establishing. These soon transformed the valley into a Moose's smorgasbord.

The Moose were quick to multiply. By 1940 more than a thousand animals inhabited the valley. Not that they dined on valley-bottom browse all year long: during the summer months their appetites carried them 500 to 1000 m higher to the rolling terrain of the adjacent highlands – lush, roomy and, above all, cool. Only with the deepening snows of autumn and early winter did the Moose reluctantly straggle into the fire-scarred landscape that provided an essential wintering grounds.

By the early 1950s, wildlife biologists were on the scene, studying the Moose herds, now nearly 3000 animals strong, and later attempting to manage both the herds and the hundreds of hunters who were now converging on the park every autumn.

In both assignments the biologists, led by Yorke Edwards and Ralph Ritcey, were assiduous: they tracked Moose, tagged Moose, counted Moose droppings, performed autopsies on Moose, evaluated Moose parasites, weighed Moose browse, and even sat out lonely vigils watching Moose eat, timing every mouthful from dawn to dusk.

WHITE HORSE BLUFF TRAIL
4 hr (11 km) return.
Elevation change: 200 m.

- VOLCANO PROBING
- HAWK WATCHING
- WILLOW BROWSING

White Horse Bluff is a volcano, albeit a peculiar one. More resembling a breached hydro dam than a volcanic cinder cone, the bluff juts westward from the flanks of Green Mountain, terminating at a point some two-thirds of the way across the Clearwater Valley. Flowing serenely past, more than 250 m below, is the Clearwater River.

The trail to White Horse Bluff leaves the Green Mountain Road from a sharp bend at km 2.6, and is clearly signposted. Carry drinking water and mosquito repellent. An alternate trail, which adds 1 km to the hiking distance, but shaves 150 m off the elevation change, commences at the Placid lake trailhead (km 36.5).

Over most of its length the trail keeps to an old grader track. At first the route is fairly level, but after some 30 minutes from the trailhead the track forks (keep right here), then descends steeply through a pleasant forest of Paper Birch and Trembling Aspen. This is good Black Bear and Mule Deer habitat. A half

Out of these studies came the somber realization that the park's Moose, each of which consumes up to 20 kg of browse every day, were in danger of eating themselves out of existence. At densities of up to 19 animals per square km during the winter months, the Moose were already consuming at least three-quarters of the year's growth. Thus it appeared that if the Moose were allowed to multiply further, the whole support system would collapse, and the Moose with it.

For this reason, a major advertising campaign was undertaken to attract even more Moose hunters to Wells Gray. Soon the park would become renowned as one of the finest hunting grounds in North America. And so, apparently, it was: in some years more than 300 Moose were shot here.

The overall effect of the hunters, however, was simply to forestall the final decline of Moose in Wells Gray. Though effective in controlling Moose populations themselves, hunting could do nothing against the innumerable conifer saplings which, 30 years after the fire, were now established throughout the winter range. As the conifers – Spruce, Pine, Douglas-fir and others – grew to overtower the shrubs on which the Moose had browsed, they began to choke them out. Forest succession was now in its second phase, en route to a conifer climax which, in time, would certainly all but eliminate Wells Gray's erstwhile mascot.

In response, a decision was made to set fire to the regenerating forests. From 1966 through 1971, ten fires were lit in the park, consuming a total of 1700 ha. The McLeod Hill burn of 1967 is clearly visible from the Viewing Tower.

In general, the plan worked. Two decades later, the burns still support healthy thickets of Willow and other browse species. The park's Moose population is also healthy, and has stabilized at about 900 animals, most of which now winter on these man-made clearings.

White Horse Bluff is the remnant of a volcano that began as cataclysmic explosions under an ancient lake. (TG)

Broad, rounded wings. Rust-coloured tail. The adult Red-tail is among the most easily recognized of hawks. (TG)

hour later, and about 200 m lower, the trail finally eases onto White Horse Bluff. Good views to the north.

The trail now crosses to a fork along the south rim of the bluff. Here the view gives out southward over the west flank of Green Mountain. Lining its base, you'll notice a narrow bench of flat-lying lavas. This is a remnant of the volcanic outpourings that once extended across the valley, encasing much of White Horse Bluff, and perhaps helping to preserve it.

From here the main trail turns left, and slowly descends, over the next 2.5 hours, to the Clearwater River. Instead, take the right fork for an easy ten-minute stroll to the snout of the buff. Along the way, watch for Red-tailed Hawks and Bald Eagles playing the thermals above you.

As already mentioned, White Horse Bluff is a volcano with a difference. That difference has to do with a lake that occupied the Clearwater Valley 600,000 years ago. White Horse Bluff erupted from under that lake.

Just why a lake occupied the valley at that time may never be known. Perhaps it formed when lavas flowing down Hemp Creek Valley dammed the Clearwater River just downstream. Or maybe the lake backed up behind a tongue of glacial ice. What is certain is that the lake was deep, its surface some 250 m above the present valley floor.

As the incandescent magma rose to the surface of the earth, it encountered water-saturated sediment at the bottom of the lake; the resulting explosions shattered the lava, sending billowing clouds of steam and debris high into the air. The particles eventually settled, depositing a layer of shattered basaltic glass at the bottom of the lake – only to be blasted upward

(Left) The Rock Roses are really remnants of dykes that fed the final phases of eruption at White Horse Bluff. (TG)

(Right) Here author Cathie Hickson examines the lower edge of a dyke that erupted through an already deposited layer of tuff breccia. (TG)

again by another explosion, as yet more magma was erupted. That process – eruption, shattering and deposition – was repeated over and over, building up layer upon layer of tuff breccia.

As the volcano grew, the rising magma cut dykes through the newly deposited layers. Because the layered material was relatively cold, it caused the margins of the dykes to harden into small columns. Today, these columns – the internal plumbing of the volcano – have been exposed through erosion; view them from below the snout of the bluff, where they form intricate starburst patterns locally called Rock Roses.

To reach the Rock Roses, first descend through a (steep!) gully along the south edge of the bluff, just west of where the trail forks. Then carefully make your way along the base of the cliffs to the snout. Allow another two hours return. Take care to avoid the Poison Ivy (*Toxicodendron rydbergii*) that grows on the slopes just below the base of the cliffs.

In keeping with the warm, south-facing slopes, the vegetation contains outliers from the dry interior. Rocky Mountain Juniper (*Juniperus scopulorum*) grows at the snout of the bluff, and the groundcover is composed mostly of Bluebunch Wheatgrass (*Agropyron spicatum*). The sandy soil here was up-blown onto the bluff by high winds during deglaciation.

On the branches of the nearby Douglas-firs, look for various "dry belt" lichens, including impressive brownish tresses of Edible Horsehair Lichen (*Bryoria fremontii*: once an important winter staple of the province's inland native peoples, and bright yellow tufts of Wolf Lichen (*Letharia vulpina*).

Wolf Lichen (Letharia vulpina) *contains vulpinic acid, and is mildly poisonous. In Scandinavia it was once mixed with ground glass, and sprinkled over wolf bait – apparently to good effect. Hence the name.* (TG)

GREEN MOUNTAIN RIVER TRAIL
13 hours (27 km) return.
Elevation change: 580 m.

Hike this trail in early spring, when the Cottonwoods are fragrant with burgeoning buds. Or again in autumn, when the Aspen leaves hang yellow and apricot. Be sure to carry water with you.

The distance and elevation given above are based on a loop hike from the White Horse Bluff trailhead to the south flank of Green Mountain, then back again along its crest. Shorter (and in some ways more interesting) routes are also feasible. If there are two vehicles in your party, consider leaving one of them at the Grouse Creek Trailhead (km 22.2); doing so abbreviates the hike to 9 hours and 19 km (total elevation change: 350 m), and makes for a satisfying, albeit rather lengthy, day hike.

The Green Mountain River Trail is a continuation of the White Horse Bluff Trail (page 87). From the south rim of the bluff, the trail swings southeast across a sandy slope, and onto the rim of a volcanic escarpment. Flowing past in the valley below, the Clearwater River seems tantalizingly near. Even so, it is still more than two hours distant by trail. Be patient, enjoy the views, the birds, the Moose droppings. . . .

These slopes were set on fire in 1971, in an attempt to create wintering habitat for Moose. Nowadays the most common woody plants are willow and Trembling Aspen – the Moose's favourite winter browse. Conifers have taken longer to get established, in part because their seeds are heavier, and not as easily carried into the centre of the burn.

Had you been standing here during the late 1940s, the view would have looked much the same. Then too the valley was recovering from fire. In those days, however, willow covered not just these recent burns, but some 540 square km of the lower Clearwater Valley.

In 540 square km of slowly healing burn grew a hundred million willow bushes. Every year these produced about two and one-quarter million km of new growth, one and one-half million km of which were consumed by 2000 Moose, each eating about 22 kg of willow stems a day. This ecological relationship between willow and Moose was the secret of Moose abundance in the valley [see: MOOSE UNLIMITED].

The Clearwater River passes directly beneath the snout of White Horse Bluff. Note the man-made burn on Green Mountain, upper left. (TG)

Moose Unlimited

In about 540 square km of burn, the most common woody plant was willow. Over most of this large area it was difficult for a Moose to stand anywhere that was more than six m from a vigorous willow bush. In each of those square kilometres, willows were producing about 4300 km of new stems per year and Moose were eating, each year, about three-quarters of this annual growth.

Late each winter the heavily browsed pastures were composed of battered and broken willow bushes thoroughly clipped by the hungry animals. They missed no accessible bushes. Yet the willows thrived on it, and this annual mutilation stimulated them to produce even more growth the next summer.

Think of it. Ninety-one thousand kg of Moose were built, repaired and powered by the partial conversion, daily, of 45,000 kg of vegetation, most of it tender, but woody, willow stems.

R.Y. Edwards

Redstem Ceanothus has three-veined leaves that are sickly sweet when crushed. (NONC)

Keep an eye and nostril open for thigh-high Ceanothus shrubs of two species. Both have oval, three-veined leaves that are sticky and sickly sweet. Snowbrush (*Ceanothus velutinus*) leaves are evergreen and glossy, whereas Redstem Ceanothus (*Ceanothus sanguinarius*) leaves are deciduous and dull. These shrubs depend on fire for germination: only when heated does the seed coat become permeable to water. Their presence reminds yet again that fire swept these slopes not long ago.

Ninety switchbacking minutes from White Horse Bluff, the trail forks; here keep left – unless you'd like to preview the river at a primitive campground five minutes upstream, or explore the base of the bluff, 30 minutes farther. (Hint: perfectly obvious along this trail is the reason for the name "White Horse Bluff"; disregard whatever competing theories you may have heard.)

Otherwise, keep left. Ten minutes later, the trail begins to climb. Here watch for sign of a small Beaver pond on the left. At time of writing the Beaver are gone, apparently for want of Trembling Aspen and Black Cottonwood, their favourite foods. The dam has broken, and the resulting change in water level seems to have favoured Western Spotted Frogs and especially Western Toads. In early summer the pond teems with their tadpoles, and by late July the surrounding forests are peppered with thousands of froglets and toadlets dispersing.

At length the trail descends and gives onto the river at Merganser Eddy. After mid July, this is a pleasant spot to pitch a tent. Later in the season, butterfly and wildflower watching are particularly productive pas-

Having an erect, upright trunk enables the Trembling Aspen to survive in forests that will sooner or later grow up to conifers. (TG)

times here [see: THE LAST OF SUMMER]. Equally entertaining, almost, is watching whitewater rafters rafting
by down the Clearwater. Should you care to join them
on some future trip, call 604-955-2447 (fax: 604-955-
2458), or write: Interior Whitewater Expeditions, Box
24015, Scotch Creek, B.C. VOE 3LO.

Southward, the trail is never very far from the river.
It is also not far from the west flank of Green Mountain,
here and there exposed in layered metamorphic bluffs.
You are now traversing some of the warmest, driest,
grassiest slopes in the park. Look carefully here for
Badger sign: deep, lens-shaped burrows roughly 40 cm
wide. The Badger, otherwise rare in Wells Gray, is quite
at home in these dry, sandy soils.

*Many people call this a
pine cone, but really it
is the cone of the
Douglas-fir. Recognize
it by its three-pronged
bracts.* (BCP)

Forty minutes south of Merganser Eddy, the trail
forks. The right fork leads to Hemp Creek and beyond,
to km 22.2 of the park road (see page 61). To return,
however, via the crest of Green Mountain, take the left
fork and follow it onto a grassy south-facing slope. At
the Hoodoo Rim intersection, turn left again. Now begins the long snort up the flank of Green Mountain.
Watch for people-sized spikes of Mullein (*Verbascum
thapsus*) – a Eurasian weed that, with 150,000 seeds to
the plant, has had little difficulty becoming established
in barren places on these dry slopes.

From the 1000 m south summit of the ridge, the
parking lot (and your vehicle) is still nearly three
hours distant; keep right.

The Last of Summer

Come the middle of August, most of
Wells Gray's wildflowers are done for
the year. In the mountains, the timberline meadows have already been rav-
aged by frost, while elsewhere the fields
and road edges are now reduced to an
occasional aster or goldenrod. Yet here
along the river, flower season is really
just beginning. Why should this be?

Spring freshet in the Clearwater
Valley comes late, and river levels do
not begin to drop until after mid June.
Only several weeks later are the river
banks dry enough to allow the shoreline
flowers to put out their leaves and buds.
Early autumn, along the river bank, is
the height of summer.

Here are some flowers to look for:
- White-rein Orchid (*Platanthera dilatata*): ivory spikes.
- Meadow Arnica (*Arnica chamissonis*):
yellow, daisy-like flowers with a yellow centre.
- Brown-eyed Susan (*Gaillardia aris-
tata*): ditto, but with a brown centre.
- Great Northern Aster (*Aster modetus*):
mauve, daisy-like flowers.
- Fringed Grass-of-Parnassus *Parnassia
fimbriata*): white "buttercup" flowers
and a single stem-leaf at half mast.
- Nodding Onion (*Allium cernuum*): a
distinctive oniony aroma.
- Indian Paintbrush (*Castilleja miniata*):
no description required.

36.5 km
(22.7 miles)

- FISHING
- BIRD WATCHING
- BOG TROTTING
- TREE BARKING

PLACID LAKE TRAIL
2 hr (5 km) return.
Elevation change: 50 m.

THE hike to Placid Lake starts from a signed trail-head located 0.3 km beyond the Green Mountain turnoff. Carry drinking water and repellent.

The trail first passes through an old forest that escaped the great fire of 1926. The trees are enormous, and are as much as 200 years old. Being tall, they are not always easy to identify using the usual characters; leaves, buds, cones and the like. Here it helps to know something about tree bark:

- Black Cottonwood is the deciduous tree with thick, pale bark that is deeply furrowed.
- Douglas-fir is also furrowed, but has dark, cork-like bark with orange furrows.
- Western Red-cedar, enormously buttressed, has bark that shreds into narrow, interweaving strips.
- White Spruce can be recognized by its exfoliating bark flakes.
- Paper Birch has whitish, paper-like bark mistakable for nothing else.
- Subalpine Fir has smooth silvery bark bulging with pitch pockets.

Rain Forests?

To a climatologist, any region receiving less than 750 mm of precipitation each year may be classified as semi-arid. Semi-arid, however, is a term hardly applicable to these lush forests, notwithstanding that the annual precipitation here measures only 550 mm.

In general appearance, these forests seem more closely akin to coastal rain forests than to the open woodlands of the semi-arid interior, as exemplified by Kamloops. Coast forests, however, receive more than 1000 mm annually. So why a "rain forest" in Wells Gray?

The answer is June. June is a critical month for many of Wells Gray's plant species. It is in June that the trees put on much of their year's growth. And it is in June that the newly sprouted seedlings are struggling to establish.

All this activity requires plenty of available water – something Wells Gray has in abundance during that month (the wettest of the year). Add to this the relatively low evaporation rates which characterize the park in early summer (a result of the prevailing cloudiness), and it should be obvious why the forests have a lush appearance quite out of keeping with the rather modest annual precipitation: mother nature sees to it that the trees get watered when the trees need water most.

If you have a magnifier with you (or even a pair of binoculars peered through back-to-front), check the Cedar trunks for colonies of minute black "stubble" (a sort of arboreal "five o'clock shadow"). These are stubble lichens (family Caliciales): bark-loving species nowhere more abundant than in oldgrowth forests.

Eventually the trail enters a much younger, fire-formed forest. Red Squirrels and Varied Thrushes are common here. Twice the trail crosses steep ravines: glacial outwash channels carved at the end of the last Ice Age.

Forty-five minutes from the trailhead, the trail forks. The main trail continues to White Horse Bluff, still 45 minutes ahead, whereas a right-hand turn takes you through a shrubby bog (technically a fen) to Placid Lake. With luck you'll encounter waterfowl of several species, including Common Loon, Barrow's Golden-eye, Mallard and Cinnamon Teal.

Like many small water bodies formed in the hummocky terrain left behind by the glaciers, Placid Lake is in the process of becoming a sphagnum bog. Sphagnum is just another name for peat moss, a genus of wetland bryophytes best known as a source of fuel in many northern countries, especially Scotland.

Sphagnum provides a clear example of how an organism may control the ecology of its environment. As the peat mosses grow, they absorb calcium, magnesium, sodium and potassium, leaving the water highly acidic. Under such conditions, decay is slowed, and organic material begins to accumulate on the lake bot-

The Snowberry (Gaultheria hispidula) *would probably not exist hereabouts were it not for sphagnum bogs. Recognize it by its disproportionately large berries that taste of wintergreen.* (TG)

Here a pair of dragon-flies (Leucorrhinia proxima) *adopt the wheel position.* (GD)

tom. As the lake margins fill, the sphagnum grows outward from the shore as a quaking mat. At Placid, such a mat now extends some 30 m outward from the original shoreline.

So well established are the peat mosses that many other plants have advanced from the original shoreline to join them. Strange to think of mosses acting as a colonizing surface for trees and shrubs, but this is precisely what has happened at Placid.

One plant that grows only in bogs is the Round-leaved Sundew (*Drosera rotundifolia*). The Sundew is a

Of Dragons and Damsels

Dragonfly-watching has certain advantages over birdwatching. For one, everything happens in a compressed time frame. Territories are established, defended, and lost in an afternoon. A patient watcher can see several matings in an hour and watch the female lay eggs afterwards. Another big advantage is the hours dragonflies keep; unlike the birds, these are late risers!

Not all of Wells Gray's 50-odd dragonfly species are active at any one season. Little blue damselflies in early summer will likely be *Coenagrion*, whereas the green-eyed emeralds will be *Cordulia*, and the small perching dragonflies will be *Leucorrhinia*. In August, the cast will have changed (respectively) to *Enallagma*, *Somatochlora* and *Sympetrum*. But the best known of all Wells Gray's "dragons" are the blue darners (*Aeshna* spp.), which appear in the latter half of July.

Along shorelines like those of Placid Lake, most of the dragonflies you see are likely to be males. They are waiting and watching for females, which usually only visit the water for a short time to mate and lay eggs. You'll soon notice that some species are busy defending small territories, while others seem to be flying randomly about.

The former, which are called "perching dragonflies," sit on a favourite perch and dart out from time to time to challenge intruders. The latter, the "pa-trolling dragonflies," roam the bog searching for a mate. Should they meet another male, they tussle for a moment, then separate and go in opposite directions.

When finally a female comes on the scene, keep your eyes open. Male emeralds and blue darners literally carry their prospective mates off by grasping the head with their abdominal claspers. Should the intended bride prove to be, as often happens, the wrong species, she rejects the male's advances and, after a brief struggle, flies off again.

But if the male has chosen well, the female swings her abdomen up and latches onto the base of his abdomen, where he has previously stored his sperm. Thus engaged in the "wheel position," they fly united into the protection of the nearby forest. When they part, the male leaves to search for other females and the female eventually returns to the lake to lay her fertilized eggs.

In general, female dragonflies lay eggs in one of two ways. Some, like the blue darners and damselflies, use a knife-like structure, the ovipositor, to lay eggs in vegetation or rotten wood. Most others lack an ovipositor, and simply wash the eggs from the tip of the abdomen into the water. If you see a dragonfly tapping the water with its abdomen, it is laying eggs.

Syd Cannings and Rob Cannings

peatland specialty: a carnivorous plant. Because the sphagnum retains most of the available nitrogen and phosphorus, the Sundew is obliged to supplement its diet with small insects. These it captures in the gum-tipped tentacles which line the margins of its leaves. The red-tinted gum attracts the insects, and soon entraps them. Once caught, they are gradually folded into the leaves, and there digested.

MURTLE PLATEAU

37.7 km
(22.4 miles)

THREE km north of Hemp Creek, and 150 m above it, the road finally levels, and begins its traverse of the most extensive of Wells Gray's volcanic landscapes: the Murtle Plateau. Over the next several kilometres, watch for Black Bear, Mule Deer and Moose.

MURTLE RIVER

39.9 km
(24.8 miles)

THE boundaries of Wells Gray are defined largely by the watersheds of two major rivers. One of these is the now familiar Clearwater River; the other is the Murtle, visible here.

Rising from glaciers in the Cariboo Mountains, the Murtle River completes its 82 km course entirely within Wells Gray. It may be the largest river in the world to be contained within the boundaries of a park.

The trail that begins at this mileage leads to one of Wells Gray's two abandoned homesteads. Today growing up to Lodgepole Pine and White Spruce, the Majerus Farm lies only about 20 minutes from the road. Getting there, however, is not as painless as it might sound, owing to the incessant swarms of mosquitoes which patrol this trail [see: THE RED BRIGADE].

In winter, however, there are no mosquitoes. This trail then serves as a popular ski route, and in fact provides a course for the Wells Gray Loppet (see page 190). The log building at trailhead is a place to get warm on cold winter days.

As in all biting flies, only the female mosquito goes after blood. Mosquitoes do not so much "bite" you, as pierce your skin with their sword-like proboscis. (BCP)

The Red Brigade

Mosquitoes are active in Wells Gray throughout the warmer months of the year. The first "hatch" of *Culiseta alaskaensis* and *Culiseta impatiens* – slow-flying creatures, much larger than later species – takes place even as the snow is melting in early spring. These have passed the winter as winged adults, and so emerge from hibernation at about the same time the Spotted Frog does, and the Columbian Ground Squirrel.

Most other mosquitoes overwinter in the egg or larval stages. Accordingly they do not emerge as adults until the first days of June. Then, or shortly afterward, the real onslaught begins, and mosquito repellent becomes a welcome addition to every hiker's backpack.

Mosquito larvae are aquatic creatures. Some require permanent ponds, but others can do very well in small, ephemeral puddles. So it is in the flat, poorly drained volcanic plateaux of southern Wells Gray that the mosquito really comes into its own. Areas most adversely affected include the meadows of Battle Mountain, sections of the Whitehorse Bluffs and Easter Bluffs trails, the Majerus Farm, and the Dragon's Tongue. Be forewarned!

By no means all of Wells Gray is equally prone to mosquito outbreaks. Over much of the northern, mountainous half of the park these insects are all but excluded by a lack of appropriate breeding habitat. Along the shores of Azure Lake, for example, mosquitoes generally present no inconvenience at all.

The worst years for mosquitoes (that is, the best years for mosquitoes, the worst years for mosquito-haters) are those that follow one or more years of drought; then the accumulated egg reserves of two or more seasons may hatch simultaneously, activated by rising water levels.

By the second week of July, mosquito populations decline, at least at valley elevations. Soon their nuisance-value is so low that mosquito-watching may even become an engaging pastime. Anyone who has ever watched mosquitoes knows that they come in many different species (about 30 in Wells Gray), some of which are quite distinctive. Points of separation include differences in size, leg-banding, posture when feeding, and behaviour.

Flower nectar is an important food for both male and female mosquitoes. In fact they can be important pollinators for some plants. Attached to the heads of some mosquitoes are tiny, yellow club-like structures called pollinia. These are the pollinating devices of orchids, here including the Round-leaf Bog Orchid (*Habenaria orbiculata*) and the White-rein Orchid (*Platanthera dilatata*). The pollinia become attached as the mosquitoes fly from flower to flower.

Also attached to mosquitoes, usually on the thorax just behind the wings, may be minute red specks which, upon closer inspection, turn out be eight-legged mosquito mites. Just as the mosquito feeds on us, so the mite sups on the mosquito.

At treeline, mosquitoes emerge somewhat later than they do in the valley. In most years the subalpine is essentially mosquito-free until about the second week of June. By early July the mosquitoes are at their most ferocious, and from then until about mid-August only the windblown ridges and snowfields high above treeline are (usually) free of them. It is here, not surprisingly, that the Caribou passes much of its time at this season.

When you visit Wells Gray, you can considerably reduce the inconvenience caused by mosquitoes by observing a few simple rules: 1) dress in brightly coloured clothing; 2) change your clothes at least once each day; 3) bathe as often as you can; 4) avoid bananas; and 5) eat plenty of garlic.

Most people eventually develop an immunity to mosquito bites: the more they bite, the less you scratch. In the mean time, it might help to wear one of the insect-repellent jackets now available at sporting goods stores. If you must use repellent, apply it sparingly, using the backs of the hands. This leaves the palms and fingers free for picking berries, eating lunch. . . and swatting mosquitoes.

DAWSON FALLS VIEWPOINT

30 minutes return.
Elevation change: 10 m.

40.3 km
(25.0 miles)

- LAVA LOOKING
- LICHEN LOOKING

T HE lower Murtle River is punctuated by six major waterfalls. Of these, Dawson Falls is fifth in order of sequence, and second in order of grandeur. Dawson is sometimes called "Little Niagara" – a name which emphasizes its splendid 90 m wide curtain of falling water.

From the park road, the falls is only a five minute walk by trail. There are two viewpoints. Keeping right brings you to the brink of the falls, for a foreshortened view across the tumbling river. Notice that the spray supports a copious growth of tree-dwelling mosses. One of the most abundant is *Orthotrichum obtusifolium*.

The left fork leads to a face-on vantage of the entire falls. En route, watch for Soopolallie (*Shepherdia canadensis*), recognizable for its paired, copper-dotted leaves. After late June, check among the leaves for equally distinctive clusters of bright red, copper-dotted berries – very tart! Here is a species in which only some of the bushes bear fruit: male and female flowers grow on separate plants.

Dawson Falls seen from the north bank is even more photogenic than Dawson Falls from the more traditional viewpoint. See page 106. (TG)

Soopolallie. Try it. You'll hate it. (NONC)

On its south bank, Dawson Falls resembles nothing so much as a staircase of many steps. On its north bank, it is a two-runged stepladder steeply pitched. The water pouring over the top rung breaks over the edge of a layer of lava. The lava is not thick and rests on beds of sand, gravel and till which are constantly backcut by the river current. The backcutting undermines the lava, causing it to break away in large, neat chunks.

The vertical distance between the rungs is about eight m; at the base of each, the spray has carved a recess backward into the mud. The lower of these recesses is the Cave-of-Winds. In low water, and at some risk to life and limb, you can slip in behind Dawson Falls, and watch the water cascading in sheets in front of you; see page 106.

40.8 km
(25.3 miles)

DAWSON FALLS CAMPGROUND

Don't neglect to watch the road edge for wildlife large and small. Pictured here is a Green Comma Butterfly (Polygona faunus) keeping company with a fly. (HK)

WITH only ten camping places to its name, Dawson Falls Campground is the smallest of four public camping places in the Clearwater Valley. It is also the only one without running water. Be prepared to use a hand pump.

Here you'll find plenty of good hiking. Areas accessible by foot include the Majerus Farm (and beyond), Helmcken Falls brink (and beyond), Pyramid Mountain (and beyond), the Mushbowl, and the Cave-of-Winds.

HELMCKEN BRINK TRAIL
3 hr (8 km) return.
Elevation change: 50 m.

41.1 km
(25.5 miles)

- WATERFALLING
- MUSHROOMING
- ORCHID LOOKING

HELMCKEN Falls is Wells Gray's grandest statement: a 145 m exclamation mark drawn endlessly. Yes, you can drive there (check km 42.5), but for a real sense of what Helmcken is about, take the trail beginning at this mileage. (Parents beware: there are no fences here.)

The trail sets out across a series of glacially arranged hummocks. Here the forests are open, and support a vigorous understory of various shrubs, including Falsebox (*Paxistima myrsinites*), one of few evergreen shrubs in the park. Look for its toothed, oval, leathery leaves much like those of the garden Boxwood, to which it is not, however, closely related. Early in the season the leaves conceal tiny flowers, four-parted and crimson red. Falsebox is a preferred winter browse of Wells Gray's Moose – when they can find it under the winter snow.

After 15 minutes, the trail descends to the Murtle River, and at the same time passes the original location of Dawson Falls, now 1.3 km upstream. Dawson first formed at this escarpment, which appears to be the edge of a lava flow.

As you proceed, watch the bases of the trees for dense clusters of creamy brown mushrooms. If the caps are scaly, and the stems are each encircled near the top by a whitish ring, you're probably looking at the Honey Mushroom (*Armillaria mellea*). This parasitic fungus feeds on living trees, which it eventually kills.

Once the host tree is dead, the *Armillaria* penetrates the wood, thus initiating decay. Dispersal is primarily via shoestring-like structures called rhizomorphs; these spread outward through the soil from the infected tree, causing further infection. (Good news for the woodpeckers that thrive for a time on insects attracted to the dying trees.)

Even if you don't see the mushroom itself (it may be too early in the season), chances are good you'll notice evidence of it, for it causes its host trees to exude pitch from their trunks. Beneath the bark of affected trees grow broad mats of tiny fungal threads (mycelia). When eventually the tree dies, and the bark sloughs

Falsebox has waxy, evergreen leaves. (NONC)

*Honey-hued Honey Mushrooms (*Armillaria mellea* group) come in several flavours – and digestibilities! Take care.* (TG)

off, the mats may for a time be seen to glow at night with an eerie phosphorescence.

Another mushroom to watch for is the Fly Agaric (*Amanita muscaria*), with its red, soap-flaky cap, white spores and whitish ring around the stalk. This is the mushroom that Alice ate prior to growing very, very small; it is definitely not recommended for consumption.

Fungi come in three groups, according to diet. To the first group belong the parasites. These, like the Honey Mushroom, feed on, and eventually kill, their hosts. The second group are the saprophytes. Their food is nonliving matter – fallen branches, logs, needles – which they thus help to decompose. The third group,

The Conifer Connection

Trees are often perceived as rugged individualists – woody versions of John Wayne. The truth is, however, trees depend for their strength on mushrooms. With these (and other fungi), trees have entered into a symbiotic relationship, each partner depending intimately on the other. Take their fungal partner away, and trees are not particularly rugged at all. A Lodgepole Pine, for example, would be a sickly stem hardly three m tall.

The partnership takes place underground, where the fungi grow as a network of fine threads. In some cases the threads surround the individual plant cells within the root tips of the appropriate tree partners, whereas in others they actually penetrate the cells. Sometimes the root tips resemble fingers in a coloured glove made of fuzzy fungal material. Together, the roots and the fungi are called mycorrhizae, that is "fungus-roots."

The fungus helps the tree by extracting phosphorus and other fertilizing nutrients from the soil, while the tree pays for its upkeep by providing sugar to the fungus. In the autumn, many of these symbiotic mycorrhizal fungi use much of the energy thus gained to produce fruiting bodies: "mushrooms" when they grow above ground, and "truffles" when below. The fruiting bodies bear the spores of the next generation.

Some conifers can enter partnerships with as many as 100 different fungal species. In different forest types, of course, different fungi are involved. But whatever the conditions, one fungus or another is always present. As many as 500 species of mycorrhizal fungi are thought to inhabit Wells Gray.

Along this trail, the Douglas-fir associates with truffle-like *Rhizopogon* species, which in autumn are dug up as food by the Red Squirrel and, especially, the Flying Squirrel. By bringing the "truffles" to the surface, these creatures ensure that the spores are released, and thus that these fungi may re-establish themselves

One common above-ground mycorrhizal mushroom occurring here is the Booted Amanita (*Amanita porphyria*), which begins by looking like an egg, but which eventually "hatches" into a tall, elegant, smooth-capped, greyish-brown mushroom having a bulb at the base. Look for it in late summer, after rain.

Mycorrhizal associations are not restricted to trees, but occur in virtually all flowering plants. Among the only truly "rugged individualists" (i.e., plants that avoid mycorrhizae) are members of the Sedge, Carnation, Mustard, Rush and Rose Families. Of these, the Swamp Gooseberry (*Ribes lacustre*) and the Baldhip Rose (*Rosa gymnocarpa*) grow along this trail.

Richard Summerbell

Lichen fungi, like mycor-rhizae, are mutualists, in this case associating with tiny algal cells which they cultivate and selectively harvest. Pictured here are Hypogymnia imshaugii *(left) and* H. occidentalis. (TG)

the mutualists, include the mycorrhizal fungi [see: THE CONIFER CONNECTION].

Another plant group entering into partnership with fungi are the orchids, second largest plant family in the world, with some 15,000 species. Common along this trail is Rattlesnake Plantain (*Goodyera oblongifolia*), an orchid more easily recognized by its leaves than by its blossoms. In fact, you may scarcely recognize the tiny, drab, greenish-white flowers (borne in a spike) as orchid flowers at all.

As for the leaves, they grow in a basal rosette, are strikingly bluish green, and generally bear a white fishnet pattern over their upper surface.

The seeds of Rattlesnake Plantain are virtually microscopic, and contain very little stored food to help the embryonic plant get started. They rely on mycorrhizal fungi for nutrients in their early stages. Orchid mycorrhizae are able to break down lignin and cellulose (the stuff of wood) into carbohydrates, and so supply these to their hosts, rather than the reverse, as in other plants.

Eventually, a sound like distant thunder begins to gather ahead of you. This is Helmcken Falls. If you have children with you, this is your cue to get them in tow.

At Helmcken Falls the Murtle River plummets into space off the edge of the Murtle Plateau. Only a few metres away, the trail leads out into a little clearing, which commands a view six seconds to the bottom! There are no handrails here; if you feel you must peer out over the canyon edge, please do so on your stomach.

In winter, the perpetual spray from the falls congeals in a wall of ice along the canyon rim, in some

Rattlesnake Plantain is neither a rattlesnake nor a plantain, though it somewhat resembles both. (TG)

years accumulating to a depth of four m. Generally this wall is slow to melt, lingering on into June, and some years into early July.

The plants encased within the ice are of course unable to begin the year's growth until long after their neighbours. For species like Oval-leaf Blueberry (*Vaccinium ovalifolium*), this results in an intriguing progression from earliest budding through to full blossoming, all in the space of four or five m. Here along the rim of Helmcken Canyon, the passage of time is made spatial and springtime can be seen to advance in terms of metres, not weeks.

MUSHBOWL HILL

41.2 km
(25.6 miles)

WHERE the road leaves the Murtle Plateau to descend to the Murtle River, it slants downward across the base of a steep embankment. As it does so, it passes successive horizontal layers of rock and till – each a separate chapter in the geologic history of the Clearwater Valley. Laid out before you is a story written by fire and ice on pages composed of soil, till, lava flows, pillows, and sediments. The story begins at the top of the hill and concludes at the bridge at the bottom.

Underneath a thin veneer of post-glacial soil lies a layer of glacial till: a compact mixture of ice-smoothed pebbles and cobbles in a matrix of clay and sand, laid down in place at the base of a glacier. Squeezed by the weight of the ice above, and cemented by the clay (actually ice-pulverized, flour-sized particles of rock), the material forms a solid grey rocky deposit – a geologic Christmas pudding! The till here dates from the middle of the last Ice Age, and was probably deposited about 15,000 to 20,000 years ago.

The till is underlain by layers of lava. The lavas vary in depth, and are in places as much as 11 m thick. They represent the same lava flows as those over which Dawson Falls falls. If you examine the rock closely, you'll see it is dense, black and flecked with green crystals. These are called olivine. Geologists refer to such iron- and magnesium-rich lava as basalt. Note how the upper portion of the basalt is pocked with bubbles, or vesicles. These result from depressurized

These bubbles (vesicles) formed when gases were trapped in cooling lava as it hardened around them. (CH)

gases within the molten lava. As the gases rise through the molten rock, they become trapped near the cooling, hardened upper surface. Further cooling "freezes" them in place forever. The fact that the vesicles are empty, rather than filled with agate or chlorite, tells us the lava here is relatively young – a mere 200,000 years old.

The lower portion of the basalt is lobed and lumpy, very different in appearance from the upper portion. Why is this? Pillows. Pillows form when lava flows into water – in this case a prehistoric creek or river. Entering the water, the lava cools quickly, and at the same time hardens into lobes. Like fresh candle wax, the lobes have a thin outer skin surrounding the still molten lava inside. Pressure within the lobes eventually ruptures the skin, thus creating new lobes as the lava oozes from the cracks. The end product is hundreds of hardened lobes, each of which bears a striking resemblance to a household pillow. Hence the name.

The till-like material at bottom of the Mushbowl roadcut was laid down by an ancient glacier, and then buried by lava. (CH)

Near the bridge, the lava overlies a second glacial deposit. Notice how much "tidier" these sands and gravels are than the till at the top of the hill. Notice also how the sands are distinctly layered. The layers tell us these sediments were deposited by meltwater streams at the close of an earlier Ice Age, roughly 400,000 years ago.

These deposits bury a still older, though possibly related, deposit, visible at the bridge. This material is grey, hard and pebbly; it closely resembles the till at the top of the section. Close inspection, however, suggests that it is actually a debris flow: a slurry of rock, sand and clay that sloughed off the melting front of a glacier. This same glacier once smoothed and polished the rock on which the footings of the bridge now stand.

Mushbowl crossing: where the bottom of a valley is really the top of a hill. (TG)

41.5 km
(25.8 miles)

THE MUSHBOWL CROSSING

- ALLIGATOR HUNTING
- RIVER CROSSING

The Northern Alligator Lizard: does she or doesn't she? (RCBM)

THE road crosses the Murtle River over an outcropping of Kaza Group schists, into which the river has carved a narrow gorge. This is the Mushbowl – a stretch of river aptly named should you happen to fall in.

Strange to say, the Mushbowl was once an elevated hillock – one of many that underlie the surface of the Murtle Plateau. Over the last half million years, lava flows have inundated this rolling landscape layer by layer. Valleys were filled and overtopped, and eventually so were the hilltops. Later the river downcut through the lava to reveal the hillock here.

The warm, south-facing outcrops on the north side of the river have in the past supported the park's only known population of Northern Alligator Lizard (*Eglaria coerulea*). This is the northernmost of all lizards in North America, and is here near the northern edge of its range. Does it still exist in the park? No one knows. Please record any sightings in the "Wells Gray Wildlife Register" at the Wells Gray Visitor Centre.

An unsigned trail to the "Cave-of-Winds" on the north side of Dawson Falls begins just upstream of the bridge, and involves a walk of about 45 minutes return. Earlier it had been possible to actually slip in behind the falls, but this is now difficult, except at low water, owing to a rock slide in the spring of 1990.

Pebbles caught in cracks in the rock were caused to swirl round and round by a rushing river current. The resulting "punchbowls" are located just downstream from Murtle River bridge. (TG)

PYRAMID MOUNTAIN TRAIL

4 hr (9 km) return.
Elevation change: 300 m.

42.0 km
(26.1 miles)

- MUSHROOM SNIFFING
- WILLOW WATCHING
- VOLCANO VIEWING
- HORSE FLY GAZING

PYRAMID Mountain is a volcano that erupted while glaciers covered this valley, some 11,000 years ago. In the geologist's lingo, it would be called a tuya. Yet unlike most tuyas, which have a characteristic crumpled stetson-like appearance, Pyramid Mountain is cone-shaped. Why? Read on.

The trail leaves the road at the top of the hill just north of the Murtle River bridge. For most of its length, it traverses the rolling surface of the Murtle Plateau; the only steep pitch is at the end, on the mountain itself. Be sure to carry water and mosquito repellent. (Beyond Pyramid, the trail continues another six km to Majerus Falls: be prepared to camp overnight in excellent Black Bear country.)

The first kilometre is through an open forest dating from the fire of 1926. Good mushroom country, this. After mid August, boletes are common, as are russulas and milk mushrooms of the genus *Lactarius*.

Milk mushrooms are easily recognized by their tendency to bleed when cut (try the gills near the stem). The "blood" (or milk) varies considerably from species to species. In the Red Hot Milky (*Lactarius rufus*), for example, the milk is whitish and, when tasted, burns the tip of the tongue (try it; you'll hate it!). By contrast, the Delicious Milky (*Lactarius deliciosus*) has a mild, orange-coloured latex. But most interesting of all is the milk of *Lactarius resimus*, which comes out white, then promptly turns yellow upon exposure to the air.

Other mushrooms can be recognized more easily by nose than by eye. Keep a nostril open for the Garlic Mushroom (*Marasmius scorodonius*). This tiny brownish parasol (growing in groups on forest litter) is sometimes smelled even before it is seen. The chlorine bouquet of the similar Alkaline Mushroom (*Mycena alcalina*) can also be experienced here, though for this you'll have to sniff a fresh cap.

Eventually the trail leaves the forest for an old burn which is now growing up to Lodgepole Pine, Sitka

The Emetic Russula (Russula emetica *group*) *looks more edible than it tastes. Eaten raw, it can induce vomiting.* (BCP)

Pyramid Mountain provides a wintering grounds for Moose, and a summering grounds for Mule Deer. The Red-cedar snags in the foreground have been standing since they were burned in 1926. (TG)

Alder (*Alnus sinuata*), Scouler's Willow (*Salix scouleri-ana*), and Bebb's Willow (*Salix bebbiana*) [see: INTRODUCING THE WILLOWS].

Understandably, this burn is a favourite wintering grounds of Wells Gray's Moose; don't be surprised if you find their droppings, affectionately known as forest glossets. The droppings come in many different sizes (depending on the size of the Moose), but only two basic shapes: pecan and walnut. On average, the former (more elongate) droppings will have been deposited by a cow Moose, whereas the latter (more chunky) ones will have been left behind by a bull.

At the foot of Pyramid, leave the trail for the final pitch up the mountain. The slopes are open here, and

Introducing the Willows

As a favourite food of Wells Gray's favourite ungulate, willow has played a major part in the destiny of the Clearwater Valley. Had there been no willows during the 1930s, there would have been no Moose; certainly the valley could not have supported what has been called one of the densest Moose populations in western North America. In that event, it is unlikely that Moose hunters (and other recreationists) would have eventually lobbied for a park here. Perhaps it is worth saying a word or two about the park's willows.

Willows are shrubby plants with bitter-tasting bark (containing salicin, the forerunner of Aspirin) and, in most cases, long, narrow leaves. Forty-three species occur in British Columbia, many very difficult to tell apart. The problem is that the species can vary not only from place to place, but also from plant to plant. Some even hybridize, producing a rat's nest of intermediate forms.

Like people, willows come in two sexes. The so-called "pussy willows" of early spring are really just the flowers (catkins) of the male shrub, which in some species are produced prior to leafing. The female flowers (aments) come out soon after (or earlier, or at the same time, depending on the species) on a nearby shrub. Later in summer, the aments break open, and a fine cottony down is released, which carries the seeds far and wide.

(*Left*) *To most plants and animals, a charred snag is an inhospitable place. To the tiny scale lichen called* Hypocenomyce scalaris, *however, it is home.* (TG)

(*Right*) *Moose browse on willow branches; so do the larvae of various insects. This "cone gall" is a cancer-like out-growth induced by a tiny gall midge* (Rhabdophaga *sp.*) *which once lived inside.* (TG)

offer one of the warmest exposures in the park. Many of the plants are specially adapted to hot, arid places. Some of them are road edge weeds: Mullein (*Verbascum thapsus*: slender, two m spikes), Yellow Salsify (*Tragopogon dubius*: oversized dandelions) and Northern Goldenrod (*Solidago multiradiata*: the name says it all). Notice how all flower like fire, with yellow blossoms.

As you climb, you're also sure to notice the sickly-sweet fragrance of Snowbrush (*Ceanothus velutinus*) and Redstem Ceanothus (*Ceanothus sanguineus*); this is one of few places in the park where both species occur together. Here too dwell warmth-loving insects like the Band-winged Grasshopper (Subfamily Oedipodinae). Listen as it flies away, never far, on crackling wings.

Because of its under-glacier origins, Pyramid is no typical volcano. Its flanks are not composed of loose boulders, as a cinder cone would be, but are compact, almost like rough cement. Walking over them produces a hollow echoing sound.

The basalt here has been quickly chilled by water, creating shiny volcanic glass. A little searching will soon reveal that the mountain is loosely covered in schist, phyllite, granite and other nonvolcanic cobbles. These rocks were deposited by the glacier through which Pyramid Mountain erupted, some time near the end of the last Ice Age.

As a tuya (that is, a sub-glacial volcano), Pyramid really ought to have a "crumpled stetson" profile like that of McLeod Hill just to the east. The fact that it is a "pyramid" instead suggests that its summit did not

Here a female Moose has briefly paused on a winter's day. In summer, the droppings are soft and shapeless, reflecting a less woody diet. (TG)

Beware the horse fly: its eyes may be alluring, but its bite is no fun. (BCP)

"Tuya" is the name given to volcanoes that have erupted under glacial ice. Should the eruption cease before the volcano protrudes through the surface of the ice, the resulting tuya is pyramid-shaped. By contrast, volcanoes that continue to erupt above the ice have a characteristic "crumpled stetson" look. (CH)

rise high enough to poke through the surface of the ice. Formed by continuous explosions in its underwater cocoon, this little volcano was confined to a tight cone by the meltwater it created.

Round the summit, and suddenly Wells Gray is laid out like a map before you. From this vantage you learn that the so-called Murtle Plateau is not really a plateau at all, but a broad ridge extending westward from the Murtle Valley into the deeper valley of the Clearwater River.

Meandering along the crest (!) of this ridge is the Murtle River. Only a few kilometres west of here the Murtle pours over the edge of the ridge as Helmcken Falls. From the summit of Pyramid, however, it is obvious that the Murtle River very nearly doesn't keep its rendezvous with Helmcken. As it rounds the base of Pyramid, the river very nearly flows southward into the neighbouring drainage of Hemp Creek. By so little is the Murtle held on track that an afternoon or two with a bulldozer and blasting caps might be enough to divert it. On so little does the existence of Helmcken Falls depend.

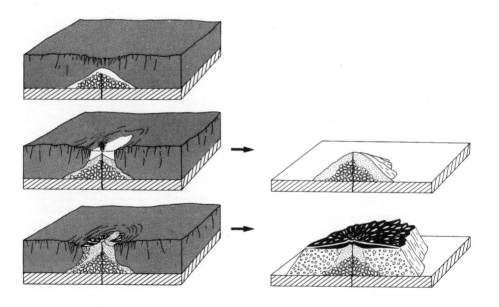

HELMCKEN FALLS ROAD

42.5 km
(26.4 miles)

• WATERFALLING

FOURTH tallest waterfall in Canada. A tremendous opening for hydroelectric power. Symbol of untouched wilderness. The very heart of Wells Gray Park. However you look at it, Helmcken Falls is a stunning display of the power of water. It is a must for anyone visiting the park.

The Helmcken Falls road is clearly signposted, and leads four km to the western rim of the Murtle Plateau. En route it parallels the Murtle River, and provides an occasional glimpse of what is here a broad, shallow stream. No sign of the vertical column to come.

About 500 m from the turnoff at km 42.5, the road passes an open wet meadow. Prior to 1985, this was a Beaver pond. The old Beaver lodge still occupies the centre of the opening, though the Beaver themselves have moved on to wetter pastures. They abandoned this area when they had finished cutting down, and eating, most of the available Cottonwood and Trembling Aspen trees.

At road-end you'll find a canyon-edge viewing platform and, nearby, picnic tables and outhouses. A fine place for a picnic, but bring your own drinking water.

The spray from Helmcken Falls continuously carves away at the adjacent canyon, and in so doing undermines the falls. (TG)

Helmcken Falls, situated about one mile above the junction of the Murtle and Clearwater Rivers, has a perpendicular drop of 465 feet, and from the basin into which the main falls drop are a series of smaller falls and rapids. These falls present a very beautiful sight when the sun is in the west, for then a large rainbow spans the canyon from wall to wall. The spray rising from these falls can be seen for miles.

summarized from
R.H. Lee (1913)

The beauty of Helmcken resides partly in the single clean arc of its fall, partly in the deep, dark cavern which backdrops it, and partly again in the graceful sweep of canyon walls that frames it. All of these characteristics tell a story.

The story of Helmcken Falls began roughly half a million years ago. It was then, as already mentioned, that volcanoes hereabouts began to erupt tens of cubic km of molten lava from deep within the earth's crust. This lava flowed into the existing river valleys, filling them and producing thick, resistant layers of lava which were later covered by Pleistocene glaciers.

Most of the sculpting of the Murtle Plateau by the Clearwater and Murtle Rivers occurred at the close of the last Ice Age, when enormous volumes of silt- and sand-laden waters were carried down from the snouts of dying glaciers. Rivers of water poured braid-like across the lap of the Murtle Plateau carving like a sander down through the heavy mantle of glacial till and into the underlying volcanic rock.

A few centuries later the glaciers had retreated to their strongholds in the Cariboos. Helmcken Canyon, meanwhile, had already been excavated to much the spectacle of today – a stupendous gap 200 metres deep, by 300 metres across, by 1800 metres in length.

The headwalls of the canyon are still being eroded. Erosion nowadays takes place mostly in winter, when the spray from the falls freezes on the nearby canyon walls. The ice then works its way into the cracks between the columns, loosening them and adding to their weight. Every so often, whole sections of the ceiling are brought down in this way. The most recent collapse occurred during the winter of 1983; look for the brightly coloured rock to the right of the falls. Who can say how long it will be until the roof caves in, and the falls relocate some tens of metres farther upstream.

How is it, by the way, that the Murtle carved a canyon, and not just a steep-sided valley? The answer is columns. As each layer of lava rock cooled, it developed vertical fractures inward from the top and bottom. If you could examine the fractures from above, you would see they are actually polygonal columns all fitted together like the cells of a honeycomb. Wind, rain, ice and snow cause the columns to weather away, but instead of crumbling grain by grain, they fall away in slabs, like slices of bread, leaving the cliff face intact.

The Violet-green Swallow can be identified by its white "coat tails." (BCP)

Meanwhile the river below, acting as janitor, carries the rubble away.

Attempt to approach the brink of the falls from the viewing platform, and you'll find your way blocked by a 75 m deep canyon. Nowadays that canyon is occupied by Cougar Creek, which drains into Helmcken Canyon over a waterfall about 20 m tall. It was not always thus. Prior to 11,000 years ago, this canyon carried the glacially swollen waters of the Murtle River (or its predecessor); it was these waters that carved the canyon in the first place. With the eruption of Pyramid Mountain, at around 11,000 years ago, the drainage pattern altered, and the Murtle was obliged to find a new point of entry into Helmcken Canyon. It is owing to the eruption of Pyramid Mountain that Helmcken exists at all.

The White-throated Swift is a recent arrival at Helmcken Canyon. Stay tuned for its excited, but descending, "jejejeje." (TG)

At the same time as it downcut into the Murtle Plateau, the Murtle River effectively opened a public archives to the history of the Clearwater Valley. It is easy to read the story recorded in these canyon walls: how when the first volcanoes erupted, 200,000 years ago, they buried a valley with a gravelly river bed; how afterward the lavas poured forth at least 20 times; and how then finally – or not finally, but only most recently – the glacial till of the last Ice Age capped the latest outpourings.

During January and February of every year, the canyon nurses an enamel-blue cone of ice in its lap. Although dwarfed by the falls itself, the Helmcken ice cone, in a cold winter standing taller at its crest than a 20 story building, is quite possibly the most impressive sculpture of its kind.

The north wall of Helmcken Canyon is interrupted by a layer of steam gravels – evidence that the lava flows were deposited over an extended period. (TG)

- CANYON
  VIEWING
- PELTIGERA
  PROBING

HELMCKEN RIM TRAIL
30 min (1.5 km) return.
Elevation change: 25 m.

The trail that follows the viewpoint fence west, or away from the falls continues about ten minutes to a fine overlook of the confluence of the Murtle and Clearwater Rivers. This little stroll is highly recommended, but keep in mind that you are still skirting the rim of a canyon; once you pass beyond the fence you are on your own.

The plants along the rim of Helmcken Canyon are to some extent reminiscent of the interior dry-belt. Clumps of Bluebunch Wheatgrass (*Agropyron spicatum*) – here probably at its northern limits in the Clearwater Valley – intermingle with trailing stems of Kinnikinnik (*Arctostaphylos uva-ursi*). A single Rocky Mountain Juniper has also caught hold not far from the viewing platform. Good drainage and full exposure to the summer's rays have contributed to the development of this little enclave of semi-desert life.

At canyon edge, the trail passes various ground-dwelling lichens at home in the semi-open conifer forest. Watch especially for colonies of Pelt Lichens (*Peltigera* spp.), of which the easiest to identify is the Freckle Pelt (*P. aphthosa*): an emerald green "scatter rug" (turquoise when dry) whose upper surface is faintly speckled with numerous tiny "freckles" (technically cephalodia).

The Freckle Pelt is not, as it would seem, a single plant; rather it is made up of three quite unrelated

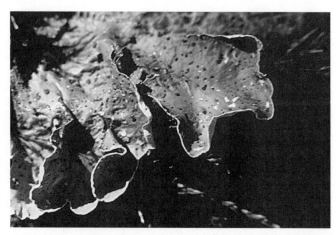

The Freckle Pelt (Peltigera aphthosa) *is only one of 24 species of Pelt Lichens that inhabit the forest floor in Wells Gray.* (TG)

This picture is worth a thousand words. (TG)

organisms, namely an alga (accounting for the green-ish upper surface), a fungus (the cottony lower surface), and a cyanobacterium (the cephalodia). Each of these partners derives from a separate kingdom of life. The only kingdoms not represented here are the plant and animal kingdoms.

At the overlook, Helmcken Canyon forms a T-junction with the much larger Clearwater Canyon. From here it is easy to imagine how the lavas of the Murtle Plateau once extended across the entire valley, but have since been cut into by the rivers. The cliffs below you fall away about 150 m.

The trail continues north beyond this point, and will eventually lead, as a very rough route, to a splendid worm's-eye view of Helmcken Falls. Allow about five hours return, and be prepared to dodge falling rock.

At the confluence of the Murtle and Clearwater Rivers, you'll have no trouble imagining a time when lava flows extended right across the valley. (CH)

44.9 km
(27.9 miles)

SNAKE HILL

SINCE entering Wells Gray, nine km south of here, the road has traversed the rolling surface of the Murtle Plateau. Now at the plateau's northern edge, the road begins a long four km descent to the Clearwater River, 150 m below.

46.8 km
(29.1 miles)

CARIBOO MOUNTAINS LOOKOUT

RISING along the northern skyline at this hillside pulloff are the Cariboo Mountains. The Cariboos are Wells Gray's cloud makers. At their north-western edge they intercept the eastward moving clouds, causing them to rise and thus to drop their excess moisture. So it is that the weather gets wetter as you continue northward to Clearwater Lake.

49.2 km
(30.6 miles)

REDSPRING

AT this roadside picnic site, named for a nearby mineral spring, the park road finally touches down on the Clearwater River – the first time it has done so since leaving the Yellowhead Highway. Southward, the river is confined in narrow basalt canyons. Northward, it winds instead through sands and gravels laid down by glaciers.

In mid summer, watch the park road for kamikaze butterflies. Most will be the Comma Tortoiseshell (Nymphalis vau-album). (HK)

DEER CREEK

O VER the next five km, heading north, the road passes through an important feeding and rest- ing area for Mule Deer and Black Bear. In late spring Moose may also use this part of the Clearwater Valley for calving; usually at least one of these animals is resident here during the summer months. Other creatures sometimes seen include Coyotes, Columbian Ground Squirrels, Red Foxes and, more rarely, Wolves and Grizzly Bear.

Large mammals are most abundant along the road during May and June. In May especially, the green, burgeoning road edges provide a welcome feeding area. It is said that young grass shoots may contain as much protein as an equivalent amount of cheese.

Here as everywhere, roadside animals sometimes fall victim to passing vehicles. At present, such inci- dents are comparatively rare in Wells Gray – probably owing to the fact that the gravel surface of the park road results in slower traffic. Not everybody, is pleased at having to travel a gravel road. It seems only a matter of time until the lobby to pave the road achieves its goal. But at what cost to Wells Gray's wildlife? Faster and smoother is not always better.

On the Road

For most of the summer, driving the park road usually involves more time spent looking at the passing scenery than at the road itself. However, from late July through mid August, the situa- tion is likely to be reversed, for then the Comma Tortoiseshell (*Nymphalis vau-al- bum*) is flying.

Actually the Comma Tortoiseshell (also called the Compton Tortoiseshell) flies at two periods during the warmer months. The first appearance is in early spring, when the adults of the previous summer – now almost nine months old – emerge from hibernation. Shortly af- terward the butterflies mate, lay their eggs, and then die.

Once the larvae emerge, they feed for the next several weeks on the leaves of birch, willow, rose, raspberry and other shrubby plants. Watch for them near water: green caterpillars, very gregari- ous, and readily recognized by their dis- tinctive assemblage of white dots, pale stripes, and spiny head.

Eventually they pupate, and then emerge as the orange-and-brown butter- fly so common during mid and late sum- mer. Like other butterflies, the Comma Tortoiseshell needs as much warmth as it can get (it takes energy to fly, and warmth is energy), and this can some- times be difficult in the cool, montane forests of Wells Gray. Thus, on sunny days (and even during sunny periods on cloudy days!), it congregates by the hun- dreds on the warm park road.

Helen Knight

54.0 km
(33.5 miles)

THE HORSESHOE

As a rule, the Clearwater River is a river in a hurry. At the Horseshoe, however, it slows to inscribe a series of meanders, the most impressive of which occurs at this mileage. Here the river doubles back on itself, describing an almost complete circle three km in circumference.

The unconsolidated sands and gravels which underlie these meanders, and make them possible, were deposited 11,000 or 12,000 years ago by the meltwaters of stagnating glaciers. Since then the Clearwater has

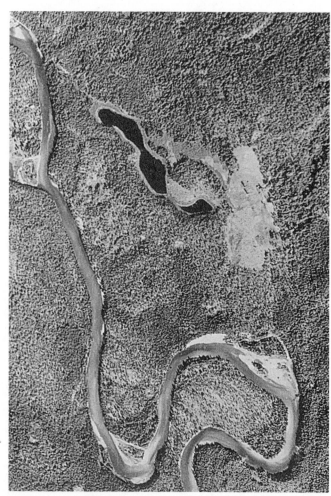

This aerial photograph of the Horseshoe, the Ray Farm, and Alice Lake predates the park road. Moose Meadows is located on the tongue of land to the west (left) of the Horseshoe. (BCE: BC 78099 087)

snaked to and fro across this giant sandbox, at each pass wearing a little deeper into the valley floor. To date the river has entrenched itself at least 40 m into the gravels.

Because the gravels are extremely pervious to water, the soils which cover them tend to be well drained and very dry. In places this can make it difficult for forest trees to establish. At the Horseshoe you'll find some of Wells Gray's largest lowland open spaces. Of these, Moose Meadows, at roughly ten ha in size, are the most accessible.

HORSESHOE LOOKOUT TRAIL
30 min (.5 km) return.
Elevation change: 25 m.

- RIVER WATCHING
- HAZELNUTTING

The walk to Horseshoe Lookout is a pleasant ramble along a high bank overlooking the Clearwater River. A few metres from the road the trail forks. Take the right-hand fork, following the trail as it first climbs, and then descends over a series of ever-lower benches. Each bench represents an old riverbed, left behind from an earlier pass of the river as it cut through the glacial deposits.

The Lookout is located about ten minutes from the road, and is unmarked; it offers a fine view over the Clearwater River and, to the south, Pyramid Mountain (left) and Mosquito Mound (right).

Even today the river continues to shift and change. Running faster on the outside of the horseshoe bends, and slower on the inside, the current is simultaneously cutting away at the former bank and depositing on the

A bend in the ever-changing Horseshoe. Willow colonizes the newly available shoreline. (TG)

Hazelnut nuts usually come in pairs. (RBCM)

latter – a process clearly visible here. Notice how the vegetation on the inside of the bend is composed of such early colonizers as willow and various herbs; these reflect the constantly changing shoreline.

Continuing thus, the river will in time cut through the neck of the Horseshoe, now roughly 100 m across; when it does so it will have left behind a sausage-shaped lake called an oxbow.

The well-drained soils provide ideal growing conditions for the Hazelnut (*Corylus cornuta*), a shrub here at its most abundant in the Clearwater Valley. The leaves of the Hazelnut resemble Birch leaves, but are lightly furry. Also characteristic are the eared fruits which, once husked, resemble the familiar European filbert, to which they are closely related. Every August, the Red Squirrel harvests and stores the Hazelnuts for winter use.

Over the water fly Rough-winged Swallows and Vaux's Swifts, the former nesting in the sandbanks above the river, the latter probably nesting in dead Cottonwoods near Moose Meadows.

• FLOWER POKING
• ANIMAL TRACKING

MOOSE MEADOWS ROUTE
2 hr (3 km) return.
Elevation change: 50 m.

The hike to Moose Meadows leads past some fabulous river scenery, but involves both bushwhacking and direction-finding. Carry a map and compass for this one. Mosquito repellent wouldn't hurt, either.

From the Horseshoe Lookout, another 15 minutes along the top of the cutbank will bring you to an obvious opening on your right (i.e., away from the river). This is the first of two large clearings which together make up Moose Meadows. Pay attention as you enter it; doing so may help you to find your way out again.

Moose Meadows provide habitat for several drought-tolerant plants elsewhere found mostly in disturbed sites. Among the most common are Arctic Lupine (*Lupinus arcticus*), Spreading Dogbane (*Apocynum androsaemifolium*), Kinnikinnik (*Arctostaphylos uva-ursi*), Bastard Toad-flax (*Geocaulon lividum*) and Blueleaf Strawberry (*Fragaria virginiana*). Also growing here are many shrubby species, including Soopolallie

(*Shepherdia canadensis*), Oregon Grape (*Mahonia aquifolium*) and Saskatoon (*Amelanchier alnifolia*).

Look also for extensive mats of reindeer lichens (*Cladina* spp.). In northern Canada these pale, shrublike lichens provide an important winter food for hundreds of thousands of Caribou. In Wells Gray the reindeer lichens are sparse, and so the Caribou depend instead upon tree-dwelling hair lichens (*Alectoria* and *Bryoria*).

Although the river lies just west of Moose Meadows, it is largely concealed by a curtain of Black Cottonwood and White Spruce, growing in response to the wetter ground along the river's edge. Penetrate this curtain, and at low water the river shoreline makes for a rather pleasant walk.

Here watch for the drooping flowerhead of the Nodding Onion (*Allium cernuum*) – a species readily identified by its familiar aroma. Other riverside flowers include the Meadow Arnica (*Arnica chamissonis*) and the Streambank Butterweed (*Senecio pseudaureus*), whose daisy-like flowers can be found blooming any time after early July. Opening at the same season are the five-spurred blossoms of Red Columbine (*Aquilegia formosa*).

The sand bars are also a good place to look for animal sign, including Black Bear tracks, Canada Geese droppings, Beaver workings and perhaps the shed antlers of a Moose. In September and October, Chinook Salmon spawn in the river here. And then die. Their rotting bodies attract all manner of carrion feeders, especially Black Bear, Foxes, Coyote, Bald Eagles and Ravens.

*The reindeer lichens (*Cladina spp.*) come in four species in Wells Gray. Nowhere are they more abundant than at Moose Meadows.* (TG)

*How did the Nodding Onion (*Allium cernuum*) find its way to the banks of Clearwater? Could it be an artifact from early Indian encampments?* (TG)

No track more resembles a human footprint than that of a bear. Here a Black Bear has crossed paths with a Mule Deer. (TG)

54.5 km
(33.9 miles)

- BIRDWATCHING
- FLOWER
  LOOKING
- PERRIER SIPPING
- MAMMAL
  TRACKING
- BATTING

RAY FARM TRAIL
1 hr (1 km) return.
Elevation change: 20 m.

THE Ray Farm, only a ten minute walk from this mileage, provides a satisfying focus for an afternoon outing.

Acting as focal centre to the farm are the mineral springs just north of the trail below the farm house. The springs are a bright orange gash in the earth, out of which flows a steady stream of water. Anyone who tastes this water is unlikely to forget the experience: you sip it; it sips back.

To the local wildlife, these springs are a kind of

The Farm that John Built

John Bunyan Ray, born in North Carolina in 1878, arrived on the scene west of here in about 1909 – just in time to help the Canim Lake Indians overcome a serious outbreak of measles. John's advice to the band – to keep the afflicted in bed in a darkened room – was apparently efficacious. In gratitude the chief of the Canims gave him the band's traditional hunting grounds on the Clearwater and Azure Rivers.

John was not long in settling on the Horseshoe area as the future location of his wilderness homestead. Here he found abundant game, storybook fishing, fertile soil, and good growing conditions on a warm southwest-facing hillside. By the early 1920s, his farm would consist of six ha of pasture, a large vegetable garden, and about 30 ha of natural hay meadow.

Things went along quietly for this crusty bachelor until the early 1930s when, in rapid succession, he applied for Canadian citizenship, filed for ownership of the 130 ha on which his farm is located, and, in 1932, at the age of 53, married 20 year-old Alice Ludke.

For the next 14 years John and Alice lived on the farm, raising three children, and maintaining a self-sufficient life style much in the tradition of British Columbia's earliest pioneers. Ducks, cows, goats, sheep and chickens are

only a few of the animals they kept on their farm. The old garden plot and orchard near the house can still be recognized by the grapes, asparagus, raspberry bushes, strawberry plants, and apple trees of several varieties that grow there. A few metres away stands a lilac bush, still providing a fragrant accent every spring.

Of course the Rays also took advantage of the "edible wild." In spring, they sometimes tapped Douglas Maple (*Acer glabrum*) and Paper Birch as a source of syrup. In summer they picked berries: first Blueleaf Strawberries (*Fragaria virginiana*); then Saskatoons (*Amelanchier alnifolia*); later Bitter Cherries (*Prunus emarginata*) and Dwarf Blueberries (*Vaccinium caespitosum*); and finally, in October, Bog Cranberries (*Vaccinium oxycoccus*).

Many stories have grown up around John Ray. Most are probably apocryphal, embroidered and expanded upon over years of telling. Yet all reveal John as a shrewd, practical man, perhaps not always easy to get along with, but never lacking in originality and plain horse sense. For more, check the appropriate pages in the books by I. Dekelver, H. Hogue, H.E. Johnson and R. Neave, listed in Appendix 1, page 213. All should be available at the Wells Gray Visitor Centre.

The roof of the Ray farm house was modelled on the traditional kekuli, or pit house, of B.C.'s interior native peoples. (TG)

wilderness drug store. According to need, Mule Deer, Moose, Black Bear, and others come here to supplement their diets with such essential minerals as calcium, sodium, magnesium and iron. Look for their telltale tracks in the mud.

Also attracted to the springs are various birds, especially finches. Finches are primarily seed eaters; lacking certain important minerals, they flock to the springs in great numbers. Evening Grosbeaks, Pine Grosbeaks, Pine Siskins and Red Crossbills are a few of the more common finches to watch for.

The springs themselves are broadly encased in deposits of a white, chalky rock called travertine. Travertine forms when the calcium present in the water precipitates out to encrust the mosses (*Cratoneuron commutatum*) that are so abundant here. As the moss grows it tends to dam the water, so causing it to rise and thus encrust more of the moss. The result is a series of terraced pools. It is even possible to find patches of travertine which still preserve, in crude outline, the original stems of the moss.

John Ray is said to have considered these springs his fountain of youth. Today visitors are sometimes inspired to tone down its bicarbonic bite with the addition of flavour crystals. The result, in small quantities, is a refreshing Wells Gray "soda pop." In large doses, it is a marvellous natural laxative.

Just north of the springs, a wet meadow provides habitat for some interesting wetland plants. Among the more conspicuous is the White-rein Orchid (*Platanthera dilatata*), whose knee-high spikes of ivory flowers release, in mid July, a delicate perfume surely as fragrant

These pocked muds suggest a steady clientele of Moose, Mule Deer and other animals at the Ray Farm mineral springs. Such places are sometimes called "mud newspapers." (TG)

The waters in these springs have travelled many kilometres under lava flows, and over Kaza Group Limestones; the dissolved minerals they contain impart a distinctive effervescence. (TG)

as any in nature. Nearby, another treat for the nose is the familiar scent of Field Mint (*Mentha arvensis*).

The drier meadows above the springs support scattered colonies of Columbian Ground Squirrels. Recognize these "Mountain Prairie Dogs" both by their abrupt, ear-piercing barks, and by their rusty underparts, here colour-matched with the orange mounds at the entrance to their burrows.

Just north of the springs stand two Black Cottonwoods – favourite perches of the Red-tailed Hawks which hunt the Ground Squirrels, and which raise their young just to the east of here. As they soar overhead, listen for their husky, sibilant "CLEerr CLEerr," repeated over and over.

Another focus is provided by the old farm house, which provides an annual nesting site for Wells Gray's northernmost colony of Barn Swallows; the nests are orange in colour, having been built of mud scooped

Through these windows fly Barn Swallows by day and Little Brown Bats by night. The Ray farm house provides shelter for both. (TG)

from the mineral springs. Add a little grass, mix with spittle, and voilà: home for the summer.

Also living in the house is a colony of Little Brown Bats; look for them in the peak of the roof directly above the pile of bat droppings that grace the centre floor. In dry weather the bats are well hidden among the shingles, but when it rains they crawl out for protection onto the rafters, where they can easily be seen. Theirs is a strange, toothy grin.

Continuing from the farm house, the trail leads north past a small creek and then crosses the upper end of the farm to connect, half an hour ahead, with the Ray Mineral Spring trail (see km 56.1). Just beyond the creek, a short spur trail climbs the hill to a grave site. Here lie John and Alice Ray: buried beneath the land they cleared, and among the conifers now growing up to reclaim it.

ALICE LAKE

55.8 km
(34.7 miles)

- BIRD WATCHING
- FLOWER LOOKING
- PERRIER SIPPING
- MAMMAL TRACKING
- BATTING

J UST north of the Ray Farm, the park road descends to the outlet of Alice Lake, named for John Ray's wife. A short spur road provides an entry point from which to launch a canoe.

On the evening of July 13, 1977, a Beaver dam broke at the outlet of Alice Lake. The flood thus released swelled Alice Creek to an angry river which uprooted trees and washed out the bridge at this mileage. By 10:00 that night the lake had dropped two m, and traffic on the park road was blocked by a chasm nine m across and three m deep.

Some time later the Beaver left the lake. They had in any case been subsisting on a scanty fare of shrubby plants (especially Hardhack [*Spiraea douglasii*]), and now with their lodges high and dry there was little reason for them to remain. The dam was not rebuilt, and the lake has held to its dam-break level ever since.

Two m of vertical drawdown translated to as much as eight or ten m of exposed lake bottom. This new shoreline was soon providing habitat for a myriad of herbaceous plants, including Hemp Nettle (*Galeopsis tetrahit*), Stinging Nettle (*Urtica dioica*) and, to take the sting away, Bracken (*Pteridium aquilinum*). All of these can be found here to this day.

Latterly the herbs have been losing ground to shrubby thickets of Hardhack (with its spires of tiny

The Barrow's Goldeneye
(RBCM)

In time, the shoreline of Alice Lake will once again support stands of Black Cottonwood; and when it does, the Beaver will return. (TG)

pink flowers), Thimbleberry (*Rubus parviflorus*, with its large "maple" leaves) and, in places, Red Elderberry (*Sambucus racemosa*, with its compound leaves). The pre-1977 shoreline is, however, still easily seen.

Every summer the thickets beside the lake come alive with birds of many different species, including Yellowthroats, Song Sparrows, Wilson's Warblers and, less easy to see, Catbirds. A pair of Common Loons and another of Barrow's Goldeneyes nest on the lake itself in most years.

Growing in the shallows of the lake itself are two aquatic plants with snow-white flowers. The first of

Toad on the Road

Like Wells Gray's Grizzlies and Wolverine, Western Toads (*Bufo boreas*) can be ferocious predators, though they tend not to hunt the same prey. And, like the Caribou and Moose, they "range" from the forested valleys to the open meadows of the subalpine. Some toads have even been noted at 2500 m, near the summits of the Trophy Mountains. Maybe they were sightseeing.

A good reason for the Toad's success is its undemanding nature. Toads require but few things in life: soil or leaf litter to escape the hot sun and the winter cold; shallow, still bodies of water in which to lay their eggs; and insects small enough to be crammed down their throats. Their tough leathery skin offers some protection from the sun, so they

can venture farther from water than other amphibians.

Toads begin breeding as soon as the lakes (e.g., Alice, Shadow and Placid) are relatively ice-free. You'll recognize the males by the feeble whimpering sounds they make at this time. Breeding is their only social activity of the year; the rest of the time they are solitary hunters.

It is hard to avoid the feeling that toads are ugly – and proud of it. To confirm this, you may wish to examine one. Note the short, squat body, the undersized legs, and the numerous unsightly warts and glands on the leathery skin. Then ignore these features; they are simply the characteristics that distinguish toads from the closely related frogs, which possess smooth skin and large,

these is Water-plantain (*Alisma plantago-aquatica*), easily identified by its "plantain" leaves and spray of
rather showy, three-petalled blossoms. The second is
Water Buttercup (*Ranunculus aquatilis*), with its small,
five-petalled flowers floating star-like upon the surface
of the water. By what means did these plants find their
way to lonely Alice Lake? One likely possibility is that
they flew in on the muddy feet of migrating ducks.

In mid July the year's hatch of tadpoles, very abundant in Alice Lake, metamorphose into thousands of
young Western Toads. In some years the adjacent park
road then becomes peppered with their flattened bodies [see: TOAD ON THE ROAD].

The Western Toad (Bufo
boreas) *is a survivor.* (BI)

powerful hind legs.

Now pick the Toad up. It will not bite.
Nor will it cause warts. Hold the Toad at
face level with the front end towards
you. Here is an expression that only the
owls can compete with for pure arrogance. As you study it, the Toad will
doubtless pee on you. Many herpetolo-
gists suggest that this is a defence behaviour, but it is hard to avoid the feeling that it may also be an expression of
contempt.

You will probably have noted that the
Toad inflated itself while you were
holding it, but you may not have noticed that it at the same time released a
whitish secretion all over your hands.
DO NOT taste this secretion, nor rub it in
your eye to see if it feels good. This is
poison – not life-threatening, but a poison nonetheless. Always wash your
hands after handling toads.

If you happened to have gripped the
Toad gently behind the front legs, you
may have heard a rapid chirping or
clicking noise. This is a release click; the
only way that male Toads can let other
equally near-sighted and undiscrimi-
nating male Toads know that they have
just proposed marriage – or something
similar – to another male Toad. In more
natural conditions, the offending Toad
would release its grip. If you do not
hear a release click, inspect the Toad's
expression carefully. What you see may
be more than just arrogance and contempt. It may be love.

Harry Parsons

56.1 km
(34.8 miles)

- PERRIER SIPPING
- LICHEN
  LOOKING
- BIRD LISTENING

RAY MINERAL SPRING TRAIL

1 hr (2.2 km) return.
Elevation change: 25 m.

THE waters that emerge from the cone-shaped Ray Mineral Spring, alias "the Soda Fountain," are often favourably compared to Perrier or Vichy Water – bottled in Europe for the connoisseur. On the other hand, they are also sometimes likened to Eno or Bromoseltzer. According to taste, therefore, you'll either bend down for a second sip, or else stand up and make faces.

This hike can be completed either as a return trip or as a circle loop. Should you decide to go the latter, allow at least two hours, and be prepared to come out at the Ray Farm (km 54.5), and then to walk the shores of Alice Lake 1.4 km back to your vehicle.

For the first 100 m the way is steep, but soon the trail levels off, traversing a broad sandy bench. Nearby is Lone Spoon Creek; here listen for various cascading bird songs, including those of the American Dipper, the Winter Wren and, especially, the Northern Waterthrush: "Wheatwheatwheat Sweetsweetsweet Chewchewchew." A more breakfast-cereal-commercial-like song would be hard to imagine.

About 20 minutes from the road, the trail enters a forest of enormous White Spruces: some of the most ponderous in southern Wells Gray. On their branches, and no less ponderous in their own right, grow copious quantities of Lung Lichen (*Lobaria pulmonaria*).

To the uninitiated the Lung Lichen could easily be mistaken for the leaves of a maple tree. In fact, the Lung Lichen is not a plant at all. It's a lichen: a sugar-hungry fungus living in permanent association with a sugar-producing alga.

The lobes of the Lung Lichen (Lobaria pulmonaria) *resemble lettuce leaves.* (TG)

Most lichens die when subjected to urban air, especially air high in sulphur dioxide. The most sensitive species – including the Lung Lichen – falter at SO_2 levels as low as 30 micrograms per cubic m; by comparison, SO_2 levels in cities may average many times this concentration. Apparently the resulting greater acidity blocks the photosynthesizing activity of the algal partner, leaving the fungal partner with no source of energy. The superabundance here of Lung Lichen guarantees that the air is very pure. Breathe deep.

Eventually the trail forks. To reach the Soda Fountain, take the left fork and follow it into a clearing a few metres beyond. The right fork continues to the Ray Farm, now about 30 minutes ahead.

The Soda Fountain, like the springs farther south on the Ray Farm, owes its existence to the glacial and river sediments which underlie the lava on the hillside above. These porous sediments allow the ground water to percolate over great distances. As it does so, it dissolves various minerals from the sediments. Having reached the erosional edge of the lava flow, it bubbles to the surface with much the mineral flavour and colour of the local rocks.

In 1928 the geological survey party of J. R. Marshall investigated the mineral properties of the spring on the Ray Farm just south of here. The following materials (in parts per million) were found to be present in the spring water: sodium, 157.69; calcium, 243.00; magnesium, 86.00; iron, 2.20; aluminum 0.53; bicarbonic acid, 1499.73; sulphuric acid, 37.32; chlorine, 27.90; silica, 1.00; and oxygen for aluminums, 0.47. Given the similarity in taste between that spring and the Soda Fountain, a similar chemical composition doubtless applies here.

Rose galls are induced by the larvae of cynipid wasps (Diplolepis *sp.*) *In autumn, the leaves fall to the ground, where the pupae overwinter. They emerge the following spring as winged adults.* (TG)

BAILEY'S CHUTE TRAIL
1 hr (2 km) return.
Elevation change: 15 m.

57.0 km
(35.4 miles)

MYANTH FALLS TRAIL ....PAGE 133

• SALMON
  JUMPING
• PLANT
  WATCHING

AT Bailey's Chute the Clearwater is at its unforgiving best. Here the current is accelerated to firehose intensity by a constricting nozzle of canyon walls. Here, too, the slate-green waters toboggan down a 30 m ramp of riverbed, then explode into a witch's cauldron of spray and thunder.

From Bailey's Chute, the trail continues upstream to Marcus Falls and Myanth Falls; allow an additional 30 minutes or 90 minutes, respectively, for a return hike.

The first 100 m of the Bailey's Chute trail hugs the park road; where the trail diverges, you'll notice an old abandoned road, last used in the early 1970s, and now colonized by a colourful weed garden. Look for Bracken

Unsurpassable Bailey's Chute (BCP)

Like all members of the Pea Family (Fabaceae), the Arctic Lupine (Lupinus arcticus) has distinctive butterfly-like flowers. (RBCM)

(*Pteridium aquilinum*), White-flowered Hawkweed (*Hieracium albiflorum*), Spreading Dogbane (*Apocynum androsaemifolium*), and Arctic Lupine (*Lupinus arcticus*). Taken together, these are the advance guard of forest succession. Already they are giving way to young shrubs and trees.

Certainly the most attractive of these early colonizers is Arctic Lupine, with its slender stems, its long finger-like leaves, and, rising above them, its raceme of blue and white "sweetpea" flowers. The Lupine inhabits open sites from valley bottom to treeline; nowhere, however, is it more at home than on sandy road edges that have lately been scoured by a passing grader blade. Lately means within the past six or eight years.

Like other members of the Pea family – vetches and peavines for example – the Lupine enriches the soil in which it grows: clinging to its roothairs are tiny bacterial nodules (*Rhizobium* spp.) which take nitrogen from the air (where it is very abundant), and introduce it into the soil (where it is relatively scarce). As the soil's fertility thus improves, other plants take hold, and eventually these replace their benefactor.

A number of other native flowers are also favoured by disturbance; one you'll certainly notice is the Columbia Lily (*Lilium columbianum*), with its tall stems topped with orange, nodding lily blossoms. Later these are replaced by upright seed pods, which resemble salt shakers.

Shortly the trail crosses Mink Creek; check here for the bright orange flowers of Touch-me-not (*Impatiens capensis*). After early August, try gently touching one of the swollen seed capsules; if ripe, it should explode at your fingertips. By such means the Touch-me-not disperses its seeds across the windless forest floor.

A little farther on, watch for the aptly named Corn Lily (or False Indian Hellebore: *Veratrum viride*). Its man-high stems, long, pleated leaves, and (in July) green, six-petalled flowers are a familiar sight in mountain meadows. In the valley, however, it is quite rare. Could its high country ancestors have been carried here by Mink Creek?

The Columbia Lily, also known as the Tiger Lily, has spots, but no stripes. (RBCM)

Reaching for the Top

From mid August through September, Chinook Salmon can be seen attempting to wrestle their way past Bailey's Chute. Early morning and late evening are the best times to watch them leap from the water, bodies quivering, only to be swept downstream again by the overpowering current.

Chinook are the largest of the Pacific Salmon, weighing in locally at between 8 and 22 kg. Those here were born four to six years ago on the gravel bars of the Horseshoe, a few kilometres downstream. They have passed the last several years ranging the Pacific Ocean as far north as the Aleutian Islands. About a month ago, they entered the Fraser River near Vancouver, and have since fought their way some 600 km upstream.

For most of the 4500-odd Chinook that return to the Clearwater River, it is enough to have reached the Horseshoe or other gravelly stretches suited to the production of a new generation. There they dig their nests (or redds) in the gravel, deposit and fertilize their eggs, and then die.

A few of the spawners, however, invariably overshoot the Horseshoe, and continue north until they are stopped by Bailey's Chute. These are the Simon Frasers of the salmon world; when the river has finally carved a navigable channel through the Chute, it is their kind that will be on scene to establish a new spawning ground somewhere above. Without them, salmon runs would never have returned to the Clearwater at the end of the Ice Age.

Skunk Cabbage or Swamp Lantern? A name is more than just a name. (RBCM)

The tiny central flowers of the Dwarf Dogwood (Cornus canadensis) open by means of a "popgun" mechanism. Check for this by carefully touching one with a small twig. (RBCM)

The lily family (Liliaceae) contains many poisonous species, and the Corn Lily is one of the deadliest. It is a witch's brew of steroid alkaloids; when ingested, these may cause vomiting and diarrhoea, and drastically lower the blood pressure. In controlled concentrations the Corn Lily has medical applications, but uncontrolled it can kill. Remember: lilies are for funerals.

As the trail descends to the river, another plant catches the eye. This is the Skunk Cabbage (*Lysichitum americanum*), with its enormous fan-like leaves. It is a member of the Arum Family, but despite this distinctly tropical lineage, it is also among the hardier plants growing in Wells Gray. Its enormous yellow spathes push up even before the snow has melted in early spring.

The Skunk Cabbage is said to be edible at certain times of the year; eating it in mid summer, however, can be a painful experience, owing to the thousands of tiny calcium oxalate crystals contained in the leaves and roots. These may lodge in the mucous membranes, causing intense irritation and burning.

At Bailey's Chute the river is in uproar. The reason for all the commotion is the underlying bedrock, here similar to the Kaza Group phyllites and schists already discussed in connection with Trout Creek Canyon (km 29.9).

The sunken "punchbowls" below the viewing platform were carved by the constant churning of pebbles caught in cracks in the rock. They are similar both in appearance and in origin to those at the Murtle River crossing (km 41.5).

Despite the tumult, the river bed is by no means devoid of life. If the water is low, scan the rock for splashes of colour: oranges, creams, greys and browns. These are crust lichens of various genera, including *Lecidea*, *Huilia* and *Porpidea*. Though submerged for much of the year, they hug the rock substrate, and so escape the worst of the current. At times, it is difficult to tell where the rock ends and the lichens begin.

MYANTH FALLS TRAIL
2.5 hr (5 km) return.
Elevation change: 20 m.

- PLANT
  WATCHING
- MUSHROOMING
- WATERFALLING

North of the Chute lie Marcus and Myanth Falls. After a few preliminary ups and downs, the trail levels to an easy hike through mature forests of Western Hemlock and, in wet spots, Western Red-cedar.

Along the way, watch for the glossy, heart-shaped leaves of Wild Lily-of-the-valley (*Maianthemum canadense*), a plant not known to occur elsewhere in the park, and apparently at or near the southern edge of its range. It seldom flowers in Wells Gray; when it does, look for a diminutive raceme of even more diminutive white flowers. This is the lily after which Myanth Falls is named.

At Marcus Falls the Clearwater River, here about 100 m wide, effects a short but impressive drop over a low escarpment. The viewpoint is fenced.

Centuries of undisturbed forest conditions have encouraged the establishment here of a full complement of mushrooms, conks, puffballs and other fungi. This fact becomes obvious after about the middle of August (later in dry years), when the fungi are fruiting [see: THREADS THAT BIND, page 134].

At trail end, the path emerges from the forest just below Myanth Falls onto a pebbly, but secluded, foreshore called Shingle Beach. Here is one of few good places in Wells Gray to soak up a little sun. While doing so, notice that many of the pebbles on the beach are arranged as though they were dominos that had just fallen over. Having been rounded and flattened by

Shingle Beach. Notice the holes (vesicles) in the water-rounded lava cobbles. (TG)

their journey downstream, each pebble rests on the back of the next pebble. This is called imbricate layering and is typical of stream- or river-lain pebbles.

On the river itself, stay alert for the American Dipper, Harlequin Duck, Spotted Sandpiper, and Common Merganser.

For the return hike, you may wish to head inland along the trail that threads past bear-beloved West Lake.

Threads that Bind

Fungi are everywhere. Even early in the season (before the fruits appear), you can demonstrate this to yourself by simply picking up a handful of decaying needle litter. Examine it, and you'll soon discover it is interlaced with innumerable branching threads. Some are white in colour, others orangish. All are fungi. For this is what fungi most resemble most of the time: tiny threads.

Technically the fungal threads are called hyphae; it is they that make up the mushroom "plant." Every now and then the hyphae mate, and soon thereafter produce what is commonly called a "mushroom," that is, the fruiting body of the fungus. If you could view a mushroom through a microscope, you would see that it is composed entirely of tiny hyphae: a remarkable job of biological knitting.

The sole purpose of mushrooms is to produce spores. Spores are microscopic seeds; so tiny are they that 10,000 might fit inside a bubble the size of a pea. A large puffball (for example, *Calvatia gigantea*, which grows at the Ray Farm, km 54.5) is said to release 1,500,000,000,000 spores. If placed side by side, these spores would circle the earth some 15 times, yet possibly only one or two of them will ever manage to produce a new puffball.

Given such astronomical quantities, it is not surprising that certain insects have evolved to feed upon the spores. Rove Beetles (*Bolitochara* spp. and *Gyrophaena* spp.) are among the most common of the spore-eaters. Check the gills of any old, delapidated mushroom for these tiny, brown insects, with their short wings and long, flexible abdomens.

In an aged forest such as this, wood-eating fungi have a field day. Because many of them feed on lignin – the woody stuff of trees – they are themselves of a hard, woody texture. And being woody, their fruiting bodies persist much longer than those of mushrooms, often several years. They also tend to lack stalks; emerging from tree trunks, they have no need to elevate their spore-producing surfaces into the air. Thus they resemble shelves or horse hooves, and are called shelf fungi, or sometimes bracket fungi or conks.

Perhaps the most easily recognized of the conks is the Indian Paint Fungus (*Echinodontium tinctorium*), here found growing from the trunks of old Western Hemlock trees. Look for a hoof-shaped fungus, the upper surface of which is blackish and copiously cracked, while below hang numerous long, densely packed teeth. If you carefully break off one of the teeth, you'll find it is a brilliant orange colour inside. Formerly this fungus was used by various native peoples as both face paint and insect repellent.

Another common conk is the Red-belted Polypore (*Fomitopsis pinicola*), usually found on dead trees. Here the upper surface is concentrically banded, with the outermost band a brilliant yellow-red. Each band represents a single year's growth, and for this reason it is easy to establish the conk's age. Notice the thousands of tiny pores which pit the pale lower surface; it is through these that the spores are released. If the conk is fresh, try detecting its sour, tobacco-like aroma.

GLACIAL ESKERS

57.1 km
(35.5 miles)

O VER the next seven km, heading north, the park road becomes a veritable rollercoaster as it weaves over and around a series of glacial eskers and kettle holes. Eskers are under-glacier riverbeds of sand and gravel laid down in meltwater channels. Because they usually form while the glacier is still active, they tend to be destroyed by later movements of the ice. The eskers here, however, were formed under a dying glacier which had already ceased flowing, and so the eskers were preserved.

The kettle holes originated somewhat later, when blocks of down-wasting ice were buried beneath heaps of glacial debris. The last blocks to melt left behind steep-sided depressions which may now be filled with water. You'll notice several of these kettle holes along the park road.

SHADOW LAKE

60.7 km
(37.7 miles)

S HADOW Lake is one of Wells Gray's hidden gems. Although directly abutting the park road, and affording a fine mirrored view of 2900 m Garnet Peak, it seems to attract little interest. A pity, and for two reasons.

First, the lake is actually much larger than it would seem. By paddling to what appears, from the road, to be its northern end, you'll reach a narrow channel, beyond which the lake opens up again. Here a small island invites exploration.

Second, the stream that feeds Shadow Lake rises, not in mountain snowfields, but in the surrounding forests. For this reason it carries a rich charge of nutrients: abundant nourishment for diatoms, insects, fish, amphibians, and, higher up the food chain, Otter, Beaver, Mink, Black Bear and Moose. None of Wells Gray's larger lakes support, in so little space, such diversity of living things.

Watch for rafts of Yellow Pond-lilies (*Nuphar polysepalum*) on the surface of the lake, easily recognized by the characteristic large green pads interspersed with butter-yellow flowers standing slightly above.

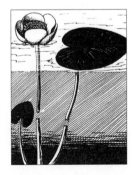

Yellow Pond-lily (RBCM)

Looking north from Shadow Lake reveals the snow-clad summit of Garnet Peak, deep in the Cariboo Mountains. (TG)

The Ruby-crowned Kinglet sings a bright, pert "Chur, chur, chur, look-at-me, look-at-me, look-at-me." (TG)

The leaves are covered – cactus-like – in a thick, waxy coating. Here, however, the wax serves to keep the water out, not in. What appear to be the petals of the flowers are actually the coverings of the flower bud, technically called sepals. The true petals are small, wedge-shaped flaps near the centre of the flower.

Shadow Lake is a lake of glacial origins, formed as the Ice Age glaciers here melted away in place. The glacial meltwaters were channelled along the edges of the valley, where they cut into the bedrock. When the ice finally disappeared altogether, these side channels were left behind, later to become long, linear lakes.

NORMAN'S EDDY TRAIL
1 hr (2 km) return.
Elevation change: negligible.

64.0 km
(39.8 miles)

- FISH WISHING
- BERRYING

A PPROACHING the south end of Clearwater Lake, the road descends a winding hill – the northernmost of the eskers discussed at km 57.1 – and then unexpectedly straightens out: yet another volcanic bench: the northernmost in the Clearwater Valley.

At the foot of the hill, a pull-off announces the Norman's Eddy trail. Allow about 20 minutes each way and, until late July, be sure to carry mosquito repellent.

Norman's Eddy is a widening in the Clearwater River, beloved of fish and fisherpeople, and named after Jack Norman, an early park ranger. Northward the Clearwater River has been narrowly confined within a small canyon of vertical lava walls. At the south end of the lava flows, the river suddenly widens; that widening is Norman's Eddy.

Here the forest canopy is open – a fact which has allowed various understory shrubs to establish and prosper. Two are especially common along this trail, and both are much sought after by Black Bears and park visitors alike.

Tall Mountain Huckleberry (*Vaccinium membranaceum*) and Oval-leaf Blueberry (*Vaccinium ovalifolium*), though closely related, are readily distinguished: the leaves of the former are medium green, faintly notched along the edges, and taper at the tip to a sharp point; in the latter, the leaves have a distinctly bluish cast, and are smooth-edged and rounded-tipped.

When ripe, the berries can also be distinguished by their colour: blackish blue in the Tall Mountain versus dusty blue in the Oval-leaf. Look carefully, and you'll notice a distinct circular imprint at the distal end of the berries. This, the flower scar, can be thought of as its "stamp of approval"; in British Columbia, feel free to eat any berry having one. (Except those of the Western Yew (*Taxus brevifolia*) – a needle-leaved, evergreen shrub quite different from the broad-leaved vacciniums).

Are the bushes heavily laden? If so, then doubtless the weather at flowering time was just right: no killing frosts; not too much rain; and lots of warm weather allowing the Bumblebees and other pollinators to perform their magic.

Aspen bark expands laterally, but not vertically. In time these bear cub claw marks may be taken for those of a full-grown Black Bear. (TG)

The Common Merganser in a characteristic pose (RBCM)

Because vacciniums bloom at different times at different elevations (at treeline the flowers are approximately two months later than in the valley bottom), a plentiful harvest along the Norman's Eddy trail by no means ensures a plentiful harvest everywhere. The best berry crops are usually restricted to a narrow elevational zone that moves up and down the mountainsides from year to year. And as the berry zones shift, so shift the bears that crop them.

By the way, what's the difference between a Huckleberry and a Blueberry? Answer this for yourself by picking an Oval-leaf Blueberry, and then carefully rubbing it.

65.2 km (40.5 miles)

FALLS CREEK CAMPGROUND

65.5 km (40.7 miles)

CLEARWATER LAKE CAMPGROUND

WITH 73 sites, Clearwater Lake Campground (including Falls Creek Campground) is the largest camping area in Wells Gray. Firewood, drinking water, sani-station and outhouses are provided, as are a picnic area and picnic shelter.

To explore Clearwater and Azure Lakes, you'll have to go it by boat or canoe. Canoes can be rented from Clearwater Lake Tours, situated at the north end of the campground. Boat tours are also available and leave daily for Rainbow Falls (at the east end of Azure Lake). It is even possible to rent a canoe on Hobson Lake; again, check with Clearwater Lake Tours.

If you're reading this book, you must be interested in learning about Wells Gray. Perhaps you should consider taking part in the naturalist programmes offered here every summer. Watch the bulletin boards for details.

Osprey Falls is a thin white curtain of water that spills over the edge of a lava dam. Northward lies Clearwater Lake. (CH)

The campground is located on a small lava flow that entered the Clearwater Valley about 7600 years ago along Falls Creek. After the flow cooled, the creek deposited a layer of sand over it. The resulting level surface has permitted the construction of two campgrounds here.

Birdwatchers will find much to keep them busy. Watch especially for a pair of American Dippers nesting behind Falls Falls on Falls Creek. Dippers spend their lives living in, on, adjacent to and under swiftly flowing water. Everything about these grey, rounded, pebble-like birds is geared to life in the fast lane. Their movements are hurried, jerky, and involve endless "knee bends," as you'll soon discover. Their song is a loud, bubbling cascade, calculated to be heard above the noise of the river.

Dippers eat the same kinds of aquatic insects as fish do, and must dive into the fast-moving water after them. Often you can see them walking quite happily underwater, foraging in currents that would topple a human. Sometimes they literally fly underwater using powerful wingbeats.

All of this raises the question whether Dippers ever experience silence.

Another specialty of the campground is the Merlin, a bird likely to be heard before it is seen. Merlins are jay-sized falcons easily recognized in flight by the pointed wings and long banded tail. They have nested in the campground area every year since about 1975.

Throughout the day the adults, concerned for the welfare of their young, utter an endless, ear-piercing "ki - ki - ki - ki - ki - ki - ki - ki - ki - ki - ki - ki - ki -

The Wells Gray naturalist programme is a fine way to learn more about the out-of-doors. Here a younger Trevor Goward tells all. (TG)

Black Bears are a common sight along the park road in early summer. Don't feed them. (BCP)

ki. . . ." Once heard, especially just after sun-up, this call is not soon forgotten.

Like the Peregrine Falcon, its larger and more famous cousin, the Merlin is a highly streamlined bird, adapted for rapid flight. It feeds primarily on other birds, which it often seizes in mid air after a high-speed chase. At one time, the Merlin was known as the Pigeon Hawk.

Black Bears also frequent the campground. Their season is predominantly mid July through mid August, when the berries are ripe. Some of their favourites include Soopolallie (*Shepherdia canadensis*), Saskatoon (*Amelanchier alnifolia*), Thimbleberry (*Rubus parviflorus*) and, finally, Red Elderberry (*Sambucus racemosa*). Fortunately, the bears normally cause few problems – a fact which perhaps attests more to the good behaviour of the campers than of the bears [see: BEAR PAUSE].

Other common mammals include Moose, Mule Deer, Red Squirrel, Flying Squirrel, Marten, Varying Hare and Columbian Ground Squirrel. Moose and Mule Deer are most readily seen along the park road at twilight, either dawn or dusk. Early summer is most productive; drive slowly, and keep your headlights on low beam. An early morning walk around the campground can also reveal wonders.

Bear Pause

Black Bears are common throughout the lowlands of the park. As soon as they emerge from hibernation, they seek out the Skunk Cabbage swamps and damp meadows. In the early spring their diet appears to consist of herbs, grasses and ants. As soon as the berries ripen the bears turn to them as their main food. According to local residents, there is a definite movement of bears to the Clearwater River in autumn, where they feed on spent salmon.

One hundred and seven bear scats were examined [in 1950 by P.W. Martin]: 12 contained ants; 14, fibrous vegetable material; and 81, berries. Logs and stumps were frequently seen that had been ripped open by bears for the ants and grubs they harboured. No animal material was identified in the scats apart from the aforementioned insects.

The abundance of bears appears to be largely correlated with the abundance of berries. The berry crop of 1949 was a complete failure owing to early frosts. Not a single cub track was seen during 1950; in all probability this was due to the fact that the bears entered the winter in poor condition and failed to produce young.

Summarized from P. W. Martin (1950)

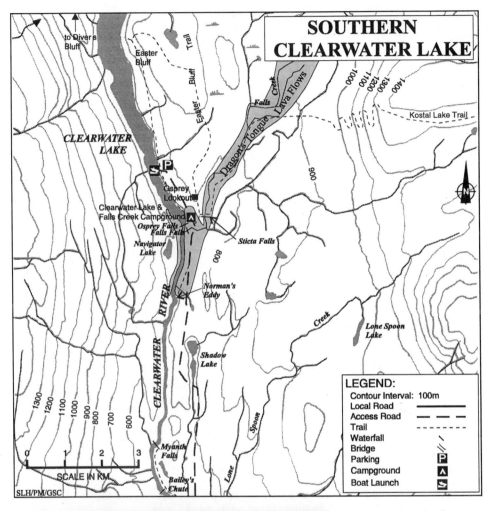

SOUTHERN CLEARWATER LAKE

to Diver's Bluff

Easter Bluff

Easter ___ Bluff ___ Trail

CLEARWATER LAKE

Falls

Creek

Dragon's Tongue Lava Flows

Kostal Lake Trail

1000
1100
1300
1400

900

N

Osprey Lookout

Clearwater Lake & Falls Creek Campground

Osprey Falls
Falls Falls

Sticta Falls

Navigator Lake

800

Norman's Eddy

Creek

Lone Spoon Lake

CLEARWATER RIVER

Shadow Lake

Spoon

LEGEND:

Contour Interval: 100m	
Local Road	
Access Road	
Trail	
Waterfall	
Bridge	
Parking	P
Campground	A
Boat Launch	S

1300
1200
1100
1000
900
800
700
600

0   1   2   3

SCALE IN KM

Myanth Falls

Lone

Bailey's Chute

SLH/PM/GSC

As you explore the clear waters of Clearwater Lake, keep in mind the unforgiving river that drains it. Pictured at left is Bailey's chute. (BCP)

- FORESTING
- LANDFORMING
- LIFE ZONING
- BEAR DENNING

OSPREY LOOKOUT TRAIL
2 hrs (3 km) return.
Elevation change: 250 m.

The rugged Cariboo Mountains rise not far to the north of Clearwater Lake Campground, but to catch a glimpse of them you'll have to climb 250 m to the Osprey Lookout.

The trail begins from km 65.3 of the park road, immediately north of Falls Creek bridge. Be ready for some steady ups and, later, some steady downs.

For the first half km, the trail switchbacks steeply through a youngish forest of Paper Birch, Douglas-fir, Lodgepole Pine and Trembling Aspen. Charred stumps along the way reveal that fire once swept this slope. The earliest accounts tell of fire as well: "From the southern end of Clearwater Lake, we travelled south-easterly through six miles of rolling fire-swept country, most of it gravel" (F.C. Green, 1914) [see: GROWING UP].

Fifteen minutes from the road the trail rounds onto a broad ridge at a signposted junction. Turn left at the junction, and continue upward along the ridge for another 20 minutes. As you climb, the ridge becomes narrower, and more exposed, resulting in stronger cross winds. Fog is also relatively frequent here, owing to the

---

Growing Up

Ever since fire swept this slope, nearly a century ago, it has been growing up to successive waves of vegetation: first weedy perennials like Fireweed (*Epilobium angustifolium*); then willows and alders; and finally the trees which currently occupy it. Today there are signs that a new generation of forest trees is preparing to assert itself.

Western Red-cedar and Western Hemlock already dominate in the forest understory. They are, in fact, the only trees now colonizing here, the seedlings of other species having been excluded by the deepening shade. Yet Red-cedar and Hemlock actually require this shade in order to establish on this warm, southwest-facing hillside; earlier, the ground was simply too dry to support them.

These trees are fast growers. In time they will outstrip the older trees, and, having done so, will cast a shade of their own. Eventually the Birch, the Douglas-fir, the Aspen and the Pine will all die, and the forest will convert entirely to Red-cedar and Hemlock. This process is called forest succession; when complete, the forest will be called a climax forest.

Climax is forever. Once established, it will be disrupted only by another round of fire, or disease, or other destructive agent. An excellent example of a climax Cedar-Hemlock forest can be explored at the Boat Launch, at km 68.5.

upslope winds which, as they rise, cool, and so condense into cloud: ideal growing conditions for at least a dozen species of hair lichens, which are apparently the lichens favoured by rapid cycles of wetting and drying.

After mid July, watch for clumps of Indian Pipe (*Monotropa uniflora*), a ghostly waxen flower which in profile resembles a corncob pipe. Different from most flowering plants, it lacks chlorophyll (the sugar-producing pigment that gives plants their green colour), and is unable to manufacture its own food. Part of its sustenance comes from decaying matter in the soil. The rest, with the help of fungi, derives indirectly from tree roots. The fungi (*Boletus* spp.) allow organic compounds to pass from the tree roots to the roots of the Indian Pipe.

Eventually the trail once again branches; this time take the right-hand fork, continuing around one last switchback to a clearing in the forest: this is Osprey Lookout.

The lookout is situated on the upper surface of what was once part of the Murtle Plateau. The Clearwater River has downcut into the plateau on the west, while Falls Creek (and its predecessors) have dissected it to the east. Today the only remnant of the original surface is the narrow ridge on whose summit the lookout is located.

Osprey Lookout takes its name, of course, from Osprey Falls, over which it provides a commanding view. Here the Clearwater River has been carving backward into a 600 m wide portion of the lava dam upon which the campground is situated.

Now nearing the northern edge of the lava (a fact readily observed from the lookout), the river can be expected to breach this natural dam within the next few centuries. When this happens, the surface of Clearwater Lake will drop by about three m, and the lake's shoreline will be changed forever.

On the valley wall across the lake, two different forest zones can be seen, each distinguishable by colour. The lower (medium-green) zone occurs below about 1300 m. It is called the Interior Cedar-Hemlock Zone (ICH), a name which emphasizes the two tree species that dominate in older, climax forests, though in younger stands these trees are not always present. The ICH Zone is widespread in Wells Gray at lower elevations.

Take a moment to consider how much life goes on above your head. More than 75 different kinds of lichens colonize the trunks and branches of Wells Gray's trees. (TG)

When crushed, the needles of Western Red-cedar are refreshingly fragrant. (BCP)

To the Red-breasted Nuthatch, up is down.
(BCP)

Above, the Engelmann Spruce-Subalpine Fir Zone cuts in, with its much darker colouration. In part, the colour reflects the darker needles of the trees (possibly an adaptation to the cooler conditions at higher elevations: dark surfaces absorb more heat than light surfaces). Part of the darker colour also comes from the enormous loads of black hair lichens which hang from the branches here. This forest zone extends upward to treeline, and is composed almost exclusively of the two tree species for which it is named.

Beyond the Osprey Lookout, the trail describes a pleasant, ten-minute loop. The right-hand fork soon brings you to a second lookout, this one giving northeastward onto the edge of the Cariboo Mountains. None of the 2400 m summits ahead has yet been named, though collectively they are known as the Goat Peaks.

Beyond the lookout, the trail crosses to the central portion of the ridge. Watch on the left for an obvious cavity among the roots of a fallen tree. Years ago this was excavated by a young Black Bear as a winter denning site.

From here the trail gradually loops back to the Osprey Lookout; en route, you'll notice a fork leading north (right) to Chain Meadows Lake and Easter Bluffs.

• LAVA LOOKING
• LICHEN LOOKING
• WATERFALL WATCHING

STICTA FALLS TRAIL
1 hr (1.5 km) return.
Elevation change: 90 m.

So well concealed is Sticta Falls that finding it is always a surprise. On hot, muggy afternoons it is also always a delight, for here is one place where you can escape not only the heat, but also the biting flies.

The trail begins at the Kostal Lake trailhead, just north of the Falls Creek bridge on the park road. From here it winds upward about 60 m to the crest of a broad ridge, 15 minutes ahead. This ridge is a volcanic remnant; as you climb, watch for lava boulders along the trail. The pocked rocks have been deposited by retreating glaciers; notice how rounded they are, a fact suggesting they have been repeatedly tumbled in glacial meltwaters.

Metamorphosed marine sediments of the Kaza Group have cracked and shifted along the fault visible in the centre of the photograph. (TG)

Rounding the ridge, the trail passes a signposted junction; here proceed straight ahead and down the other side of the ridge to a rushing stream. This is Falls Creek. If it seems to you the creek is flowing in the wrong direction relative to its intersection with the Clearwater River, don't worry: it is. Just downstream from here, it will describe a sharp bend, thus veering back to its rendezvous with the Clearwater.

From here the main trail crosses the creek on a wooden bridge, continuing thence to the Dragon's Tongue. Just before the bridge, turn right down a narrow path signed Sticta Falls. Be prepared to negotiate a few rather steep pitches.

Sticta Falls is named for the small, black lichen, *Sticta fuliginosa*, which inhabits tree branches near

False Solomon's Seal (Smilacina racemosa) is a lily with rose-scented flowers and, later, red-speckled berries. (NONC)

here. The genus *Sticta* is much more common in the tropics than in Canada, where it occurs primarily along the oceanic coasts. Roughly comparable conditions are met in southern Wells Gray Park only in the spray zones of waterfalls.

At Sticta Falls, Falls Creek tumbles stepwise into a narrow canyon. In the canyon walls just downstream, look for a fine exposure of foliated metamorphic rock of the Kaza Group. Running diagonally through the middle of the cliff is a fault line. A fault occurs where the rocks move relative to one another. Look closely, and you'll see that the banded rock on either side of the fault has been offset to left and right.

• LAVA LOOKING

DRAGON'S TONGUE TRAIL
2.5 hr (4 km) return.
Elevation change: 100 m.

Campers at Clearwater Lake seldom guess that buried beneath their camping pads lies the business end of a river of lava: the tip of the Dragon's Tongue.

7600 years ago this lava flow, then a river of fire, was erupted from the throat of Dragon Cone, a volcano northeast of here near the headwaters of Falls Creek. Channelled by the narrow defile of Falls Creek Valley, the lava flowed some 15 km until it poured out across the Clearwater River, there fanning out and creating a broad dam three m in height.

Today the roar of Osprey Falls, adjacent to the campground, is really nothing more than the grumbling of

The Dragon Cone is the volcano that erupted the Dragon's Tongue on which you are camping at Clearwater Lake. (The lower snowpatch marks the volcano's crater.) (CH)

the tongue-tied river as it gradually dislodges the Dragon's Tongue from the mouth of Clearwater Lake. Osprey Falls is, of course, the cutting edge of that process.

From the campground it is only 30 minutes by trail to a much more pristine portion of the Dragon's Tongue. Here the lavas present a broken, precarious aspect – in places nearly as open, and barren, as the summit of a high mountain; be sure to wear sturdy footwear.

From the trailhead (just north of the Falls Creek Bridge at km 65.3), the trail switchbacks to the crest of a ridge, then winds down the other side to Falls Creek, about 20 minutes from the road.

A change in the rock just beyond the creek announces the volcanic Dragon's Tongue, which can be seen in a bold, cavernous cut-away called The Grotto. The Grotto has formed where the flowing lava covered loose, hummocky glacial debris. Later, the creek cut downward through the lava, and carried away the underlying glacial sands and gravels, leaving a hollow which has since been eroding inward.

Although this lobe of the Dragon's Tongue comes right to the edge of Falls Creek Canyon, there is no evidence that it went any farther. The lava that was eventually to reach the Clearwater Valley (and Clearwater Lake Campground) apparently got there via a tributary valley some distance downstream.

Beyond the Grotto, the trail climbs briefly, then descends to a smooth lava floor. Notice that the rock here is pocked with numerous tiny holes. These are trapped gas bubbles, frozen in place as the cooling lava crystal-

The fragrance of the Twinflower (Linnaea borealis) is well worth going down on hands and knees for, but can only be detected when the flowers are growing en masse. (TG)

The upper surface of the Dragon's Tongue is a landscape of lava fragments. Take care not to turn an ankle. (TG)

lized around them. The bubbles are oriented roughly at right angles to the trail, suggesting that it was in this direction that the lava was moving as it cooled.

Contrasting with this level surface is the jumbled mass of lava that looms ahead, at the end of a short spur trail. Here the Dragon's Tongue has buckled, cracked, crimped and cluttered, like piles of broken crockery. The piles formed at the time of the eruption, when the hardening surface was jostled from below by the still-liquid river of lava. Such rock is technically called aa, a name which supposedly derives from the sound uttered by barefoot Hawaiians as they walked across similar lava flows in their homeland.

Near the edge of the aa, you may notice large vertical and, in places, diagonal caverns in the lava rock. Called the Dragon's Teeth, these are imprints of trees which were growing at the time of the eruption, and then engulfed by the surging river of lava. Look carefully, and you may also notice that the walls in some of the cavities are smooth, suggesting that the original trees may have been Trembling Aspen.

Not far away the lava buried a bed of peat laid down along the edge of an earlier version of Falls Creek. Geologists have recovered some of this peat, and subjected it to radiocarbon dating in an attempt to estimate the age of the Dragon's Tongue. The result: 7560 years, give or take 110 years.

To explore the Dragon's Tongue further, either proceed directly ahead, through willow thickets browsed by wintering Moose, or else (and better) backtrack a few metres to the main trail, and continue for another ten minutes. Eventually you should notice a clearing in the forest some distance to the right of the trail. This is your cue to head cross-country onto the middle of the flows.

Here is a landscape both hot and dry: an open wound only now being assuaged by the salve of Raspberry canes, Fireweed thickets, Birch trees and Dwarf Juniper. Very gradually the forests are colonizing inward from the edges, but until they meet in the middle, here is a home for the Common Garter Snake and its major prey, the Pacific Treefrog and Western Toad. Watch for them.

(Note: Because the trail hugs Falls Creek, you should have no trouble finding your way back; simply listen for the sound of rushing water.)

The Pacific Treefrog is easily recognized by its black face mask and knobby fingertips.
(NONC)

KOSTAL LAKE TRAIL
2 days (48 km) return.
Elevation change: 600 m.

- FISHING
- DEVIL CLUBBING
- VOLCANO
  PROBING

The words that best describe the trail to Kostal Lake are mud, brush and sore feet. As for the lake itself, with its attendant volcanic cone and lava flows, the operating word is wilderness.

This eight to ten hour slog is definitely not a hike for the faint-of-heart. Allow at least four days: one to get there; a second to explore the surrounding volcanic features; a third to walk out again; and a fourth to recuperate.

The first two km of the Kostal Lake trail doubles as the trail to the Dragon's Tongue, just described. Continuing, it winds for several kilometres across a rolling volcanic plateau clothed in second-growth forests. Along this section of the hike there may be little or no drinking water, and the mosquitoes can be merciless; be prepared.

About two and one-half hours from the road, and now at 900 m, the trail finally reaches the east wall of the Clearwater Valley, and begins to climb. Twenty-six switchbacks later, it levels at about 1200 m in an east-west valley forested in oldgrowth Subalpine Fir and Engelmann Spruce. Two small campsites will be encountered over the next several kilometres, each adjacent to a small stream.

The terrain eventually becomes very wet, and supports copious colonies of Devil's Club (*Oplopanax horridus*), a species with which the hiker soon becomes all too familiar. You'll easily recognize the long, procumbent, spine-covered stems and, at their tips, the maple-like leaves, equally spiny and 25 cm across.

About seven or eight hours from the road, the trail briefly emerges from the forest into a large opening, created by a blowdown in the early 1970s. The blowdown, about ten ha in size, provides strong evidence that Wells Gray may not be entirely immune to tornadoes. The severity, extent and type of damage seen here can scarcely be explained in any other way (unless, perhaps, a small meteoritic explosion).

Prior to the "blow" the forest here was densely stocked, fully mature and apparently healthy; afterward, scarcely a tree was left standing. Many were up-

The swampy ground was densely covered with a tough-stemmed trailing plant, with leaves as large as those of the Rhubarb plant, and growing in many places as high as our shoulders. Both stem and leaves are covered with sharp spines, which pierced our clothes as we forced our way through the tangled growth, and made the legs and hands scarlet from the inflammation of myriads of punctures.

summarized from Viscount Milton and W.B. Cheadle (1865)

The leaves of Devil's Club (Oplopanax horridus) *are enormous solar panels adapted to intercept as much sunlight as possible in shady woods.* (TG)

(*Left*) *A view west over Kostal Lake from the volcano.* (TG)

(*Right*) *The Kostal Volcano was breached at the time of eruption by a river of lava.* (CH)

rooted. Others were snapped off at the butt. Examining the now decaying logs reveals that most were apparently thrown outward from a common centre, an observation further suggesting that swirling winds might have been involved.

Long before the trail reaches Kostal Lake, you'll probably wonder whether you might have somehow passed it without noticing. Be assured this is impossible, for the lake is a primary terminus for the trail, offering one of the park's most magical camping places.

It is difficult to explain the magic of Kostal Lake. Certainly there is nothing obviously spectacular about its setting: the surrounding mountains are low, gradual and undistinguished; and the lake itself is roughly circular, with no obvious bays or juts of land to redeem it. Even so, no one who once visits Kostal Lake ever quite forgets its quiet, haunting mood.

Until recently, the lake contained no fish. In 1987, however, it was stocked by the B.C. Ministry of Environment with 30,000 Rainbow Trout. Good luck.

Kostal Volcano rises sharply from the east shore of the lake [see: FIRE MOUNTAIN, p. 177], roughly 30 minutes from the campground at lakeside. Crowning its 1450 m summit is a forest of Western Red-cedar, here somewhat above the usual elevational limits of this species. Some of the trees are enormous, measuring as much as four m in circumference. Red-cedars doubtless grow slowly at this elevation; there is reason to suppose that these forest giants may be among the most ancient trees in Wells Gray. Might they date to a time shortly after the volcano erupted?

LAKESIDE TRAIL
2 hrs (4 km) return.
Elevation change: negligible.

- BUTTERFLYING
- ROCK READING
- BIRD WATCHING
- LICHEN LOOKING

The Lakeside trail is signposted as Clearwater Lake Boat Launch, and begins from the picnic area, at the north end of the campground. Here is a trail combining easy grades, fine lakeside scenery, varied plantlife and great wildlife viewing.

The picnic area is a good place to see Osprey. Formerly known as the Fish Hawk, the Osprey is perhaps the completest of the "compleat anglers." Its hawk eyes may discern the least shadow of a fish from 20 m above. Its angled wings enable it to hover above its quarry until just the right moment. At the end of each toe is a peerless "fish hook," needle-sharp and curved. Even the bottoms of its feet are suited to their task, being spine-covered so as to better grasp the slippery fish.

Most days, an Osprey can be seen holding in mid air above its namesake Osprey Falls. Here the river crosses a lava flow, and so the shallow bottom maintains the fish close to the surface. Morning is usually the best time to watch the Osprey suddenly plunge into the water. A moment later, it lifts off again and, if successful (it misses about seven times out of ten!), it holds its prey head-forward.

If you get out on the lake, watch the shores for Osprey nests – huge stick platforms atop old snags. The young remain in the nest until summer's end. Once they leave the park, they will not return until they are two years old, and will not breed until the following year.

In the mixed forests at the northern end of the campground, and beyond, various Warblers and Vireos also come into their own. Among the more conspicuous are the MacGillivray's, Orange-crowned and Yellow-rumped Warblers, and the Red-eyed and Solitary Vireos. The Solitary Vireo utters short, disjointed phrases not unlike the rain song of the American Robin, only more melodious. Listen also for the bright, lively "Thlip!" of the Dusky Flycatcher.

A few minutes up the lake, berry bushes become common. Berries are just seeds that have been wrapped up in fleshy packages. Plants that produce

The Osprey, going down. (TG)

The Eastern Swallowtail (Papilio glaucus) *is the most widespread of its genus in North America, occurring from Florida to northern Alaska.* (HK)

berries are attempting to enlist the help of birds and mammals (including hikers) in dispersing their seeds. Indeed, berries don't just sit and wait for animals to come along; they actively invite them by being colourful and, in most cases, tasty. The seeds of some species are so well adapted to passing through digestive tracts that they will not germinate in any other way.

July is berry month in the park. Coming ripe then are Swamp Gooseberries (*Ribes lacustre*: spiny and black), Soopolallie (*Shepherdia canadensis*: translucent, red and copper-spotted), Saskatoons (*Amelanchier alnifolia*: like

Puddle Parties

If it is early summer – mid June to mid July – watch the puddles and other damp areas for congregations of large black-and-yellow butterflies sporting conspicuous tails. These are Swallowtails; their congregations are called puddle parties.

As many as three species of Swallowtails inhabit Wells Gray; of these, by far the most common is the Eastern Tiger Swallowtail (*Papilio glaucus*). Keep an eye open, however, for two other easily recognized *Papilio*: the Pallid Swallowtail (*P. eurymedon*), with black-and-white markings; and the Two-tailed Swallowtail (*P. multicaudatus*), with (you guessed it) two tails on each hind wing.

Swallowtails belong to the cosmopolitan family Papilionidae, which includes the world's largest butterflies, the Birdwings, with a wingspan up to

30 cm. By contrast the local Swallowtails are a mere 10 cm – still impressive enough when you see them. And as if to emphasize the fact they are Wells Gray's largest, Swallowtails tend to rest with their wings open, not closed as most other butterflies do.

So why the puddle parties? Apparently the puddles are "butterfly salt licks." The male butterflies gather to imbibe dissolved salts and sometimes amino acids. The salts are incorporated into the male's sperm and then transferred to the females during mating, to be used in egg production. When the butterflies are puddling, they often become so engrossed that they can readily be approached – a fine photographic opportunity.

Helen Knight

miniature, blue-black apples), Thimbleberries (*Rubus parviflorus*: like oversized raspberries), and Huckleberries (*Vaccinium* spp.: see km 64.0), all of which are edible, and all of which can be found, in varying quantities, along the Lake trail.

About 15 minutes north of the picnic area, the terrain steepens. At one point the trail, now a wooden, cantilevered walkway, crosses beneath a near-vertical cliff 30 or 40 m high. This is another outcropping of the Kaza Group rocks, which originated as mud on the bottom of the ocean [see: BITING THE DUST].

The fast-moving water of Clearwater "Lake" enables certain aquatic insects to live here that are normally restricted to rivers. In early July, for example, you can watch stonefly nymphs (*Pteronarcys* spp.) crawling from the water.

You'll find the empty larval castings clinging to vertical rocks and plants along the shore. The emerged adults are large, winged, orange-and-brown creatures

A hatch of midges on Clearwater Lake. Of the 100,000-odd insect species inhabiting North America north of Mexico, only about 500 are harmful to humans. Midges are not among them. (TG)

Biting the Dust

In places – and especially on the undersides of overhangs – the cliffs are literally coated in what at first might be mistaken for a fine yellow baby powder. Upon closer inspection this powder turns out to be a living lichen. And on closer inspection still, the lichen resolves into not one species, but many. At least five different kinds grow here.

Most dust lichens belong to one of two genera: *Chrysothrix* if they are yellowish; and *Lepraria* if they are whitish.

As a group, they grow in the most barren of habitats. They require neither soil nor rain nor even direct sunlight. Their food they take from dust; their water, from the air; and their energy, in some cases, from reflected light. They even reproduce without sex. All that need happen for a new colony to get started is that a single speck of "dust" (technically a soredium) be carried to some suitable nook or cranny.

The Lakeside Trail. When does a lake become a river? (TG)

Stoneflies evolved hundreds of millions of years ago, and have changed little since then. They are insect dinosaurs. (NONC)

– for many people, the stuff of nightmares. Though it is true they may inadvertently land in your hair or take shelter up your pant leg, they won't bite you (they have no mouths!). After a few weeks the flight is over.

At intervals the trail commands a good view out over the lake; here it is worthwhile stopping for a moment to scan for water birds. In mid summer, watch for female Common Mergansers and Barrow's Goldeneyes swimming by, an armada of tiny young in tow.

Forty minutes from Clearwater Lake Campground, the trail enters an ancient woodland composed mostly of Western Red-cedar and Western Hemlock. Shortly afterward, the trail terminates at the Clearwater Lake Boat Launch. If the day is young, you may wish to continue to Easter Bluffs; see below.

68.5 km (42.6 miles) CLEARWATER LAKE BOAT LAUNCH

As you've journeyed into Wells Gray, you have shed one twentieth century convenience after another. The last gas station was left behind in Clearwater; the last grocery store at km 22.2; the last mailbox at km 28.7; the last telephone booth at km 34.6; the last vehicle campground at km 65.3. Now, at Clearwater Lake Boat Launch, you must leave your vehicle behind. Turn to page 160 for a description of the park's waterways.

EASTER BLUFFS TRAIL
3 hrs (6.6 km) return.
Elevation change: 275 m.

- TREE WATCHING
- BIRD BOOING
- MOSS MULLING
- ROCK READING

Easter Bluffs is an erosional remnant of the ancient Murtle Plateau, now separated from its southern extensions by Falls Creek. The trail to the bluffs is a steep uphill grunt. Even so, the final spectacular view over northern Wells Gray makes it all worthwhile. Carry water and repellent.

Leaving the Boat Launch, the trail enters a towering forest about 500 years old. The largest trees, at more than 50 metres tall, have died back at the crown, and now protrude above the forest canopy, beckoning like bony fingers.

Apparently the forest dates from a fire that swept this slope half a millennium ago. Afterward, the first trees to colonize would have been the same species now seen in the younger forests to the south. Gradually, however, the early colonizers were shaded out by Western Red-cedar and Western Hemlock, which today form an almost unbroken canopy.

A few other tree species do occur, however, albeit sparsely: look, for example, for the deeply furrowed trunks of Douglas-fir and Black Cottonwood. These trees certainly could not have sprouted in the deep shade that now prevails; they must have established shortly after the fire, when the land was more open. Only by rising above the average height of the forest, have they continued to survive.

Few understory plants can survive in deep shade. Those that do must use to maximum advantage what little sunlight filters down to the forest floor. This may explain, for example, the enormous leaves of the Devil's Club (*Oplopanax horridus*), which are spread out like radar discs to pick up the least ray of sunshine. Watch for it in wet sites.

This may also partly explain the Western Yew (*Taxus brevifolia*): why its limbs here are so long and so trailing. Elsewhere this shrub is an upright tree to 20 m tall. Here it has no choice but to sprawl. In the first place, its branches are weighed down every winter by heavy snow. In the second place, the only way it could benefit from an upright habit would be to overtop the surrounding trees – something it is simply not adapted to do.

Growing just north of the Boat Launch is one of few forests in southern Wells Gray to have escaped fire during the past century. (TG)

The berries of the Western Yew (Taxus brevifolia) *are coral pink and poisonous.* (BCP)

By creeping, the Yew turns a difficult situation to its own advantage. For as it creeps, year after year, it seeks out small, sunlit gaps in the forest canopy; when it finds one, it pauses and puts on more foliage, thereby storing away food reserves against a shady day. In time the gap closes, and the Yew continues on its way. Look for a dark green shrub having pointed, flat, two-ranked needles, and coral-red "berries."

Of course, even better adapted to tolerate the shade are the mosses. Although 225 mosses are known to occur in the park, much of the moss cover in this forest is composed of only a few species. Collectively these are known as feather mosses, named for their resemblance to the feathers of birds.

The Stairstep Moss (*Hylocomium splendens*) is locally perhaps the most common of the feather mosses. Identify it by its step-like stems, or "fronds," each rising from the frond below. The steps represent annual growth increments; by counting them, you can actually tell how old a particular plant is.

Mosses contribute much to the ecology of old-growth forests. On the credit side, their loose, deep mats retard evaporation, and so help maintain the water balance of the soil. On the debit side, they intercept whatever nutrients are washed from the trees, making them unavailable to other forest plants. As well, the thick mats sometimes prevent the roots of young seedlings from reaching the soil, causing them to dry out, and so die. It is likely that the mosses are partly responsible for the sparse understory in this climax forest.

Sparse here, too, are the birds. Yet one bird you are sure to see – or at least to hear – is the Winter Wren. This tiny, 9 cm dynamo is really more like a mouse than a bird. Recognize it by its movements (quick, brown, and low to the ground), and especially by its song, which is a loud bubbling stream that continues unbroken for up to 11 seconds.

The nest of the Winter Wren is difficult to locate, being squirrelled away among the upturned roots of a fallen tree, or other out-of-the-way place. Constructed by the male, it is essentially a large ball of moss and twigs, having a side entrance. The male also sometimes constructs one or more dummy nests, apparently to throw would-be nest robbers off the track. After the young have fledged, and before they leave

Easter Bluffs. These haunting shapes owe their existence to the differential erosion of bubbles (vesicles) trapped while the lava was still cooling. (TG)

their parents, you can sometimes find family groups of three or four young birds all perched together on top of a stump.

Thirty minutes from the Boat Launch, the trail enters a much younger woodland, and at the same time turns inland and begins to climb. The climb is long, and will occupy the next hour or so, bringing you some 200 m above the lake. If you've carried mosquito repellent with you, this is the time to apply it.

Shortly after the trail levels, watch for an unmarked spur path branching left. A few minutes along this brings you to a narrow volcanic ridge overlooking Clearwater Lake. Unless you are planning a boat or canoe trip up the lake, nowhere else will you enjoy such a commanding vista of northern Wells Gray.

Winter Wrens are more common in the park in summer than in the winter. Such a lot of song from such a little bird. (BCP)

The shores of Chain Meadows Lake provide a fine home for many species of sedge. (TG)

Like many other members of the Heather Family (Ericaceae), Prince's Pine (Chimaphila umbellata) has nodding flowers and evergreen leaves. (TG)

2900 m Garnet Peak dominates the skyline, flanked and fronted by the Huntley-Buchanan Ridge. Garnet may already be familiar to you from the Clearwater Valley Overlook, now 60 km south. During the last Ice Age, its summit stood above the ice sheet, and thus escaped glaciation. Its flanks, however, did not escape, but were steepened by the grinding action of the glaciers that clung to them; it was these which shaped Garnet to its present horn-like profile.

Back on the main trail again, another 15 minutes of uphill clambering brings you to a broken talus slope. Exposed here is a line of vertical basalt columns approximately seven m tall. Viewed in profile, some of the columns bear an uncanny resemblance to human faces, just as the famous megaliths of Easter Island do: whence the name Easter Bluffs.

The columns are volcanic remnants that originated with the cooling of a lava flow here. Newly solidified lava is still four times hotter than the hottest household oven; as it cools, it contracts sideways, each cooling particle pulling equally against the one beside. Cracks form, usually to make six-sided columns, but three-, four-, and five-sided columns are also common. Here the columns have been exposed by erosion.

Hikers sometimes prefer to treat the Easter Bluffs trail as part of a more extended hiking circuit – which indeed it is. From Easter Bluffs, you can continue south to Clearwater Lake Campground, en route passing Chain Meadows Lake and Osprey Lookout. Should you wish to complete the circuit, allow about three hours from this point.

PART THREE

THE LAKES

CLEARWATER AND AZURE LAKES

Elevation: 680 m.
One-way distance (time) from Clearwater Lk Boat Launch to:
- North end of Clearwater Lake: 20 km (7 hours by canoe).
- East end of Azure Lake: 46 km (2 days by canoe).

Maps: National Topographic Series (1: 50,000):
- Clearwater Lake: 93 A/1, 8.
- Azure Lake: 83 D/5, 93 A/8.

Time to allow: 4 days to 1 week.
Camping:
- 12 camping places with space for 64 tents. See map.
- purchase camping tickets at boat launch.
- Ivor Creek Campground, No Name Campground and Osprey Campground are for canoeists only.
- maximum stay: 14 days.

Hazards:
- high winds, especially at north and south ends of Clearwater Lake, and east end of Azure Lake.
- strong current at south end of Clearwater Lake, and on river between Clearwater and Azure Lakes.

C LEARWATER Lake Boat Launch (page 154) is gateway to northern Wells Gray, with its un-climbed peaks, unexplored icefields, and un-trodden valleys. It is gateway also to three of the park's five large lakes: Clearwater, Azure and Hobson. Clearwater and Azure Lakes form a water highway 50 km long, accessible to canoes, kayaks and motor boats. Getting to Hobson Lake is another matter, however, and involves a shoulder-numbing portage 13 km long.

Overnight visitors can choose among 12 camp-grounds (eight on Clearwater and four on Azure) with space for approximately 64 tents. As most camping spaces are situated on low-lying deltas at the mouths of streams, some may be unusable in high water. The most hospitable beaches (after mid July) are at Bar View, Divers' Bluff and Rainbow Falls campgrounds. Firewood is supplied at each of the campgrounds. Also supplied are picnic tables, camping pads, fire grates, pit toilets and bear caches. When using a bear cache, keep in mind that bears can climb ladders.

Sightseeing tours of Clearwater and Azure Lakes are offered daily from June through September by the op-erators of Clearwater Lake Tours. The tours leave from the mini-boat launch at the north end of Clearwater Lake Campground. Canoe rentals and water taxi ser-vices can also be arranged. For further information

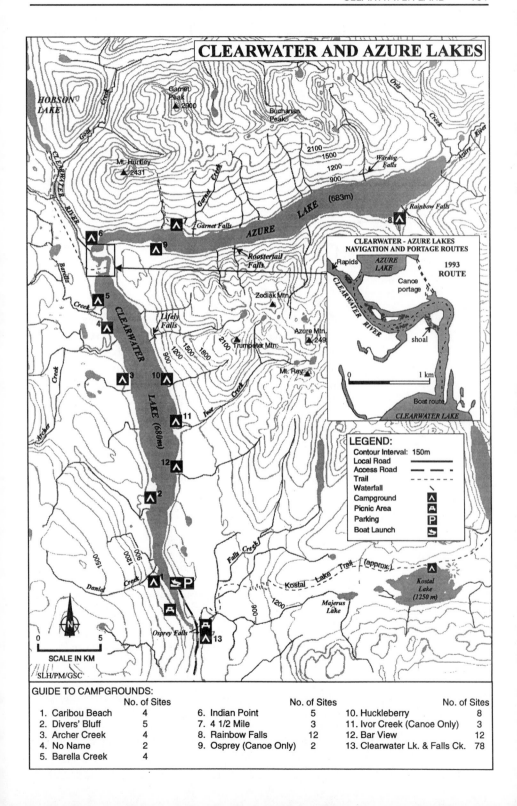

CLEARWATER AND AZURE LAKES

HOBSON LAKE

Garnet Peak ▲2900

Buchanan Peak

Goat Creek

Mt. Hurtley ▲2431

Garnet Creek

Wardog Falls

2100
1500
1200
900

AZURE   LAKE   (683m)

Rainbow Falls

Garnet Falls

7

8

Barella Creek

6

9

AZURE

Roostertail Falls

Zodiak Mtn.

CLEARWATER

5

Lifely Falls

4

2100
1800
1500
1200
900

Trumpeter Mtn.

Azure Mtn. ▲2491

Mt. Ray

Archer Creek

3

10

LAKE   (680m)

11

Pivot Creek

12

2

Falls Creek

Daniel Creek

1500
1200
900

1

P

A

Osprey Falls

13

Falls Creek

Kostal   Lake   Trail   (approx.)

Kostal Lake (1250m)

Majerus Lake

900
1200

CLEARWATER - AZURE LAKES NAVIGATION AND PORTAGE ROUTES

AZURE LAKE

Rapids

1993 ROUTE

Canoe portage

CLEARWATER RIVER

shoal

0   1 km

Boat route

CLEARWATER LAKE

LEGEND:

Contour Interval: 150m	
Local Road	
Access Road	
Trail	
Waterfall	
Campground	⛺
Picnic Area	⛺
Parking	P
Boat Launch	⬗

N

0   5
SCALE IN KM

SLH/PM/GSC

GUIDE TO CAMPGROUNDS:

	No. of Sites		No. of Sites		No. of Sites
1. Caribou Beach	4	6. Indian Point	5	10. Huckleberry	8
2. Divers' Bluff	5	7. 4 1/2 Mile	3	11. Ivor Creek (Canoe Only)	3
3. Archer Creek	4	8. Rainbow Falls	12	12. Bar View	12
4. No Name	2	9. Osprey (Canoe Only)	2	13. Clearwater Lk. & Falls Ck.	78
5. Barella Creek	4				

The Mule Deer (BCP)

write Box 27, Clearwater B.C. VOE 1NO or call 604-674-2121 or 604-674-3052.

Along the shores of the lakes, and especially along the banks of the river separating them, watch for Black Bears, Beaver, Mink, Moose, Caribou, Mule Deer, Otter, Marten, Porcupine and, of course, Red Squirrels. Plying the lakes themselves, watch for Common Loons, Horned, Red-necked and Western Grebes, Canada Geese, Mallards, Northern Pintails, American Wigeons, White-winged Scoters, Barrow's Goldeneye, Buffleheads and Common Mergansers. If you see any waterfowl not on this list, we'd like to hear about it.

Clearwater Lake

C LEARWATER Lake is a lake of transition. Not only do its waters divide the Clearwater River, above and below, into two very different streams [see: MUDWATER B.C.], they also separate Wells Gray's front country from its back country. The lake is bounded by lava flows in the south, highlands in the middle, and mountains in the north.

The lower half of Clearwater Lake is hemmed in against the western side of the Clearwater Valley by volcanic Murtle Plateau, here as much as six km wide and 250 m high. Northward, this lava obstruction narrows, and the lake gradually broadens to fill the entire valley, 2.5 km across.

Mudwater, B.C.

Where the Clearwater River enters Clearwater Lake, the Clearwater River is not clear water at all. Rather it is a milky, murky stream fresh out of the Cariboo Mountains, and laden with a heavy burden of silt. The silt is glacial flour: infinitesimal particles of rock milled by the grinding press of glaciers on the mountains of the northern park.

Twenty-three km later, the Clearwater River exits the south end of Clearwater Lake as clear as glass. The lake, a settling pond for the river, has transformed it from mudwater to clearwater. Azure and Hobson Lakes are also settling ponds, of course, but it is in Clearwater Lake that the settling process finally comes full term.

The silt that gets left behind in the lake is gradually filling it up. The only reason Clearwater Lake still sounds at 197 m deep is that the infilling began only 11,000 years ago; prior to that, the lake's bottom had been freshly dredged and scoured by glacial ice.

Must we then look forward to eventually losing our beloved Clearwater Lake? Not to worry: long before glacial sediments will have succeeded in infilling the lake, the coming Ice Age is sure to have dredged and scoured it once again.

As you paddle or putt-putt uplake, scan the eastern skyline for the reddish summit of 2050 m Ray Mountain. Ray Mountain is a volcano: the most northerly volcano in the park. It erupted approximately 20,000 years ago, at a time when the Clearwater Valley was filled with glacial ice to a thickness slightly deeper than the summit of the mountain. At first the up-welling lava merely melted a watery peephole upward into the ice, but soon it was fire-fountaining high into the chill air. After the eruption ceased, the glacier closed once more over the summit of the mountain. Today this story of fire and ice is easily read in the red, oxidized cinders clearly visible from the lake.

A line of three successive cliffs jutting westward into the lake marks Diver's Bluff Campground, with its sandy beach and cove-like setting. The beach consists in part of small, flat, shiny pebbles of schist, as well as occasional larger boulders in which reddish crystals of garnet are embedded. Though the forests hereabouts date from a forest fire of roughly 50 years ago, a few grand old Douglas-firs are also to be seen. Recognize these "vets" by their thick, corky bark – the same bark that helped preserve them from fire. At the base of the cliffs, watch among the ground cover for the egg-shaped, evergreen leaves of Kinnikinnik (*Arctostaphylos uva-ursi*). Besides being a member of the Heather Family, Kinnikinnik is one of the longest palindromes in the English language. Late in the season, its bright red berries and will dry your mouth. Try one.

Beyond Diver's Bluffs, the Cariboo Mountains fill the skyline. To the north, watch for the claw-like summit of Garnet Peak (2900 m), tallest of Wells Gray's mountains. To the northeast rises the pyramidal profile of Azure Mountain (2500 m). During the last Ice Age the summit of both these mountains were "pencil-sharpened" by small mountain glaciers clinging to their flanks.

Rising east of Clearwater Lake north of Ivor Creek is 2300 m Trumpeter Peak – so named because it "trumpets in" the Cariboo Mountains. Here an open burn provides an obvious route to the summit. The ascent is dry and approximately eight hours one way; only experienced backpackers should attempt it.

Apart from the campgrounds, there are few obvious stop-overs along the lake. Two to watch for are the small natural harbour just north of Divers' Bluffs

Divers' Bluff: numb's the word. (TG)

Kinnikinnik has pink bell-shaped flowers, later replaced by bright red berries to dry your mouth. (NONC)

The Bald Eagle (top left), the Osprey, the Common Loon and the American Dipper are four conspicuous birds to watch for above, on, in and around Clearwater Lake. (TG) (BCP)

(apparently a submerged kettle hole, formed where a buried block of glacial ice melted in place); and ten m high Lifely Falls (see map).

Along the shores of Clearwater Lake, Paper Birch, Black Cottonwood and Trembling Aspen are all conspicuous; not so along Azure Lake where deciduous trees are rare or absent. This difference reflects different stages in forest succession, the forests of Clearwater Lake being much more prone to wildfire, and hence much younger.

- OLDGROWTH
    OGLING
- WOLFING
- WILDERNESSING
- NOT FISHING

HOBSON LAKE TRAIL
8 hr (26 km) return.
Elevation change: 180 m.

IN keeping with its wilderness billing, Hobson Lake is not an easy place to get to. The only approach from southern Wells Gray involves a 13 km hike originating at the north end of Clearwater Lake. Actually there are two trailheads: one at the northwest corner of the lake (among avalanche-derived deadheads and log jams), and the other on the west side of the Clearwater River, about 100 m north of the top end of the lake. Either way, the hike to Hobson divides roughly into an hour of bottomland meandering through green hectares of Devil's Club, and four hours of sidehill climbing and gouging through forests primeval.

To judge from the frequency of scat along the trail, the Gray Wolf is a regular visitor here. Wolf scats are similar to dog do-do's, but are usually fur-filled and often bleached white (crunched bones perhaps contain more calcium than kibbles do). Further evidence of Wolves can be deduced from the occasional bright lime-green algal crusts growing at the bases of trees. These crusts are nitrogen-lovers; their growth is favoured every time a male wolf raises a hind leg to mark territory. Look for similar algal crusts along a boulevard near you.

At Lickskillet Creek (three vista-less hours from Clearwater Lake), the trail drops 50 m into a small canyon. The creek signals not only the end of the uphill portion of the trail, but also the one truly grand prospect this hike affords. To reach it, cross Lickskillet Creek and continue to the canyon rim opposite. Here turn right off the trail and head downstream along a narrow ridge. At ridge end is a view (unfenced, unsafe, unofficial) encompassing both the great maw of Sundt Falls, and the crazy crags and hanging glacier of Goat Creek.

From the creek, the trail continues another six km (two hours one way) through immense oldgrowth Cedar-Hemlock forests to Hobson Lake. At trail end, a rustic overnight camp on the shore of the lake is a pleasant possibility, with space for about three tents. But unless you've carried an inflatable canoe with you, or made arrangements to rent a canoe here through Clearwater Lake Tours, this is very much the end of the trail.

Responsible anglers will be delighted to learn that Hobson Lake has not been artificially stocked with fish. Its ecosystems are therefore wild to a degree unmatched by any of the park's other large lakes [see: FESTIVAL OF LOONS, page 172]. Clearwater River below the lake is currently impassable to fish; the Redside Shiners and Largescale Suckers that presently inhabit Hobson must have entered it at a time when its waters had merged with those of either Quesnel Lake to the west, or Clearwater and Azure Lakes to the south. A well-placed Ice Age ice lobe would have sufficed to produce either effect. Evidence that lake levels were higher in the past than they are today can be seen also in the gravelly terraces along the northwest corner of Clearwater Lake, including the elevated floodplain on which the Hobson Lake trail begins.

Mountain Goats are at home in the Cariboo Mountains. (BCE)

(*Above*) *Despite its glacial origins, Clearwater Lake is inhabited by leeches of several species. Look for them on the undersides of stones along the shoreline.* (TG)

(*Below*) *The mountains surrounding Azure Lake are cloaked in oldgrowth forest.* (TG)

Azure Lake

O CCUPYING a deep gash in the Cariboo Mountains, Azure Lake provides a glimpse of the mountainous majority of Wells Gray. It is a wild, windy, raw-boned place, bounded by steep, forested mountainsides culminating in sawtooth ridges where Mountain Goats clamber at will.

The 2.3 km stretch of river linking Clearwater Lake with Azure Lake is navigable to motorboats equipped with a ten-horse engine or greater (check page 61 for route). Canoeists will prefer to take the portage trail on the right bank a short distance upriver. The portage, roughly 500 m long, traverses a wet area productive of mosquitoes, thus accelerating the portage process. Watch here for Skunk Cabbage (*Lysichiton americanum*, also called Swamp Lantern): an olfactory delight bearing leaves as large as a three year old.

The return journey is an easy, invigorating paddle downriver, but do beware the strong current where the two rivers meet, and please, **please, PLEASE** keep well away from the shore-line sweepers (leaning trees).

At Azure, with 58 streams over 56 km of shoreline, the sound of falling water is everywhere. Waterfalls to watch for include Roostertail Falls (splashing directly into the lake), Garnet Falls (doubling in winter as an avalanche track), Wardog Falls (set back from the lake) and Rainbow Falls (see page 168).

In the vicinity of these and other waterfalls, watch for three ferns uncommon elsewhere in the park: Maidenhair Fern (*Adiantum pedatum*), with its glossy blackish stems and ginkgo-like terminal "leaves," or pinnae; Anderson's Holly Fern (*Polystichum andersonii*), with its evergreen pinnae and brown-chaffy stems; and Long Beech Fern (*Phegopteris connectilis*), with its strongly down-turned pairs of lower pinnae.

Wildfires are rare on the shores of sodden Azure, where the trees are accordingly often sizable. On the slopes above the north shore of the lake, Red-cedars to 44 m tall and eight m in circumference have been reported. Such trees, which can usually be recognized from a distance by their spike tops, were already in place long before the days of Christopher Columbus. The forests supporting them may be much older still.

Roostertail Falls: Azure Lake always has something emphatic to say. (TG)

Recognize the Sitka Alder by its sharply serrated leaves.
(RBCM)

Recognize alders by their fruiting cones, or strobiles, which resemble miniature pine cones. (RBCM)

Oldgrowth forests are notable not only for the age and size of their trees, but also for the unbroken green carpet of feather mosses they support. Recognize four common feather mosses from their names: Electrified Cat's Tail Moss (*Rhytidiadelphus triquetrus*), Big Redstem (*Pleurozium schreberi*), Stairstep Moss (*Hylocomium splendens*), and Knight's Plume Moss (*Ptilium crista-castrensis*).

In the non-forested spaces surrounding the lake, dense alder thickets thrive. Alder roots bear nitrogen-fixing colonies of cyanobacteria (readily seen as small-ish nodules), and so help to fertilize the water-soaked, water-leached soils in which they grow. Two species of alder grow at Azure. Mountain Alder (*Alnus tenuifolia*) has somewhat rounded serrations on the margins of the leaves, and is restricted to the shore of the lake. Sitka Alder (*Alnus sinuata*) has much sharper serrations, and forms unbroken colonies up and down the avalanche paths.

At Rainbow Falls Campground, sandy beaches and mountain scenery constitute popular attractions, but no less engaging is the "rain forest" trail to Rainbow Falls. Here a fine mist of spray supports grand old Red-cedars and Hemlocks which in turn support thick, branch-draping balls of *Antitrichia curtipendula* – a moss more typical of coastal localities.

En route to the falls, the trail also passes close by a sandy ridge laid down by a stream at the base of a glacier. Different from most streams, which sooner or later erode downward into their streambed, under-glacier streams actually "erode" upward into the glacier on an inverted streambed. When the glacier melts, this streambed is left behind as a sinuous, sandy ridge, or esker. The esker here has disrupted local drainage, creating a small pond and bog bedecked with Yellow Pond-lilies (*Nuphar polysepalum*), Round-leaved Sundew (*Drosera rotundifolia*) and Dwarf Cranberries (*Vaccinium oxycoccus*).

Every so often, Woodland Caribou are seen swimming the lake just west of the campground. Exactly where they are coming from, or going to, nobody knows. Still, the relative likelihood of catching a glimpse of a caribou thus engaged provides a fine excuse to pull up a log on the beach, and sit awhile. If you have binoculars to hand, you might also scan the peaks north of the lake for Mountain Goat.

HUNTLEY COL ROUTE
7 hours (7 km) return.
Elevation change: 1300 m.

- THICKET THREADING
- GRIZZLY GAWKING
- MEADOWING
- GARNET GAZING

MOUNT Huntley and Buchanan Peak are end-points along the 13 km ridge running west and east above the north shore of Azure Lake. The low point in this ridge, Huntley Col, is one of few alpine destinations that can be explored from Azure as the labour of a day. At 2050 m, the col offers, among other things, a northward vista of Garnet Peak's vaguely Matterhornesque summit.

Grizzly Bears are at home among the avalanche tracks and alder thickets approaching treeline. Reassuring though it might be to reflect that nobody has yet been hurt by a bear in Wells Gray, that record could be broken any day now. As you climb and descend this route, announce your progress with plenty of noise. Try whistling Dixie, for example. And do carry water with you – to wet your whistle.

The Huntley Col Route begins at Four-and-a-Half Mile Campground, and is steep and steady all the way. For the first few hours, the going is easy enough, but near treeline, at 1750 m, the way becomes obscured by thickets of Mountain Rhododendron, False Azalea and Sitka Alder. Here work your way gradually westward (to the left) into a thicketless gully, and continue upward into the land above the trees.

As you climb, notice how restricted the subalpine meadows are on these slopes. By comparison, the meadows of southern Wells Gray (page 43) seem to roll on forever. Both these meadows (in the Cariboo Mountains) and those meadows (in the Shuswap Highlands) do in fact span a similar vertical interval. In the Cariboos, however, the slopes are steep, and narrowly compress the meadows between forest and heath. A few minutes of upward mobility, and they're behind you.

From this point on, the way to the ridge is a veritable alpine rock garden. Tending the garden are the Hoary Marmot (alias "the Whistler") and the Pika (with its nasal "Eep"). Listen for them.

Grizzly Bears are at home on these slopes; pay them the respect they deserve (and demand). (BCP)

MURTLE LAKE

Elevation: 1067 m.
One-way distances from canoe launch at Murtle Lagoon to:
- South Arm: 1.5 km (30 minutes by canoe).
- West Arm: 20 km (7 hours by canoe).
- North Arm: 26 km (10 hours by canoe).

Maps: National Topographic Series (at 1: 50,000): 83D/4, 5.
Time to allow: 3 days to 2 weeks.
Camping:
- 22 camping places with space for 85 tents: see map.
- except for 4 sites at west end of Murtle Lagoon, campsites are accessible only by canoe.
- purchase camping tickets in Blue River.
- maximum stay: 14 days.

Restrictions:
- internal combustion engines prohibited.
- no dogs allowed.
- no cans or bottles allowed.
- no fires permitted at treeline.
- overnight camping prohibited on Fairyslipper Island.
- firewood available only from wood corrals.

Hazards:
- sudden and strong winds, especially on north arm.
- shallow, rocky bottom in west arm.
- swift current near outlet of lake.

The north arm of Murtle Lake penetrates deep into the Cariboo Mountains. (TG)

O N a majority of the world's larger lakes, outboard motors are an accepted, and perhaps acceptable, fact of life. Not so on Murtle Lake. Here internal combustion engines have been banned since 1968, and visitors have been paddling their own canoes – in perfect silence – ever since. According to an unofficial survey conducted in the late 70s, Murtle is the largest lake in North America to be set aside entirely for paddlers.

Quillwort (Isoëtes *spp.*) *is an aquatic "fern." An autographed copy of this book goes to the first person who can reliably document what water bird consumes it in quantity at summer's end.*

Murtle Lake is quintessential Wells Gray: a 7600 ha wilderness lake ringed by 100 km of shoreline, and set in the midst of timeless mountain scenery. Eastward, a few token clearcuts remind us "Why Wilderness," after all.

Murtle Lake is not everybody's cup of glacier water. Biting insects can be a nuisance until about the end of July. The lake is subject to sudden and violent storms; paddle close to shore at all times. In case of emergency, rangers are on duty from early June through late September; they can be located at the ranger station along the south shore of the west arm.

With three separate arms radiating south, west and north, Murtle Lake offers three separate solitudes. As measured from their point of intersection, the south arm is 6 km long, the west arm 14 km long, and the north arm 18 km long. Each gives a quite different impression of the lake.

The south arm is a gentle place of clean, sandy beaches and shallow, translucent waters. Lake waters here are relatively warm (18°C in August), and attract sunbathers and swimmers in numbers perhaps unexpected at 1050 m, at least after mid July, when lowering lake levels expose the beaches. A special feature of the south arm is nearby Murtle Lagoon, with its calm demeanour and frequent offerings of Beaver, water fowl and Moose.

Most visitors to Murtle spend a majority of their time exploring the west arm. Besides the usual fishy attractions, this portion of the lake abounds in islands, bays, peninsulas and, not least, hiking trails. Also at hand are numerous sandy beaches (see map); but because lake waters are cool here (12°C in August), and biting insects numerous, water sports are not popular.

Lining the shores of the west arm are blocky basalt boulders derived from (an earlier version of) Kostal Volcano, 12 km to the northwest. The boulders were

Where there are Clarke's Nutcrackers, there are also Whitebark Pines. And vice versa. (RBCM)

The Common Loon: call of the wild, or of human intervention? (TG)

originally transported by glacial ice, but have since been rafted onshore by lake ice, and now encase the lower shoreline of the islands, which they thereby protect from erosion.

Other west arm specialties include 1) the hundreds of red-bodied Kokanee (land-locked Sockeye Salmon) that spawn in File Creek from mid August through late September; 2) the dozen-odd Osprey nests that line the shores (look for big stick platforms in the crowns of broken trees); 3) the wrack of Quillwort that strews the beaches every summer's end; and 4) the ever-present laughter of Common Loons [see: FESTIVAL OF LOONS].

Festival of Loons

If it is true that wilderness has many voices, then the voice of the Common Loon is certainly among them. All summer long Murtle Lake ripples with loon music. During June and July, the music has mostly to do with defining and maintaining breeding territories; maniacal yodels and falsetto wails are common refrains at this time. Later, as territorial instincts mellow, and the resident loons are joined by birds from smaller lakes nearby, the music takes a turn for the subdued: tremulous tremolos are a typical sound of late summer. By September, as many as 300 birds have gathered, all jostling in loose flocks: a festival of loons.

There is reason to believe that Common Loons have not always been present at Murtle. When Joseph Hunter, a surveyor with the Canadian Pacific Railway, first visited the lake in 1874 (naming it, we are unreliably assured, after his birthplace in Scotland), there were no fish in Murtle. And so, presumably, there were no fish-eating loons either.

Ever since glacial times, fish had been barred from entering Murtle by a downstream obstacle course of six impassable waterfalls, including Helmcken Falls. Then in 1928 and 1929, the Canadian Department of Fisheries overruled the waterfalls by introducing 40,000 Rainbow Trout to Murtle Lake. Not to be outdone, the B.C. Game Commission later stocked the lake with 100,000 Kokanee. By the late 1940s, Trout had become so plentiful at Murtle that the Seattle Fish and Game Club, for example, was moved to construct a fishing lodge – still standing – near the lake's outlet.

Almost overnight, the twin-engine roar of aircraft landing and taking off became a familiar sound here. Familiar too were the sounds of motor boats being revved, of cabins being built, and of trails being cleared. It was surely also during these years that the fish-loving Common Loon first favoured Murtle with its haunting calls. But unlike the sounds of planes and motorboats, which have a distinctly 20th century flavour, loon music quickly became emblematic of Murtle Lake's essential wildness.

By an order-in-council, passed in 1968, planes and motorboats no longer come and go on Murtle. But the loons still come and go. Their presence, like that of Mergansers, Osprey and Bald Eagles, is therefore really an emblem as much of wildness as of human tampering. For better or worse, the decision to introduce fish to Murtle Lake has disrupted 11,000 years of ecological tradition, setting its ecosystems down a new path altogether.

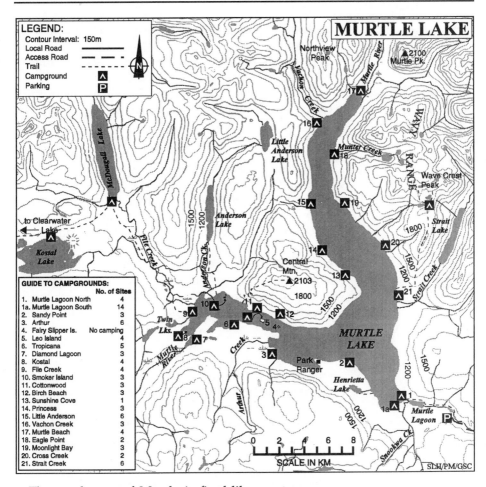

LEGEND:
Contour Interval: 150m
Local Road
Access Road
Trail
Campground
Parking

GUIDE TO CAMPGROUNDS:

		No. of Sites
1.	Murtle Lagoon North	4
1a.	Murtle Lagoon South	14
2.	Sandy Point	3
3.	Arthur	6
4.	Fairy Slipper Is.	No camping
5.	Leo Island	4
6.	Tropicana	5
7.	Diamond Lagoon	3
8.	Kostal	4
9.	File Creek	4
10.	Smoker Island	3
11.	Cottonwood	3
12.	Birch Beach	3
13.	Sunshine Cove	1
14.	Princess	3
15.	Little Anderson	6
16.	Vachon Creek	3
17.	Murtle Beach	4
18.	Eagle Point	2
19.	Moonlight Bay	3
20.	Cross Creek	2
21.	Strait Creek	6

    The north arm of Murtle is fjord-like, austere, re-
mote. Its main attraction lies in the rugged beauty of
the pencil-sharp mountains towering above. The water is cold (7°C in August) and milky blue, and supports few fish, except at the outlets of some of the
larger streams, which also furnish the only beaches of
any size.
    Watch the north arm for numerous lakeside stands
of five-needled Whitebark Pine to 18 m tall (often at-
tended by crow-sized Clarke's Nutcrackers). In the
wetlands at the north end dwell Canada Geese in the
hundreds, while in Strait Creek watch for spawning
Kokanee. The waters off Strait Creek, at 333 m deep,
are the deepest waters in Wells Gray.
    The forests surrounding Murtle Lake are arranged
elevationally in obvious zones. Engelmann Spruce and
Subalpine Fir dominate at lakeside, and can be recognized from a distance by their dark bluish cast. Typical

of mountain climates, these trees have presumably been favoured in the valley bottom by nighttime ponding of cold air. Higher on the slopes, and reflecting slightly warmer temperatures, Douglas-fir, Paper Birch, Western Hemlock, Western Red-cedar and other species more typical of lowland forests are common.

HOW TO GET TO MURTLE LAKE

The gravel road to Murtle Lake leaves the Yellowhead Highway at Blue River, 110 km northeast of Clearwater. The turnoff is located just south of the Blue River bridge. Be sure to study the notice board at the foot of the road for the latest crop of regulations and restrictions. From here the road leads westward 25 km, hugging the south wall of Blue River Valley. Though passable to motorhomes and other low clearance vehicles, the Murtle Lake Road is bouldery in places, steep in others, and narrow in others still; watch for logging trucks.

An hour later, and 400 m higher, the road crosses a low pass (elevation: 1100 m), formerly the outlet of Murtle Lake. Here the road enters Wells Gray Park, and then abruptly terminates in a parking lot doubling as the trailhead to the Murtle Lake portage. The lake is still about 30 minutes distant – or seemingly farther if you're loaded down with canoe, paddles, life jackets, tent, food, extra clothing, fishing rod, camera, binoculars, maps, rock hammer, lichen field guides, and other paraphernalia of survival.

The portage trail is gravelled and graded, but be prepared to negotiate a few minor hills. Should you have a canoe with you, avail yourself of the canoe rests erected along the trail for that purpose. While resting, consider that Phyllis Lake and the unnamed pond beyond it are kettle holes: depressions left behind after buried chunks of glacial ice melted away. Farther on, watch for the tallest Spruce trees in the park, aged 250 to 300 years. In June through mid July, listen here for the thin zi-zi-zi-zi-zi-zi-zi's of the Blackpoll Warbler: a song more common farther north. In late August, check the bushes beside the trail for Canada Blueberries (*Vaccinium myrtilloides*), the choicest of Wells Gray's berries of whatever colour.

Look for the velvety leaves of the Canada Blueberry. And among the leaves, look for berries as tasty as they are blue. (RBCM)

Paddlers can put in at the east end of the Murtle Lagoon (Murtle Lake itself is another half hour by paddle). Hikers, however, may wish to continue another 30 minutes farther to the only camping spot accessible by foot.

In the space remaining, we briefly sketch a few of Murtle's more well-appointed hiking trails; the rest we leave to your discovery.

CENTRAL MOUNTAIN TRAIL
7 hr (9 km) return.
Elevation change: 1000 m.

- HUCKLEBERRYING
- PERSPECTIVE TAKING
- GROUND SQUIRREL HUNTING

Central Mountain is the hinge on which the west and north arms of Murtle Lake turn. From here as nowhere else the lake is an open book.

The trail to the 2100 m double summit starts from the north shore of the west arm, roughly 1.5 km west of Leo Island. After traversing a fine old forest of Red-cedar and Engelmann Spruce, you'll enter a regenerating burn from the late 60s. Here, as elsewhere, the going is often hot and dry; be sure to carry drinking water with you, and perhaps a sun hat. Come late July, it is pleasant to dawdle in the burn awhile, picking Tall Mountain Huckleberries (*Vaccinium membranaceum*) as you go. At length the trail enters a sweet-scented forest of Subalpine Fir – only to emerge, half an hour later, at treeline.

Encircling the double summits of Central Mountain are subalpine meadows reminiscent of the Trophy Meadows (page 43). The summits themselves are rocky places – upholstered, if at all, in sedges and heaths. Here live small mammals of several species, including Hoary Marmots, Pikas, Yellow Pine Chipmunks, and, not least, Golden-mantled Ground Squirrels. The last-named species, at 30 cm long, resembles an outsized chipmunk. Golden-mantled Ground Squirrels are near the northwestern edge of their range in Wells Gray, and are here very localized.

If any of this moves you to words, you might want to record your thoughts in the hikers' register in the cairn on the west peak.

The Yellow Pine Chipmunk, at 23 cm long, resembles an undersized Golden Mantled Ground Squirrel. (NONC)

- CREEK PADDLING
- LAVA LOOKING
- LICHEN LOVING
- VOLCANO
  VIEWING

FILE CREEK PORTAGE TRAIL (KOSTAL VOLCANO ROUTE)

6 hr (11 km) return (2 days [28 km] return). Elevation change: negligible (175 m).

The File Creek Portage trail is turnstyle to the Kostal Lava Flows and, beyond, to the volcano that spawned them. This is Wells Gray at its geologic best. The return trip to the lava flows can be completed in a day, though reaching the volcano is quite another matter. In either case bring plenty of drinking water, and don't forget the mosquito repellent. For an alternative entry to Kostal Volcano, see page 150.

The portage portion of the trip begins at File Creek Campground, and ends, about 40 oldgrowth minutes later, along the shrubby shores of meandering File Creek. If you happen to have a canoe on your shoulders, launch it here.

As you now begin to paddle upstream (keeping always to the right), the shoreline presses inward with tall willow bushes alive in season with the songs of Yellowthroats, Yellow Warblers and Song Sparrows. Listen also for the occasional slap of a beaver tail striking water. An hour (four km) later, a log jam marks the end of navigable water. Here cache your canoe on the west (left) bank, then hike the marked trail 15 minutes to the open, jumbled moonscape of Kostal Lava Flows [see: FIRE MOUNTAIN, page 177].

This ribbon bomb twisted like taffy as it was thrown from the crater of an erupting Kostal Volcano. (CH)

Congratulations. The easy portion of the journey is now behind you. From this point on, be prepared to trudge for hours on end over ankle-busting, boot-shredding lava cakes on end. The going is softened only by mosses (*Rhacomitrium*) and lichens (mostly reindeer lichens [*Cladina*] and froth lichens [*Stereocaulon*]) colonizing the otherwise barren rocks. Five km later, watch for a large white sign marking a fork in the route. Here bear left (the right fork leads to McDougall Lake, still about an hour distant), and continue another three km to the volcano, and thence to your waiting camping spot beyond. Estimated time from Murtle Lake to the Kostal Lake campsite (see page 150) is six hours.

On the return trip, you will doubtless prefer to carry your canoe the final distance back to Murtle, than to risk scraping bottom on rocky File Creek.

McDOUGALL FALLS TRAIL

3 hr (9 km) return.
Elevation change: 40 m.

- WATERFALLING
- DEVIL'S CLUBBING

McDougall Falls is the first of six basalt stairsteps maneuvered by the Murtle River on its 30 km journey across volcanic Murtle Plateau. (The final, and most acclaimed, stairstep is Helmcken Falls.) It provides an inspired destination for a late afternoon walk, when sunshine accentuates the commotion of falling water.

The trailhead is clearly signposted, and is located halfway along the south shore of Diamond Lagoon (see map), well back from the outlet of the lake. The trail more or less hugs the Murtle River, offering occasional views of its raging progress. Especially common at trailside is Devil's Club: a maple-leaved member of the Ginseng Family bearing copious long, inflammatory spines. You can't miss it.

Nor can you miss 15 m tall McDougall Falls, which can be heard long before it can be seen.

Fire Mountain

The Kostal Lava Flows date from only a few thousand years ago. Your first impression is likely to be one of chaos, as though the earth's crust had shattered into thousands of fragments, and the fragments stood on end. In fact that is exactly what happened on the day of eruption. As the surface of the still-moving lava cooled and solidified, it broke into rafts like ice floes in a fast-flowing river. In places these rafts have been piled into pressure ridges, oriented at right angles to the direction of flow.

You may notice that the blocks increase in size in the direction of the volcano. In places, you may also notice large plasticine-like splatters of lava, all lumped and clumped together. These were flung aloft by the erupting volcano. The technical name for this type of lava is agglutinate, though some geologists refer to it as "chicken splat."

The flanks of the Kostal Volcano itself are composed of loose lava clinkers and blocks. These were ejected from the central crater in a fire fountain. Later, molten lava ponded within the cone to form a fiery lake. Eventually this lake breached the north wall in a cascade of molten rock, at the same time excavating the narrow cleft still visible today. Below the cleft, watch for large blocks of lava that have been up-ended and rafted onto even larger blocks of agglutinate. In the crater itself, a most impressive feature is the dome of lava which hardened as it welled up through the central vent: the last gasp of eruption.

Near the summit of the volcano, you may notice green crystalline fragments in some of the broken blocks. These are peridotite: a rock carried upward from as deep as 60 km below your feet.

Paul Metcalfe

WAVY RANGE TRAIL
8 hr (16 km) return.
Elevation change: 1000 m.

The Wavy Range is a small knot of peaks defining the western edge of the Cariboo Mountains. The "Wavys" can easily absorb a three-day back-packing trip, though the following account is written for day-trippers. Carry water, either way.

Reach the trailhead at the north end of the Strait Creek beach. For the first 30 minutes, the trail passes upward through a magnificent 500-year-old Red-cedar and Hemlock forest. The "undercuts" in some of the larger trees once held leghold traps set for Pine Marten and Fisher, still not uncommon here.

Approximately 40 minutes from the lake, the trail forks. The right fork leads to avalanche-wracked Strait Lake, still 45 minutes distant. To reach the Wavy Range, take the left fork, climbing steeply onto the back of a broad, dry, south-facing ridge.

As you climb, notice how Red-cedar and Hemlock forests here extend upward to at least 1600 m, owing in part to the southerly aspect. Above this elevation, these trees give way to forests of Engelmann Spruce and Subalpine Fir.

Eventually the trail eases above the trees onto a narrow ridge that culminates, some distance later, at a cairn with the usual hikers' register buried inside. This is an admirable terminus for the day hiker, for whom the view should be reward enough for any hardship endured thus far. The Trophy Mountains ripple the skyline to the south. Strait Lake occupies the valley to the east. To the north, still two hours distant, rises 2250 m Wavecrest Peak.

The little valley to the west contains three small ponds that seem to spell the letters COS. On the shores of these, the Cosine Tarns, is a scenic, sheltered, but perhaps somewhat buggy camping place for hikers with overnight intentions.

Wavy Ridge: winter snow drifts shelter trees on either side of the ridge, but not on the ridge itself.

MAHOOD LAKE

Elevation: 630 m.
One-way distance from west end to east end: 21 km (5 hr).
Maps: National Topographic Series (at 1: 50,000): 92 P/15, 16.
Time to allow: 1 to 3 days.
Camping:
  • 40-unit vehicle campground at west end of lake.
  • 6 rustic lakeside camping places with space for about
      19 tents; no charge. See map.
  • maximum stay: 14 days.
Hazards:
  • sudden strong winds, especially at east end of lake.
  • swift current at the outlet.

MAHOOD Lake is the warmest and most livable of Wells Gray's five large lakes. Its rugged scenery has rightly inspired a 28 km westward extension of the park in a long narrow taper.

Vehicle access to the western terminus of this taper, three km west of Mahood Lake, converges from three directions: northeast from 100 Mile House along 88 km of good gravel road; north northeast from Little Fort along 132 km of road, half paved and half good gravel; and northwest from Clearwater along 66 km of logging road (ask for directions at the Wells Gray Visitor Centre: 604-674-2646).

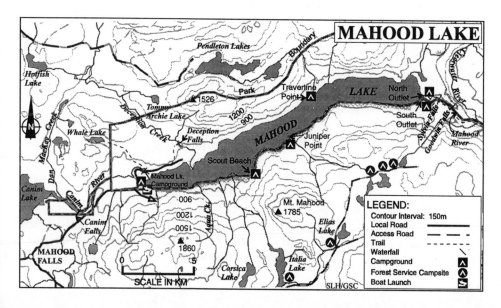

A 40-unit vehicle campground is located at the lake's west end. Provided here are camping pads, picnic tables, pit toilets, firewood, fire grates, a children's playground and, nearby, a pebbly beach. More primitive camping areas also exist (see map), but are accessible only by boat. Allow at least six hours to paddle the lake from end to end. Be prepared, in fair weather, to share Mahood with motorboats and waterskiers.

Mahood Lake is distinctive for the variety of beach sands and gravels lining its shores – sign of a complex geology. The shingle beaches at Scout Beach, for example, are composed of blue-grey phyllite – flat rocks unsurpassed as skipping stones. At the east end, the South Outlet is sandy, whereas the North Outlet is composed of rounded, marble- to egg-sized cobbles, many of which originate from looming granitic bluffs part of the Raft and Baldy Batholiths exposing the north and south shores of the lake. At Travertine Point, the beaches are strewn with porous, white, limy boulders: evidence of a calcium-rich seepage somewhere on the bluffs above. Elsewhere look for ice-rafted basalt boulders, best viewed in late summer, when lake levels are low, and beaches exposed.

Two of the park's hallmark trees – Subalpine Fir and Western Hemlock – are all but absent at Mahood Lake, whereas Douglas-fir takes their place as the tree of choice. Mahood's drier climate also appears to have favoured extensive wildfires: this is the only lake in Wells Gray whose shores lack any trace of oldgrowth forest whatsoever.

The volcanic history of the area can be seen in the basalt outcrops at both ends of the lake. At North Outlet Campground, for example, watch for remnants of an earlier basalt plateau, rising abruptly 100 m above the lake, and skirted below by a well-developed talus slope. The lava to west of the lake has been cut into by the Canim River at Mahood and Canim Falls (see page 181).

Mammals to scan for along the shores of Mahood Lake include Coyote, Red Fox, Mule Deer, Mink and Otter. On the surface of the lake itself, keep an eye open for Mallard, Northern Pintail, American Wigeon, Surf Scoter, White-winged Scoter, Barrow's Goldeneye, Bufflehead, Common Merganser and Ruddy Duck. Beneath the waters swim Rainbow Trout, Lake Trout, Longnose Suckers, Kokanee and Burbot, among others.

Parsley Fern
(Crypto-gramma crispa)
looks the part, but doesn't taste it. Check the talus slopes for this two-toned oddity. (RBCM)

CANIM FALLS TRAIL

1 hour (2.5 km) return.
Elevation change: negligible.

- GORGING
- WATERFALLING

Between Canim and Mahood Lakes, the Canim River has carved impressive gorges in basalt. Mahood Falls and Canim Falls are the cutting edge of these gorges. The trailhead is located along the park road approximately five km west of Mahood Lake Campground. A ten minute walk brings you to 15 m Mahood Falls, and 15 minutes farther you are standing before 20 m Canim Falls. Watch your children well. A rough trail continues from Canim Falls to Canim Lake, another 20 minutes farther still.

WHALE LAKE TRAIL

3 hours (8 km) return.
Elevation change: 250 m.

- SNAILSHELL PEERING
- RAINBOW CHASING

The trail begins just over the bridge on the Canim River, roughly one km north of Mahood Lake Campground. From here it climbs steeply, terminating at Whale Lake, west of the park boundary. In outline Whale Lake somewhat resembles Moby Dick. It is rich in calcium, and supports snails by the tens of thousands. Stocked with Rainbow Trout in the early 70s, Whale Lake is popular with anglers. A Beaver dam blocks the outlet of the lake.

DECEPTION FALLS TRAIL

35 minutes (2 km) return.
Elevation change: 125 m.

- WARBLER WONDERING
- RICE GRASS GAZING
- CATARACT CONCENTRATING

This is arguably the most agreeable of Wells Gray's woodland ambles. The trailhead is located at six km from Mahood Lake Campground, along the park road on the north shore of the lake. The road terminates a short distance beyond, at the gate of a private inholding signposted as "Deception Point."

The trail climbs gradually, but continuously, wending through an open forest of Aspen (smooth, chalky, pale olive-coloured bark), Paper Birch (papery white bark) and Douglas-fir (corky brown bark with orange furrows). In summer these trees confer a filtered green light, and the forest then chimes with birdsong – mostly Warblers and Vireos. The forest floor at trailside is dominated by Indian Rice Grass (*Oryzopsis asperifolia*), with its raspy leaf blades and ricy florets. The trail terminates abruptly with a view of 35 m Deception Falls, fanning outward as it cataracts.

The name "deception" dates from exploratory railway surveys of late last century, when this creek was twice mistaken for the Clearwater River.

- HOGBACKING
- WATERFALL AH-ING
- GLACIAL TILLING

SYLVIA FALLS TRAIL
3 hours (6 km) return.
Elevation change: 100 m.

Sylvia Falls is only one of several points of interest along the trail leading from the east end of Mahood Lake down the Mahood River to its confluence with the Clearwater River. The entire hike is roughly five hours (14 km) return.

The trail begins from South Outlet Campground, and is rough and dry. For the first km or so the trail traverses various hogbacks of slaty blue phyllite. It then eases south along the south wall of the valley which it hugs for most of the remaining distance. At the halfway point, watch for an open Lodgepole Pine forest that might serve as a comfortable campsite; the river, at this point, is only five minutes distant.

Sylvia Falls resemble a scaled-down version of Niagara Falls (the American side, not the Canadian). The falls are roughly 20 m high and 100 m wide, and tumble over glacial till: the unsorted material laid down at the base of a glacier. The till here is very compact (owing to the weight of the glacier), and is cemented together by clay particles. When wet, however, the clay expands, and so breaks the till apart. For this reason, Sylvia Falls is eroding upstream faster than any other waterfall in the park.

Sylvia Falls is Wells Gray's most rapid cascade. (TG)

PART FOUR

THE PARK IN WINTER

THE RIVERS AND WATERFALLS

I N winter, Wells Gray contracts. Snows deepen, trails disappear, campgrounds close, roads go un-ploughed. From the point of view of motorists, ac-cess shrinks to roughly 10% of what it was only a few months before. Yet what does remain accessible is, for many, 90% of the reason they come to the park at any season: the waterfalls.

Rising above Helmcken Falls in winter is a wispy column of mist. On cold days this column, which is known as the "Bookmark," may gather to 300 m or more, making it possible to pinpoint Helmcken from

Winter by winter, the Helmcken ice cone enlarges the cavern that backdrops Helmcken Falls. (TG)

In winter, the Dawson Falls Cave-of-Winds becomes a cave-of-ice. (BCP)

great distances. One place to watch is along the park road just north of Spahats Creek; here the Bookmark (still 25 km away) is visible in the gap at the south (left-hand) end of Green Mountain.

All winter long, the mists of Helmcken Falls congeal into ice. Ice coats the surrounding canyon walls. Ice accretes on the canyon rim, building up into a long, low ridge which may persist well into June. Here and there you'll notice icy stalactites – icicles – hanging 15 m in length. Even the falls itself is partly encased in ice: above, an ice bridge spans the Murtle River; and below, an ice cone gradually builds.

The Helmcken ice cone can only be described as stupendous. Although dwarfed by the falls itself, it rises, in a cold winter, taller than the total height of Niagara. The cone is at its best in early March; by the middle of the month, the warming spring weather causes it to collapse inward. Over the following weeks, the canyon reverberates with the sound of falling ice, and the parabolic headwalls of the canyon amplify that sound. Listening, it is hard to escape the sensation that the waterfall is alive, and is speaking to you.

The fast-flowing Murtle River resists freezing – except at its edges. (TG)

Another ice cone forms around the base of Spahats Falls. Here, however, the word "cone" is not entirely appropriate: "stocking" would be more descriptive: a long, icy blue knee-sock, the rim of which, in cold winters, reaches all the way to the top of this 75 m waterfall.

In winter, Dawson Falls too takes on an entirely new demeanor. Only months before, it was an exploding wall of whitewater. Now it is an icy mask, behind which still rumbles the ventriloquist voice of cataract.

In cold winters, the ice mask completely conceals the waterfall – a massive blue wall 100 m wide by 18 m high.

Many who view Dawson Falls in its winter incarnation are struck by the fact that parts of the river remain open just upstream. Though you might expect that weather cold enough to freeze a waterfall would also be cold enough to freeze a river, actually it is Dawson Falls that freezes first.

Why? In winter the atomized water droplets associated with the falls are jetted into the subfreezing air, and so lose whatever heat they contain. Soon they have begun to coat nearby surfaces in ice, and before long the Dawson ice mask is in progress. Upstream, by contrast, the river is considerably less turbulent, and retains a much greater fraction of its latent heat.

During the coldest days of winter, watch the riverbed for "bottom ice": pale green ice patches that seem strangely out of place beneath the swiftly flowing water. A good viewing place is just below the Mushbowl at km 41.5.

WHERE TO STAY AND WHERE TO GO

A master of voices, the Steller's Jay mimics the calls of such diverse birds as the Common Loon, Pileated Woodpecker and Red-tailed Hawk. Don't be fooled.
(RBCM)

WINTER camping is not everybody's cup of chilblains. But for those with the right equipment, southern Wells Gray invariably provides a few good spots to set up tent or trailer. Check with the good people at B.C. Parks for this year's assortment of designated winter camping areas; call 604-587-6150 (fax: 604-587-6200), or write: Box 70, Clearwater, B.C. VOE 1NO. Tell them Trevor sent you.

Back-country skiers may wish to avail themselves of the privately operated Wells Gray Backcountry Chalets. Located on Trophy, Table and Battle mountains, these rustic cabins offer hut-to-hut skiing both vigorous and breath-taking. The Trophy Mountain and Fight Meadows chalets are identical structures, sleeping 12, and equipped with dishes, mattresses, lights, heat, propane range and sauna. The Table Mountain Cabin is a refurbished log building that sleeps six. For rates and other information, call 604-

587-6444 (fax: 604-674-3997), or write Wells Gray Back-country Chalets, Box 188b, Clearwater, B.C. voe 1no.

More traditional accommodations are available both in Clearwater and at the Helmcken Falls Lodge, at km 34.6. In addition to providing warm rooms and hot meals, the Lodge rents cross-country ski equipment. Be sure to call or fax ahead for reservations (604-674-3657).

In winter, the main park road is ploughed only as far as Helmcken Falls; north of the turnoff at km 42.5, the road is closed to traffic between November and May. The park road is now under the jurisdiction of B.C. Highways and is usually sanded and salted, salted, salted. Even so, it's a good idea to carry chains.

If you intend to travel any distance off road, you'll need to do so by ski or snowshoe. On the Murtle Plateau, starting north of the park entrance, a number of ski routes are feasible, some groomed, others not. Here are some routes to consider, arranged in order of increasing technical difficulty:

The Hairy Woodpecker thinking (TG)

- The Redspring Glide. An easy ski across the Murtle Plateau and down to the Clearwater River. Follow the park road north from the Helmcken Falls turn-off at km 42.5. The ski is 13.4 km return, and involves a 150 m descent to the picnic site at Redspring, at km 49.2. Allow roughly four hours return.
- The Pyramid Bay Roller Coaster. Start at the Warming Hut (km 39.9), and allow about 2.5 hours return. Elevation change is negligible. Gorgeous river scenery, with views of volcanic Pyramid Mountain.
- The Blackwater Scream. Start at the Warming Hut (km 39.9), and turn right at the Majerus Farm; allow about 3.5 hours return. Elevation change: 175 m. Most happily organized using two vehicles, the second of which can be parked at the park entrance, or Helmcken Falls Lodge.
- The Green Mountain Grunt. A 300 m uphill ski to the summit of Green Mountain. Start at the Green Mountain turnoff (km 36.2). Allow about two hours return, and be ready for some sharp switchbacks. Fine views of the park, and a 3.5 km return glide. Not recommended under icy conditions.
- The Wells Gray Loppet. A challenging voyage of discovery. The Loppet Trail is usually track-set by

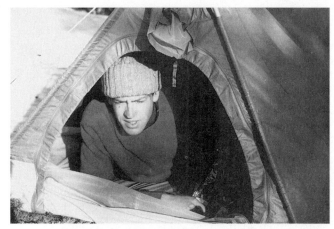

Winter camping is not everybody's cup of chilblains. (TG)

late December, depending on conditions. Start at the Warming Hut (km 39.9), and allow five hours return for this 26 km circuit. Be prepared to come in dragging, but pleased with yourself. Further details on page 190.

Also beloved of cross-country skiers is the alpine. Choose from among three approaches to the high country. None is for the inexperienced or the unprepared. For word on latest conditions, contact either B.C. Parks (604-587-6150) or Wells Gray Backcountry Chalets (604-587-6444).

- The West Trophy Mountain Tour. This is a long day outing or, more satisfactorily, an overnight campout. Turn east off the park road (at km 11.4) onto the Trophy Mountain Road, which may or may not be ploughed, depending on logging. From here, follow the road and trail descriptions on page 39. At treeline, the terrain is gentle, and the views bracing.

- The East Trophy Mountain Tour. Take the Trophy Mountain Road as in the previous account. From the right fork at km 4, the alpine is still about five hours distant; follow the road and trail descriptions on page 53. This is heavy snow country, and spring skiing is often feasible well into May. The terrain is steep, and the views spectacular.

- The Battle Mountain access. The turnoff is at km 26.6 on the Wells Gray Road. Here again the access road goes unploughed in winter; allow nine or ten hours to the Fight Meadows Chalet: first a

The crow-sized Pileated Woodpecker is a cavity nester dependent entirely on large, old trees and snags. (BCP)

three or four hour slog to the end of the access road; then a very steep 90 minutes to Philip Lake (be sure to carry skins); and finally a more gentle four or five hours to Fight Meadows. More details on the route are given on page 63. Because the total elevation gain from the park road is about 1200 m, snow conditions can be expected to vary tremendously as you climb. If your destination is the Fight Meadows Chalet, don't necessarily count on getting there in one day: be prepared to camp out in an emergency.

A WORD OF ADVICE: Skiing is best in the high country during March and April. In the valley, January and February are the favoured months for track skiing. For off-trail valley skiing, however, March is the month of months. Call the park headquarters for up-to-date conditions (604-587-6150).

The Trembling Aspen is a Moose's best friend – especially in winter. (TG)

- MAJERUS
  FARMING
- BIRCH CLUMPING
- DEER MOUSING
- WINTER MOOSING

WELLS GRAY LOPPET TRAIL

26 km (5–6 hours) return.
Elevation change: 250 m.

T HE Wells Gray Loppet trail – mainstay of cross-country skiing in the park – provides the venue for an annual Wells Gray Ski Marathon, held each mid February. Winding across the Murtle Plateau, the trail describes a giant "A" with spurs to the Warming Hut (km 39.9) and to the park entrance (km 35.8), and secondarily to the Helmcken Falls Lodge (km 34.6). Here we describe a 26 km "Q" route beginning and ending at the Warming Hut.

From the Warming Hut, proceed northeast along the Majerus Farm trail through forest and along river. If the day is colder than, say, –6°C, watch the riverbed for pale green bottom ice; as the weather warms, this ice becomes detached and floats to the surface as ice cakes. Downstream, some of these cakes apparently lodge at the base of Dawson and Helmcken Falls.

As you step-glide into view of the Majerus Farm, 1.4 km from the Warming Hut, the trail forks. While deciding which fork to take, you may wish to pause and contemplate what kind of man would have chosen to live in the cabin that still stands a few metres away. Perhaps the views of Pyramid Mountain to the north and Battle Mountain to the south will provide insight.

Mike Majerus was a loner. Born in Luxembourg, he arrived in the Clearwater Valley in 1911, and for a time found work with the surveyor Robert H. Lee, who was then mapping the Hemp Creek and Murtle plateaus. Eventually, however, Majerus settled into the trapper's life, operating an 80 km trapline each winter. He died in 1958.

At time of writing, the Majerus cabin, barn, stable and root cellar still stand. If it is late in the season, you may notice parallel bands of ice running horizontally through the snow that covers their roofs. Each band records an individual snowfall; taken together, they provide a rough indication of how often, and how much, it has snowed these past several months.

Bull moose shed their antlers beginning in early December. (BCP)

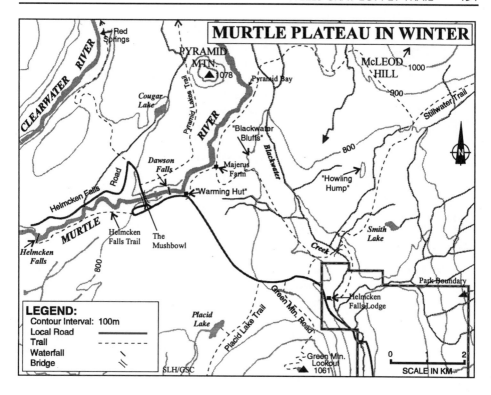

MURTLE PLATEAU IN WINTER

CLEARWATER RIVER

Red Springs

PYRAMID MTN.
▲ 1078

Pyramid Lakes Trail

Pyramid Bay

McLEOD HILL
1000

900

Stillwater Trail

Cougar Lake

RIVER

"Blackwater Bluffs"

800

Dawson Falls

Majerus Farm

Blackwater

"Howling Hump"

N

Helmcken Falls Road

"Warming Hut"

MURTLE

Helmcken Falls Trail

The Mushbowl

Smith Lake

Helmcken Falls

800

Creek

Green Mtn. Road

Park Boundary

Helmcken Falls Lodge

LEGEND:
Contour Interval: 100m
Local Road
Trail
Waterfall
Bridge

SLH/GSC

Placid Lake

Placid Lake Trail

Green Mtn. Lookout
▲ 1061

0   1   2
SCALE IN KM

(*Left*) *Valley skiing, loppet style.* (TG)

(*Right*) *Mountain skiing, free style.* (TG)

The Majerus Farm in 1979 was not what it is today. (TG)

If you intend to ski the entire Loppet, it hardly matters whether you turn right at the Majerus Farm, or continue skiing along the river; both trails return to this point. Our own preference is a counter-clockwise route. We therefore recommend taking the right fork, the Blackwater Connector.

For the first few hundred metres, the trail winds through what used to be an open pasture, now growing up to two-needled Lodgepole Pine. For an object lesson in forest succession, compare the scene as seen today with the photo at left. Soon the trail enters a somewhat older forest dating from the great fire of 1926. Here the trees are well spaced, and the shrubs sparse, probably reflecting the rather shallow topsoil. Apparently the topsoil here has been depleted by repeated wildfire. By comparison, notice how much denser the forests are along other sections of the trail.

As you up-down, up-down, up-down across 1.5 km of hummocky terrain, watch for Paper Birch, recognized by its tattered, whitish bark. Notice that while some of the Birch trees hereabouts stand alone, others are clumped. Herein is a story. Prior to the fire of 1926, the clumped trees (or rather their forebears) were probably not clumped at all. The clumping is a result of resprouting from roots that survived the fire. Most of the clumped trees thus originated as single stems that date from before 1926. By contrast, the solitary Birches have germinated from seed since then. Because Paper Birch is a pioneer tree, the presence of clumped stems tells us that forest conditions prior to 1926 were similar here to those of today.

At length the trail arrives at a fine, nestled view of the western slopes of McLeod Hill. Below the lookout is the headwall of a box canyon. This is the westernmost of a series of similar canyons collectively called Blackwater Bluffs. The Bluffs were carved by glacial meltwaters pouring off the south rim of the Murtle Plateau at the close of the last Ice Age. When snow conditions permit, a cross-country outing east along the rim of these bluffs makes for a scenic, if rather fatiguing, afternoon.

The viewpoint marks the southern edge of the Murtle Plateau. Now begins a 150 m downhill slither to Blackwater Creek, 4.3 km distant. Along the way, watch for more signs of forest conditions prior to 1926.

Occasional stumps of Douglas-fir suggest that the forests were mostly less than 100 years old prior to burning. A few large, spiky snags of Western Red-cedar (usually a late arrival in forest succession) tell of occasional stands of much older forest. Near the bottom of the trail, watch for fire-blackened trees roughly 200 years old. These trees apparently date from an intense fire that burned the valley about the time Captain James Cook became the first European to set foot on British Columbia soil.

The Deer Mouse hops, skips and scampers its short life through. (BCP)

As you puff your way 130 m up the east side of the Blackwater Valley, you may pause to wonder how such a tiny creek ever managed to carve so deep a passage into the surrounding plateau. The answer, quite simply, is that it didn't. The valley was formed by glacial meltwaters flooding off the Murtle Plateau at the close of the last Ice Age.

Back on the Murtle Plateau, the trail winds past open stands of Douglas-fir, Lodgepole Pine, Trembling Aspen and, in moister spots, White Spruce. Anyone who has ever skied the rolling Cariboo to the west of here will recognize a close kinship between that landscape and this.

There, as here, hummocky glacial till is underlain by plateau lavas. There, as here, the forest cover is relatively sparse, and the views commanding. There, however, the openness of the forest is primarily a function of dryness. Here, it is at least in part a tribute to the appetites of rodents; see the adjacent sidebar.

Obviously, there is no guarantee you'll see a Moose when you ski the Wells Gray Loppet trail. But if you don't, you probably weren't paying attention. In most winters, except when the snow is more than about a metre deep, Moose are numerous along this route. So are their sign. Whether it's the nibbled branches of a Red Osier Dogwood, or the debarked trunk of a Trembling Aspen (lacking upper incisors, the Moose rake the trunks upward with their lower jaw), you're never far from evidence that Moose have recently passed this way. Indeed, at times Moose even use the packed Loppet trail as an arterial highway, punching holes as they go.

Ahead looms the low dome of McLeod Hill. McLeod Hill is a volcano – possibly the most ancient in the Clearwater Valley. At 1250 m, it is also the most massive volcano to have survived the erosive power of

The ecology of land is complex. Who would expect that mice are a major factor in prolonging the life of good Moose range in Wells Gray Park? Mice are plentiful on these willow-covered burns. Mice eat most evergreen seeds blowing into such burns. By delaying plant succession, mice are prolonging the stay of willow and thus, too, of Moose. But they are also delaying the establishment of Western Red-cedar, White Spruce, Douglas-fir and Western Hemlock, the industrially important plants – and they are contributing to increased soil erosion. More mice means more Moose, but less timber. These are but a few of countless such relationships operating on these lands.

summarized from R.Y. Edwards (1951)

When browsing Moose remove the terminal buds of Red Osier Dogwood (Cornus sericea), *the side buds take over, and so the branches branch branchily.* (TG)

Pleistocene glaciers. Like so many of Wells Gray's other volcanoes, this is a tuya: it erupted under a glacier.

Having reached the foot of the volcano, the Loppet trail suddenly veers northwestward, and onto its flanks. The 100 m climb which ensues is the last major climb of the day. Fortunately, both Ruffed and Spruce Grouse inhabit the mixed forests hereabouts; watching for their tracks and droppings can provide, for some, a much-needed diversion.

Then it's down, and around, and through, and finally out – to the Murtle River. Along the way, you'll pass "Study Area C": one of nine areas in the park that were set on fire during the 1960s in the name of better Moose habitat. To judge from the numbers of Moose that are seen along this rather open, willow-clad section of trail, the burn was obviously a success.

Among the branches of willow and alder thickets, watch for birds' nests. Now that the leaves are off, last year's nests are easy to locate. Among the most common are the nests of Vireos, especially the Red-eyed Vireo, now wintering in the western Amazon. Look for a small hanging basket, delicately woven, and incorporating bits of grass, birch bark, hair lichens and, to fasten it, spiderweb. Unlike the more sturdy nests of Osprey, Ravens and many hawks, this one is used only during the year it is built. Fortunately, Vireo nests are biodegradable.

The trail comes out to the Murtle River at "Pyramid Bay" – a river bend named for the striking view it affords of Pyramid Mountain and landslide Little Pyramid, resting on its flanks.

Different from the bark of most other trees, Aspen bark contains small amounts of chlorophyll, and is regularly "browsed" by Moose. (TG)

If you scan these slopes for Moose, you may be rewarded. Here is also a good place to scan the river banks for Otter tracks: an entertaining patterning of paw prints and belly toboggan marks.

Tending southwest now, the Loppet trail crosses hummocky terrain; be ready to roller coaster up and down over the next three km. The hummocks were deposited as the glaciers of the last Ice Age stagnated and wasted away. At least some of this rubble probably derived from Pyramid Mountain, which was erupting at about the same time.

From here on, the Murtle River is never far away. Watch the ice for Wolf tracks. Wolves find the river ice easy going, so they often use the Murtle as a winter highway. Moose, too, are sometimes tempted to try the ice (the willows are always greener on the other side!), but here their greater weight works against them. Apparently the Murtle River claims one or more of the park's largest ungulates every winter. Take care not add a winter skier to the tally.

As you continue down river, the terrain becomes less hummocky, and eventually you once again come into view of the Majerus Farm. Ten minutes later, you are back at the Warming Hut, and your parked vehicle.

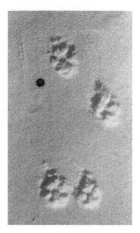

Wolves may be fierce, but they are also shy of humans; should you see more of them than their tracks, lucky you! (TG)

Here's one Wolf that definitely wasn't eating crow. Our best guess is Moose, though the Canadian quarter in the photo seems to say Caribou. (TG)

Helmcken on a humid winter day. Look for the Helmcken "Bookmark" from the Green Mountain Viewing Tower. (TG)

WEATHER WATCHING

I N winter, the park is protected from climatic extremes by two ranges of mountains. Eastward, the Rockies stem the arctic air masses of central Canada, while to the west the Coast Range holds back the sopping Pacific storms. Between these two extremes, winter is a quiet, comfortable time. By winter's end, the snow lies 70 cm deep on the valley floor, and 200 cm at treeline.

As a rule, winds are light in the park, and especially so at elevations below about 1000 m, where snow drifts are practically unheard of. In the Canyon area, however, between km 13 and km 18, winds are stronger, and here you may encounter blowing snow.

An interesting feature of the Clearwater Valley in winter – one recommending it to cross-country skiers – is its relative immunity to prolonged thaws. Once winter temperatures drop a few degrees below freezing (usually in early December), they tend to hold there. Powder snow is the rule, not the exception.

Warm winds do, of course, sometimes invade the Clearwater Valley, and when they do, temperatures may climb several degrees above seasonal values. Yet even then the winds often pass by in the tree tops, leaving pockets of cold air trapped at ground level. This phenomenon (a "crown thaw") is most pronounced over the plateaus, and especially the Murtle Plateau, where it is not uncommon for the snow to disappear from the upper branches, while only a few metres below everything remains locked in winter's grip.

"Chinook clouds" tell of a warming trend in the mountains. If they persist, the snow will soon be melting in the valley, too. (TG)

Plate

Stellar Crystal

Column

Needle

Spatial Dendrite

Snow crystal forms (TG)

SNOW WATCHING

S NOW is one of the most variable substances in nature. From the moment of its inception high in the clouds, to the moment it washes away as meltwater, snow is constantly changing. No one who really looks at snow can fail to be intrigued by its incredible variety.

Even reducing snow crystals to their basic patterns yields, according to one internationally accepted system of classification, some 80 different crystal forms. For the purposes of amateur snow watching, however, it is probably enough to recognize eight categories, namely plates, stellar crystals, columns, needles, spa-

Capped Column

Graupel

Irregular

tial dendrites, capped columns, graupel and irregular forms.

Noting what kinds of snow crystals are falling at any given time can tell you a lot about the weather in the clouds overhead. For example, stellar crystals form only at cloud temperatures around –15°C. If the branching patterns are intricate, then the air above is quite moist. Should the crystals be perfectly formed, with no missing rays, then the winds aloft must be very light. Often some of the crystals will be covered in rime; if so, they probably passed through a layer of warmer air near the cloud base.

As you study Wells Gray's falling snow, keep in mind that snow crystals are not the same thing as snowflakes: one snowflake may contain dozens of snow crystals (usually then of stellar form), all intricately locked together. Also, don't be discouraged if in cataloguing the snow crystals, you find yourself relying on the "irregular forms" category more often than you'd care to. Perfectly symmetrical snow crystals are comparatively rare in nature.

No sooner does a snow crystal touch down than it begins to change shape. On average, fallen snow crystals change shape in much the same direction as many middle-aged people, with a tendency to decrease the

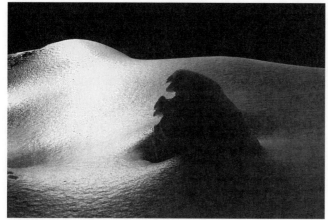

The spray-induced ice at the brink of Helmcken Falls masks a young tree. Beyond the crest is a slippery canyon rim, 150 m to the bottom. Take care. (TG)

ratio of surface area to volume. Put another way, they round out or "metamorphose."

As metamorphism proceeds, snow crystals gradually consolidate until, at the end of days or weeks, they may occupy only one-quarter of their original space. Thus, although approximately 200 cm of snow falls over the Murtle Plateau each winter, the actual snowpack averages one-third this depth.

By the end of February, the sun's rays are strong enough, at valley elevations, to cause surface melting even when air temperatures are below freezing. Thus begins a period of melt-freeze metamorphism that of course intensifies over the following weeks. Eventually the snow loses its powdery texture, and hardens into what skiers refer to as corn snow.

The strength of corn snow varies tremendously at different temperatures: in cold weather, it can be firm enough to support an adult Moose; in thaw, it can be so soft that not even a child on snowshoes may travel over it without sinking. Skiing is usually best on corn snow in the late morning or early afternoon, when the "corn" begins to soften.

Eventually, unless it melts first, corn snow compresses further into what is called firn snow. Firn snow, though a hallmark of mountain snowpacks during late spring and afterward, on occasion also develops on the Murtle Plateau toward the end of the season. Firn snow offers easy walking under any conditions, though in the early morning it may again prove unskiable.

AVALANCHE WATCHING

DURING prolonged periods of clear, cold weather, moisture contained in the snowpack near the (now much warmer) ground may be drawn upward to the surface, leaving behind a region of recrystallized snow at ground level. This is called depth hoar. Because depth hoar is composed of feathery, or plate-like crystals, it is highly unstable; indeed, in mountainous terrain, it may suddenly give way, triggering an avalanche.

Depth hoar avalanches claim lives each winter on the east slope of the Canadian Rockies. In Wells Gray's mountains, by contrast, snowpacks are generally too deep, snowfalls too frequent, and temperatures too mild to favour the development of depth hoar. Even so, other kinds of avalanches are just as deadly; when above treeline, keep away from steep slopes at all times.

WINTER IN THE MOUNTAINS

MOUNTAINS are windy places. So fierce are the winds that buffet the summits of the Trophy Mountains, for example, that even in winter, unless the snow is very wet, the wind soon carries it away. In winter, you may see evidence of these mountain winds from many kilometres away. Look for long plumes of snow streaming off the summits. Along the park road, a good viewing place is from the top of Mailbox Hill (km 28.7). Expect warming weather when the mountain winds are blowing from the south.

Where southerly gales cause the snow to overvault the peaks, snowpacks pile up deepest on the north-facing slopes. So it is that at treeline on the north slope of the Trophies, snowpacks up to three m have been recorded, whereas elsewhere the maximum depth is closer to two m. Such wind-enhanced snowpacks combine with cool northslope summers to produce permanent snowfields and glaciers.

As snow crystals get blown about by the wind, they break into bits and pieces; the resulting fragments may

For an olfactory treat, try crushing a Black Cottonwood leaf bud: sticky, but oh so aromatic! (RBCM)

be no more than one-tenth of the original crystal size. When later the fragments freeze together, they do so at many more points of contact than would a similar volume of large-particle (i.e., fresh-fallen) snow. The result is nature's very own particle board.

Battle Mountain's 52 Ridge is a winter home to Caribou and Wolverine. On the skyline are the Monashee Mountains (TG)

Covered in a few centimetres of fresh powder snow, an alpine snowdrift can offer reasonable skiing. This is a good point to keep in mind should you ever find yourself floundering waist-deep in alpine powder; heading for the windward sides of the ridges could save you a lot of effort.

When the winter wind blows the clouds around on the mountaintops, the supercooled cloud droplets quickly congeal against any surface they touch. The result is rime: a dull, white, noncrystalline "frost," which in winter gets deposited on the windward side of rocks, trees, and sometimes whole mountainsides. In Wells Gray, rime is most common at treeline and above, where it can be recognized by its lacklustre appearance. Rime is a good indicator of wind direction.

As spring advances, the trunks of the trees absorb the sun's warmth, causing the snow to melt in a circle around their bases. The Inuit of northern Canada call the dark snow-free circles "qamaniq." During the day, qamaniq are heated to temperatures several degrees above that of the ambient air only a few metres away.

Both male and female Caribou are antlered. Pictured above are two males. (BCP)

Spring comes late to the high Trophy Mountains. The last of the snow lingers in the subalpine forests until early July. (TG)

At night, the overarching conifer branches act as a roof to hold in some of this warmth. In this way, thousands of little greenhouses – one for every tree – are created in the midst of deep snows.

Qaminiq provide early-season living quarters for spiders, ants, mosquitoes, and other creatures whose metabolisms depend directly on the external warmth of the sun. They may also, for this reason, provide temporary cafeterias for the Golden-crowned Kinglets, Red-breasted Nuthatches, Brown Creepers and other small birds now returning to the high country from their wintering grounds below, and to the south.

One of the hallmark animals of the high country is the Woodland Caribou. For much of the year, the park's Caribou keep to the high, jumbled mountains of northern and central Wells Gray. Yet in winter most of them range south into the Shuswap Highlands, where as many as 40 to 60 roam the slopes of Battle, Table and Trophy Mountains.

Of the larger game animals, Caribou are the most plentiful. Herds of 30 individuals have been seen on the large snowfields. These animals summer in the alpine meadows near the snow, and winter near the lakes.

summarized from
N.F.G. Davis (1929)

Different from their barrengrounds counterparts, the Caribou of Wells Gray are remarkably erratic in their seasonal movements. Yet some general patterns can be discerned. From mid January to early April, most are in the open timberline forests of 1800 m and above. Once, however, the snows begin to soften, many move to lower elevations, where they remain until late May. Early June sees them heading into the high country again, though now they climb to above treeline, where they remain until October, when deepening snows drive them once more into the lowlands. By January, the snows have hardened somewhat, and the Caribou climb yet again to timberline [see: CARIBOU TRACKS, CARIBOU TRACKERS].

WINTER MAMMAL WATCHING

To some people, winter is a dead space, a time to be endured. To others, it is a celebration of life. Certainly no other season provides a better introduction to the mammals of Wells Gray. Whether Mouse or Moose or Marten, a thousand activities are written out daily on the winter snow.

Learning to identify Wells Gray's mammal tracks is not as difficult as it might at first seem. In the first place, of the approximately 4000 mammal species extant on earth, only about 56 occur in the park. In winter, furthermore, many species are hibernating or otherwise unlikely to be encountered; of those that do remain active, consider yourself lucky if you find the sign of

Caribou Tracks, Caribou Trackers

Historical records suggest that Caribou were once abundant in the Wells Gray area, but that their numbers declined dramatically after about 1935. Over the years, various explanations have been offered for this decline, including poaching, disease, and loss of habitat to wildfires.

However, results from a recent radio-collar study suggests that none of the above is likely to have been the major cause. Instead it appears that Wells Gray's Caribou population was decimated by Wolves.

Apparently the main link is the Moose. Moose have not alway inhabited the Clearwater Valley; in fact they arrived only in the early 1920s, that is, just before the Caribou went into decline. It now appears that these two events may be related: the presence of Moose doubtless supported greater Wolf numbers, which in turn must have led to greater predation on the Caribou.

In winter, Wolves tend to roam the valley bottoms, where Moose are their major prey. Caribou, for their part, live high in the subalpine forests, and so are protected from Wolf predation by the soft, deep snows. Only during the summer months do Wolves (and Moose) migrate into subalpine forest habitat, and so potentially come into contact with Caribou.

Prior to the arrival of Moose, Wolves would have been few in number, due to winter starvation. Their impact on the Caribou in the traditional summer ranges would have been negligible. But once the Wolf population increased, owing to the greater abundance of winter food (i.e., Moose), summertime Wolf predation on Caribou soon reached disastrous proportions.

Today things have changed. Different from earlier Caribou bands, which would have summered largely in the Shuswap Highlands, today's Caribou range northward into the rugged Cariboo Mountains. Wolves rarely follow them there because their main prey continues to be Moose, which do not migrate as far into the mountains as do the Caribou.

Although Wolf predation may have greatly reduced the Wells Gray's Caribou in the past, the remaining Caribou appear to have stabilized at about 275 animals. They are protected by a migration pattern which effectively separates them from their major predator.

Dale Seip

more than a dozen. See the table on pages 28 and 29.

The park's winter mammals can be grouped into seven categories: the shrews, the rodents, the rabbits, the weasels, the cats, the dogs, and the deer.

THE SHREWS

Tiniest of the mammals, Shrews are sometimes thought of as mice with pointed noses. In fact they belong (with the Moles) to an altogether separate order, the Insectivora – the "insect eaters."

Shrews are frenetic little creatures; most of the five species occurring in the park are active at night, when they rush about attacking and consuming insects, centipedes, spiders and other small creatures. In winter, Shrews spend most of their time beneath the snow, but may appear on surface during warm spells or when forced to vacate their tunnels owing to high concentrations of carbon dioxide. Their tracks closely resemble those of mice but are slightly smaller.

THE RODENTS

Mice. Squirrels. Marmots. Porcupine. Beaver. Although these creatures differ considerably from one another both in appearance and in place of residence, all are rodents. All possess sharp chisel-like teeth, and all make a living gnawing on plants. Nineteen species of rodents are known to inhabit Wells Gray; of these, 13 are active during the winter months, though only two, the Red Squirrel and the Deer Mouse, are at all common above the snow.

The Red Squirrel (Brown Squirrel would be a more descriptive name) is surely the most familiar of all Wells Gray's small mammals. Being short on body mass, squirrels do not thrive in cold weather; below about –15C, they retire to their nests under the snow, and there pass the livelong day drowsing and shucking cones. When the weather warms again, their trails will be found leading from tree to tree, in the manner of little highways. The individual tracks to some extent resemble those of the Varying Hare, but are smaller and proportionately scrawnier.

The Squirrel – like many other tree-dwelling rodents – tends to pair its front feet such that its tracks tend to align perpendicular to the line of travel. Ground-dwelling species, by contrast, usually offset their front feet.

The Red Squirrel is a rodent that lives in trees. (TG)

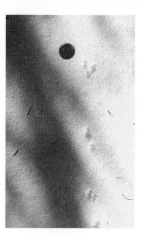

The Red Squirrel may well be the park's most visible rodent, but the most numerous is doubtless the Deer Mouse. The Deer Mouse occurs virtually wherever there are seeds for it to eat; only wet habitats are avoided. In autumn it stores away piles of seeds for the winter, carefully sorting the seeds to species. In winter it sometimes dozes in heat-conserving huddles with family and friends.

The tracks of the Varying Hare (left) are unmistakable, as are those of the Red Squirrel (centre). The tracks of the Southern Red-backed Vole, however, are much like those of many other small rodents. Canadian quarters are included for scale. (TG)

The Deer Mouse is nocturnal; business hours run from dusk to dawn. During the night it may venture from its subnivean chambers, scurrying deliberately over the snow, and leaving tracks that can later be recognized by the characteristic four-by-four hopping pattern and sometimes by a tail drag. The tracks closely resemble those of Shrews but are larger, the trail measuring 3.5 cm to 4.2 cm across, compared with the Shrews' 2.2 cm to 2.8 cm.

Sometimes the trail ends abruptly, and wing prints on the snow tell where an owl descended for a nice light snack. Deer Mice constitute an important winter staple for both owls and weasels.

THE RABBITS

Two species of "rabbits" (order Lagomorpha) occur in Wells Gray, and both are active during the winter. One – the Pika – sits huddled in darkness in alpine boulderbeds, nibbling from stored underground haystacks, and waiting for May. The other – the Varying Hare – lives above ground, and inhabits brushy forested areas at all elevations.

The Hare, though relatively common, is seldom seen: first because its white winter coat blends in well against the snow; and second because it moves about mostly at dusk and at night. By day, it keeps to itself under some sheltering shrub or log. Its primary winter food includes the buds, twigs and bark of young Paper Birch, Douglas-fir, Trembling Aspen, willow, Red Osier Dogwood and Hazelnut. The Hare's gnawings can resemble rodent work, except that they may reach as high as 40 cm above the surface of the snow.

The tracks are among the most easily identified of all mammal tracks. Often they put one in mind of a rabbit happy face: two long "rabbit ears" (the traces of the hind feet) above, and two round "eyes" (the forefeet) below. It is the hind feet, of course, which suggest the name Snowshoe Hare.

THE WEASELS

Ten species of weasels call Wells Gray home. Of these, eight are active all year long (only the Badger and the Striped Skunk sleep away the winter months). Many are inquisitive, and can sometimes be coaxed nearer by keeping very still and making high-pitched squeaking noises.

Typical mustelid tracks (e.g., belonging to the Marten, Fisher, Ermine [or Short-tailed Weasel], Long-tailed Weasel, Least Weasel and Mink) are easily recognized by their oval shape and distinct two-by-two patterning. In general, the back feet register precisely in the prints left by the front, allowing these lithe little creatures to loop over the snow with a minimum of energy. Some species, including the Ermine, Mink and Long-tailed Weasel, also sometimes dive into soft powder snow, popping up a metre or so away.

It is less easy to identify weasel tracks to species. Here size is the thing. Pay special attention to the width or straddle of the trail: Least Weasel (4 cm); Ermine (5 cm); Long-tailed Weasel (6.4 cm); Mink (7 cm); Marten (8.8 cm); Fisher (15 cm). These are, however, only averages; the larger males of one species can overlap in size with the smaller females of the next species up. It's a tough world.

The most commonly encountered weasel in Wells Gray is doubtless the Marten. Most active during the night, the Marten seldom ventures far from its perches and travel routes in mature and oldgrowth forests. Here it feeds on whatever is going. Mice and voles provide the bulk of its diet, but the Red Squirrel, too, has reason to chatter when the Marten is around.

In the upper forests, near treeline, watch for the tracks of Marten (above), Squirrel, Wolverine and Caribou. (TG)

You'll recognize it by its house-cat length, its broadly triangular face, its tree-climbing abilities, and, often, its bright orange chest patch.

THE CATS

The Bobcat, the Lynx and the Cougar all make their home in the park, though none is often encountered. Look for large, rounded paw prints having four toes that show no sign of claws. (The claws are retractable). Size differences are helpful in telling the tracks apart, the Bobcat's prints averaging five cm across, against the Lynx's and the Mountain Lion's nine or ten cm. Lynx tracks are distinctive for their lack of definition, owing to the very furry feet.

THE DOGS

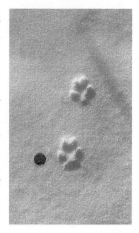

Bobcat or Fox? That's hard to say. Scale: a Canadian quarter. (TG)

Three species of canines inhabit Wells Gray: the Gray Wolf, the Coyote and the Red Fox. None of these animals is often seen, and the Fox is in fact rare here. But if it is winter, and if you're on skis, chances are good you won't ski very far without at least crossing the trail of a Wolf pack.

The tracks of all three species are dog-like, showing four toes, a heel, and (usually) claw marks. Depending on gait, the tracks may be arranged either in twos (as when trotting) or in fours (when galloping). Obviously, the largest tracks (e.g., 12–13 cm in length) belong to the Wolf, the middle-sized ones (e.g., 7 cm) to the Coyote, and the smallest ones (e.g., 6 cm) to the much rarer Fox. These measurements are estimates for tracks in shallow snow, and refer to the front feet, which are somewhat larger than the hind. (Note that canines, when trotting, move somewhat diagonal to their line of travel; the front feet register on one side of the trail and the hind feet on the other).

Wells Gray's 15 to 25 Wolves range widely during the summer months, but in winter they concentrate in the southern portions of the Clearwater Valley, typically south of the Ray Farm and north of Third Canyon Creek. Here a majority of the park's Moose and Deer also winter, so the Wolves seldom want for food. Hunting is easiest in late winter, when the snow is heavily crusted: then the Wolves lope easily over the surface while the Moose break through. Their kills provide feasts for other animals, including Ravens, Chickadees, and Steller's and Gray Jays.

A Wolf in wolf's clothing (BCP)

Our studies reveal no long-term relationship between game abundance and predator abundance. We should continue to resist any efforts to invade the park with poisoned baits.
Predators are a part of the wilderness that we are striving to maintain, and should receive protection in our parks.

summarized from
R.W. Ritcey (1958)

Much has been written about the howling of Wolves, but none of it is likely to prepare you for the experience of actually hearing Wolf music for the first time. Or even the hundredth time. It is the sound of wind blowing down the empty corridors of evolutionary time.

Wolves tend to be most vocal during the mating season, that is from roughly late February to mid March. This might be a good time to try Wolf watching (or listening) in Wells Gray. By day, scout the roads and ski trails for fresh sign. By night, drive up and down the park road, focusing on the section between Dawson Falls in the north and Third Canyon Creek in the south. If the chorus doesn't start up spontaneously, try making Wolf howls of your own. Wolves aren't particular.

THE DEER

Because the Mule Deer winters largely below the most popular ski areas, and the Caribou above, the only member of the deer family you're likely to see in winter is the Moose.

There is no mistaking the 14 cm tracks left by the cloven hooves of a Moose. In outline, they somewhat resemble arrowheads, the pointed end indicating the direction of travel. The droppings are also diagnostic, and resemble brownish "glossets." (The droppings of the Mountain Caribou more closely resemble blackish "jujubes.") The former are composed of compressed

Crying Wolf

In the past, Wolves were maligned as blood-thirsty killers. Ranchers, hunters, biologists and others have waged a continent-wide campaign to reduce their numbers – perhaps spurred on by childhood recollections of *Little Red Riding Hood*.

Today we recognize that Wolves are not so much killers as cullers. We also know that given their dietary preference for large ungulates such as Moose, they could hardly be otherwise. A healthy Moose, remember, is a powerful animal. For a Wolf pack to attempt to bring one down is, under most conditions, to risk injury to its members. A wounded Wolf, unable to hunt, is soon likely to be a dead Wolf, so it's not surprising that millions of years of evolution have favoured Wolves with a taste for weaker Moose, rather than stronger. To sick, wounded and aged Moose, however, Wolves are the Angels of Death.

The Wolf shares many behavioural traits with its descendent the Dog – man's best friend. It is a social animal, for whom the family pack is the basic social unit. A Wolf pack averages between four and seven individuals, and consists not only of parents and pups, but often also of assorted uncles and aunts that help rear and educate the young. Tail-wagging, romping, and caressing are all prominent parts of daily life.

wood and bark chips, whereas the latter reflect their origin as black hair lichens of the genus *Bryoria*.

By January, deepening snows have forced Wells Gray's Moose to descend from their summer ranges in the Shuswap Highlands. Now they gather on 150 square km of lowland burns, feeding on Willow, Falsebox, Paper Birch, Beaked Hazelnut, Red Osier Dogwood, and other shrubs and trees. ("Moose" is derived from an Algonkian word meaning "eater of twigs"). In the best ranges, where willow thickets are thickest, the Moose may now crowd at more than eight animals per square kilometre.

The bull Moose sheds its antlers some time in December or early January. Question: what happens to the antlers after they are dropped? Answer: they are transformed into rodent bones. Rodents gnaw the antlers for calcium. Later in the spring the Moose will grow a new set, weighing up to 20 kg.

Green Mountain – the low, 300 m ridge that runs like a divider down the middle sections of the Clearwater Valley – is a favourite wintering grounds with Wells Gray's Moose. Between km 31.8 and km 32.8 (i.e., where the park road gradually descends into Hemp Creek Valley), several good views of the mountain can be obtained, and it is here that you are most likely to see a Moose. Because of the distance, it helps to have a pair of binoculars or, better still, a spotting scope. Cloudy days are most productive; on sunny, warm days, check near the edges of the burn. These slopes were set on fire in 1968: browse production though still fairly high, has declined in recent years.

> *Moose can be seen browsing at any time during the day, though heaviest feeding tends to occur in the morning before about 9:30, and in the afternoon, around 2:30. Cows and calves generally feed and rest together, and the same is true of bulls, which tend to form "clubs." When feeding, Moose seldom move about very much; in most cases, they bed down within 100 m of their previous bed. The preferred bedding areas include ridges, knolls and open hillsides.*
>
> summarized from V. Geist (1960)

WINTER INSECT WATCHING

INSECT watching in winter? Strange as it may seem, some of Wells Gray's most interesting winter inhabitants are insects. You needn't worry about Mosquito bites at this season, but chances are you will encounter tiny creatures walking, running and hopping over the snow on jointed, insect legs [see: WINTER ON SIX LEGS].

Wingless Crane Fly (TG)

Winter on Six Legs

The two most conspicuous groups are the crane flies (*Chionea* spp.) and the Snow Scorpionflies (*Boreus* spp.). Because cold weather makes it difficult to generate the energy needed for flight, neither of these groups possesses wings, having lost them during the course of evolution.

Chionea (the name is from the Greek chion, snow) are related to the huge, gangly Leatherjacket Crane Flies of temperate lawns and gardens, but are much smaller and, as just mentioned, essentially wingless. They are able, however, to walk over the snow at a quite respectable gait.

Despite their ability to remain active in winter, *Chionea* freeze to death at temperatures below about −8°C. When the weather is cold, they bide their time in mammal burrows or runs, under rocks or logs, or in the airspace beneath the snow. There they are well insulated, for temperatures beneath even thin snowpacks remain constant and close to freezing. Only when the outside air moderates do they venture forth into the open, and even then they prefer cloudy days to sunny ones.

Exactly what *Chionea* are up to on their winter forays has never been conclusively determined. They don't feed, and neither do they appear to be mating. Possibly they are taking advantage of the smooth snow surface as an easy road for dispersal. Certainly they do give the impression of knowing where they are headed. They move across the snow with all the apparent unconcern of a Great Dane out checking fire hydrants.

Snow Scorpionflies, *Boreus* (from the Greek boreas, the north wind, or the north), are small, dark, glossy insects with long snouts. They are generally smaller than *Chionea*, with more slender legs. They also differ in their movements, preferring to walk with frequent hops, like a small child on the way home from school. On the males you'll notice vestigial, bristle-like wings, which are used to hold the females during mating; the wings of the females are further reduced to small scales. Both adult and larval *Boreus* live in and feed on moss.

After mid February, when the days are longer and the sunshine stronger, other insects take up snow walking. It is now, for example, that the winged Stoneflies begin to emerge. All winter long the larvae have fed voraciously in the rivers and creeks (and been fed upon, with equal voraciousness, by Rainbow Trout and American Dippers). Now the adults walk and fly about, apparently munching lichens, and mating, and eventually returning to the streams to lay their eggs.

Two common groups of winter Stoneflies in Wells Gray are the genera *Capnia* and *Zapada*. *Capnia* are small (about 5 mm long), often short-winged creatures whose abdomens sport two prominent tails (cerci). *Zapada* usually emerge later in the spring, are larger and chunkier than *Capnia*, have smoky, patterned wings, and lack obvious cerci.

Strangest of all the winter insects are the Springtails (*Collembola*). Springtails are fungus-eaters, and are as widespread as their food, occurring in moist soils the world over. Even so, they are seldom seen, owing to their minute size and generally dark or mottled colours.

On warm winter days, however, they mass in the thousands or even millions on melting snowbanks or over the surface of puddles. Because their bodies absorb the sun's heat, the snow can become cratered where they gather. Should the species be blackish in colour, as in the genus *Hypogastura*, the scene can resemble a mini oil spill.

The name Springtail derives from a unique structure possessed by *Collembola* – a tail that is bent forward underneath the body and secured by a catch mechanism. When the Springtail wishes to be elsewhere, it simply flexes its tail. This causes the catch to release suddenly, thus propelling the Springtail great distances into the air. On the snow, this habit has given these creatures yet another name – snowfleas.

Syd Cannings and Rob Cannings

WINTER BIRDWATCHING

WELLS Gray's birdlife fluctuates tremendously with the seasons. During the summer months, almost 200 species of birds inhabit the park, while in winter probably fewer than 35 species remain. Of the latter, only 20 or so are seen with any degree of regularity. (See the Wells Gray Bird Checklist, available from B.C. Parks, Box 70 Clearwater, B.C., Canada VOE 1NO).

The Common Raven is the largest of Wells Gray's songbirds, and one of very few that mates for life. (TG)

Birdwatching is most productive on the Hemp Plateau, particularly between First Canyon Creek (km 13.5) and the park entrance (km 35.8). Here you might well list 15 species in a day. Look for Winter Wrens in the canyons, Pileated Woodpeckers in the swamps, and, maybe, Great Horned and Barred Owls at the edges of the fields.

On the Murtle Plateau, bird numbers are dramatically lower. Here you'll be doing well if you see more than seven species in a day. Among the more sought-after are the Three-toed Woodpecker (check the Placid Lake trail) and the American Dipper (along the Murtle River).

Certainly the most dependable winter bird is the Raven: no matter what the weather, one or more of these outsized "crows" inevitably seems to be winging by overhead. In a sense, Ravens are the vultures of the north woods; their eyes are always open to a Wolf-killed Moose or other winter fatality. Given that they grow fat in the midst of starvation, it is not surprising that they pair early in the year, often in late February and early March, and nest not long afterward. Watch for the intricate aerial courtship displays.

As you sit down to lunch, the sound of your sandwich wrappings may well attract a little troupe of Gray Jays (otherwise known as Canada Jays, Camp Robbers, or Whiskeyjacks) looking for handouts. A few moments later a flock of 50 Common Redpolls may suddenly materialize above you in the branches of a White Birch. As they settle down to their own favourite lunch, it now begins to snow a flurry of Birch seeds around you.

On the trail again, the woodland silence may be subtly interrupted by the soft, companionable utterances of Pine Grosbeaks, or else the silvery lispings of Golden-crowned Kinglets, or again the lively chatter of Black-

The Gray Jay is well adapted to life in the north woods. An omnivore, it takes to nesting in March, when other animals are at their most desperate. (TG)

The Barred Owl may be barred on the throat, but on the belly it is definitely striped. (RBCM)

capped Chickadees, all travelling in loose bands. Often you can hold the attention of these and other birds by responding with squeaky conversational noises. Try for instance loudly kissing the back of your hand. Go ahead; no one's watching.

In late February the Barred Owl begins its haunting nighttime ululations, among them "Who-cooks-for-you – who-cooks-for-YOU-awll." This distinctive call is one of the earliest datable events leading to spring, for the Barred Owl is announcing its readiness to mate.

Strange to say, the Barred Owl was until recently a bird of the eastern and northern forests. It is a relatively new arrival into British Columbia, having first been recorded here in 1943. The first record for Wells Gray dates to November of 1955. Since then its numbers appear to have grown steadily; today it is probably the most common (and certainly the most vocal!) owl in the park. Why? Nobody knows.

AN INVITATION

The wilderness of Wells Gray is something to think about. (TG)

Where there are birds, there are bird watchers. Most years, between Christmas and New Year's Eve, one of the authors of this book (TG) organizes a Wells Gray Christmas Bird Count. The purpose of the count is to estimate the numbers of birds (individuals and species) wintering in the Clearwater Valley between Helmcken Falls (page 111) and Third Canyon Creek (page 59). If you'd like to take part in next year's count, write to T.G. at Edgewood Blue, Box 131, Clearwater, B.C. V0E 1N0 Canada. Tell him Trevor sent you.

APPENDIX I

Selected Wells Gray References

AHTI, T. 1962. Ecological investigations on lichens in Wells Gray Provincial Park with special reference to their importance to mountain caribou. Unpublished Report, British Columbia Parks, Victoria. 69 pp.

AHTI, T & R. FAGERSTEN. 1967. Mosses of British Columbia, especially Wells Gray Provincial Park. Annales Botanici Fennici 4: 422–440.

ANTIFEAU, T. 1987. The significance of snow and arboreal lichens in the winter ecology of Mountain caribou (*Rangifer tarandus caribou*) in the North Thompson watershed of British Columbia. Master of Science Thesis, Simon Fraser University.

CAMPBELL, R.B. 1963. Geology of Quesnel Lake. Preliminary Map 1. Geological Survey of Canada.

CAMPBELL, R.B. 1963. Geology of Adams Lake. Preliminary Map 48. Geological Survey of Canada.

CAMPBELL, R.B. 1967. Geology of Canoe River. Preliminary Map 15. Geological Survey of Canada.

CAMPBELL, R.B. & H.W. TIPPER. 1971. Geology of Bonaparte Lake Map Area, British Columbia. Geological Survey of Canada Memoir 363, Ottawa. 100 pp.

CANNINGS, R. 1977. Blue River area of Wells Gray Park, Wildlife recommendations. Unpublished report, British Columbia Parks, Victoria. 27 pp.

CLAGUE, J.J. 1981. Late Quaternary geology and geochronology of British Columbia. Part 2: Summary and Discussion of radiocarbon – dated Quaternary history. Geological Survey of Canada Paper 80-35. 41 pp.

COOMBES, D.M. 1985. A reconnaissance survey of Kostal Lake. A.S.A.P. No. 345001, Fisheries Branch, British Columbia Ministry of Environment, Victoria.

COOMBES, D.M. 1985. A reconnaissance survey of McDougall Lake. A.S.A.P. No. 345002, Fisheries Branch, British Columbia Ministry of Environment, Victoria.

COOMBES, D.M. 1985. A reconnaissance survey of Ray Lake. A.S.A.P. No. 345006, Fisheries Branch, British Columbia Ministry of Environment, Victoria.

COOMBES, D.M. 1991. A reconnaissance survey of Azure Lake. A.S.A.P. No. 346010, Fisheries Branch, British Columbia Ministry of Environment, Victoria. 36 pp.

COOMBES, D.M. 1991. A reconnaissance survey of Clearwater Lake. A.S.A.P. No. 346001, Fisheries Branch, British Columbia Ministry of Environment, Victoria. 61 pp.

COOMBES, D.M. 1991. A reconnaissance survey of Hobson Lake. A.S.A.P. No. 346003, Fisheries Branch, British Columbia Ministry of Environment, Victoria. 36 pp.

DEKELVER, I. 1992. The Ray Farm story. Clearwater and District Chamber of Commerce. 20 pp.

DUFORD, J.M. & G.D. OSBORN. 1978. Holocene and latest Pleistocene cirque glaciations in the Shuwap Highland, British Columbia. Canadian Journal of Earth Science 15: 865–873.

EDWARDS, R.Y. 1953. The value of moose in Wells Gray Park. Unpublished Report, British Columbia Forest Service, Victoria. 8 pp.

EDWARDS, R.Y. 1954. Comparison of an aerial and ground census of moose. Journal of Wildlife Management 18: 403–404.

EDWARDS, R.Y. 1954. Fire and the decline of a mountain caribou herd. Journal of Wildlife Management 18: 521–526

EDWARDS, R.Y. 1956. Snow depths and ungulate abundance in the mountains of western Canada. Journal of Wildlife Management 20: 159–168.

EDWARDS, R.Y. 1961. Some summer observations of a captive yearling bull moose, Wells Gray Park. Unpublished Report, British Columbia Parks, Victoria. 9 pp.

EDWARDS, R.Y. 1971. Moose heaven is a valley. Ontario Naturalist 9: 24–26.

EDWARDS, R.Y. & R.W. RITCEY. 1956. The migrations of a moose herd. Journal of Mammology 37: 486–494.

EDWARDS, R.Y. & R.W. RITCEY. 1958. Reproduction in a moose population. Journal of Wildlife Management. 22: 261–268.

EDWARDS, R.Y. & R.W. RITCEY. 1959. Migrations of caribou in a mountainous area in Wells Gray Park, British Columbia. Canadian Field-Naturalist 73: 21–25.

EDWARDS, R.Y. & R.W. RITCEY. 1960. Foods of caribou in Wells Gray Park, British Columbia. Canadian Field-Naturalist 74: 3–7.

EDWARDS, R.Y. & R.W. RITCEY. 1967. The birds of Wells Gray Park. Unpublished Report, British Columbia Parks, Victoria. 37 pp.

EDWARDS, R.Y., J. SOOS & R.W. RITCEY. 1960. Quantitative observations of epidendric lichens used as food by caribou. Ecology 41: 425–431.

FIESINGER, D.W. & J. NICHOLLS. 1977. Petrography and petrology of quaternary volcanic rocks, Quesnel Lake Region, east – central British Columbia. Geological Association of Canada, Special Paper 16. pp. 25–38.

GEIST. V. 1960. Diurnal activity of moose. Memoranda Societatis pro Fauna et Flora Fennica 35: 95–100. Helsinki.

GODFREY, W.G. 1961. First Canadian record of the black-throated sparrow. Canadian Field-Naturalist 75: 162.

GOWARD, T. 1981. Patterns of climate in Wells Gray Provincial Park and its vicinity. Typewritten manuscript. 43 pp.

GOWARD, T. (compiler). 1982. A naturalists' source book of Wells Gray Park. Unpublished Report, British Columbia Parks, Kamloops.

GOWARD, T. 1985. The Trophy Mountain Extension: a new perspective on Wells Gray Provincial Park. pp. 246–251 in P. J. Dooling (ed.), Parks in British Columbia: Emerging Realities. British Columbia Parks, Victoria.

GOWARD, T. 1989. The valley of fire and ice. Nature Canada 18: 36–43.

GOWARD, T. (compiler). 1993. Checklist of the Birds of Wells Gray Provincial Park. Third Edition. British Columbia Parks, Kamloops.

GOWARD, T. & T. AHTI. 1992. Macrolichens and their zonal distribution in Wells Gray Provincial Park and its vicinity, British Columbia, Canada. Acta Botanica Fennica 147: 1–60.

GRIFFITH, R.P. 1994. A review of lake survey information towards a fisheries management plan for Wells Gray Park. Unpublished report, British Columbia Parks, Clearwater. 37 pp.

HÄMET-AHTI, L. 1965. Vascular plants of Wells Gray Provincial Park and its vicinity, in eastern British Columbia. Annales Botanici Fennici 2: 138–164.

HÄMET-AHTI, L. 1965. Notes on the vegetation zones of western Canada, with special reference to the forests of Wells Gray Park, British Columbia. Annales Botanici Fennici 2: 274–300.

HÄMET-AHTI, L. 1978. Timberline meadows in Wells Gray Park, British Columbia, and their comparative geobotanical interpretation. Syesis 11: 187–211.

HARTMAN, F.G., 1957. Floristic descriptions of cover-types in Wells Gray Park. Wildlife Section Report 57, British Columbia Forest Service, Victoria. 36 pp.

HICKSON, C.J. 1986. Quaternary volcanism in the Wells Gray – Clearwater area, east central British Columbia. Ph.D. Thesis, U.B.C., Vancouver. 357 pp.

HICKSON, C.J. 1988. Whither the Anahim Volcanic Belt? Pacific Northwest Region American Geophysical Union, Annual Meeting, September 29–30, Victoria.

HICKSON, C.J., W.H. MATHEWS & R. HORNER. 1986. Quaternary extension in British Columbia – Is it reasonable? Neotectonic workshop, Geological Association of Canada, Pacific Section meeting, March 27, Sidney, British Columbia.

HOGUE, H. 1980. A wilderness story of fear and courage. [No publisher given.] 82 pp.

HONG, W.S. 1981. Hepaticae of Wells Gray Provincial Park, British Columbia, Canada. The Bryologist 84: 414–419.

HUNTER, J. 1877. Report on exploration from the Clearwater to the North Thompson, via Blue River Pass. pp 101–104 in Fleming, Sandford report on surveys. . . on the Canadian Pacific Railway up to January, 1877. Appendix D.

JOHNSON, H.E. 1984. Memories of a depression homestead. [No publisher given.] 60 pp.

LEA, E.C. 1986. Vegetation of the Wells Gray study area. British Columbia Ministry of Environment Technical Report 21, Victoria.

LEE, R.H. 1913. Report on surveys in the Clearwater Valley, Kamloops District. pp. 310–311 in Annual Report to Minister of Lands, 1912. King's Printer. Victoria.

MARTIN, P.W. 1950. Report on wildlife survey of Wells Gray Park 1950. Unpublished Report, British Columbia Forest Service, Victoria. 67 pp.

MAXWELL, R.E. (project coordinator). 1985. Wells Gray Biophyscial – South half. Thematic

Mapping Unit, Surveys and Resource Mapping Branch, Ministry of Environment, Victoria.

METCALFE, P. 1987. Petrogenesis of Quaternary alkaline lavas in Wells Gray Provincial Park, British Columbia and constraints on the petrology of the subcordilleran mantle. Unpublished PhD. Thesis, University of Alberta, Edmonton. 395 pp.

MILTON, W.F. & W.B. CHEADLE. 1865. The North-west Passage by land. London, Cassell, Petter, and Galpin. [Toronto, Coles Pub. Co., 1970.] 400 pp.

MURPHY, D.C. 1985. Stratigraphy and structure of the east – central Cariboo Mountains, British Columbia and implications for the geological evolution of the southeastern Canadian Cordillera. Unpublished Ph.D Thesis, Carleton University, Ontario.

NEAVE, R. 1995. Exploring Wells Gray Park. 4th ed. The Friends of Wells Gray Park, Kamloops.

NORRIS, J.G. 1991. A reconnaissance survey of Mahood Lake. A.S.A.P. No. 346004, Fisheries Branch, British Columbia Ministry of Environment, Victoria. 87 pp.

PIGAGE, L.C. 1978. Metamorphism and deformation on the northeast margin of the Shuswap Metamorphic Complex, Azure Lake, British Columbia. Unpublished PhD. Thesis, U.B.C., Vancouver. 185 pp.

RITCEY, R.W. 1955. Report on live trapping and tagging moose and deer, winter, 1955, and on moose calf tagging, spring, 1954 and 1955. Unpublished Report, British Columbia Forest Service, Victoria. 15 pp.

RITCEY, R.W. 1955. Grizzly bear studies in Wells Gray Park to September, 1955. Wildlife Sec. Rep. 51. Unpublished Report, British Columbia Forest Service, Victoria.

RITCEY, R.W. 1958. Predators in Wells Gray Park, 1950 – 1956. Unpublished Report, British Columbia Parks, Victoria. 21 pp.

RITCEY, R.W. 1961. A study of winter moose foods, Wells Gray Park, 1960 – 1961. Unpublished Report, British Columbia Parks, Victoria.

RITCEY, R.W. 1965. A proposal for moose habitat management in Wells Gray Park. Unpublished Report, British Columbia Fish & Wildlife, Kamloops. 9 pp.

RITCEY, R.W. 1981. Woodland caribou in the Thompson-Nicola resource region. Unpublished Report, British Columbia Ministry of Environment, Kamloops. 18 pp.

RITCEY, R.W. & R.Y. EDWARDS. 1956. Guide to moose hunting in Wells Gray Park. British Columbia Forest Service Publication B.44. 35 pp.

RITCEY, R.W. & R.Y. EDWARDS. 1963. Grouse abundance and June temperatures in Wells Gray Park, British Columbia. Journal of Wildlife Management 27: 604–606.

RITCEY, R.W. & F.R. RITCEY. 1990. Wells Gray Corridor wildlife viewing plan. Unpublished Report, British Columbia Parks, Kamloops. 23 pp.

SATHER, M. 1983. A creel census and fisheries evaluation of Clearwater Lake. Unpublished Report, British Columbia Parks.

SATHER, M. & G. JONES. 1984. A stratified random block moose census of Wells Gray Park. Unpublished Report, British Columbia Parks, Victoria. 34 pp.

SCHIARIZZA, P. & V.A. PRETO. 1984. Geology of the Adams Plateau – Clearwater area. Ministry of Energy, Mines and Petroleum Resources, Province of British Columbia, Map Number 56.

SEIP, D. 1990. Ecology of Woodland Caribou in Wells Gray Provincial Park. British Columbia Ministry of Environment, Wildlife Bulletin B-68, 43 pp.

SELWYN, A.R.C. 1872. Journal and report of preliminary explorations in B. C. Pp. 16–72 in Geological Survey Report of Progress for 1871–72. Montreal, 1872.

SHOOK, C. 1972. Glimpses of the past. Unpublished manuscript. 157 pp.

STRUIK, L.C. 1985. Dextral strike-slip through Wells Gray Provincial Park, British Columbia in Current Research, Part A, Geological Survey of Canada, Paper 85-1A, pp 305–309.

STRUIK, L.C. 1986. A regional east-dipping thrust places Hadrynian onto probable Paleozoic rocks in Cariboo Mountains, British Columbia. Pp. 589–594 in Current Research, Part A, Geological Survey of Canada, Paper 86-1A.

VAARTNOU, M. 1990. Horse use impact and reclamation recommendations for the Battle and Table Mountain region of Wells Gray Provincial Park. Unpublished report, British Columbia Parks, Kamloops. 148 pp.

WEBB, R. 1952. A preliminary study of small mammals and vegetation in Wells Gray Park with special reference to conifer suppression by rodents. Unpublished Report, British Columbia Forest Service, Victoria. 39 pp.

APPENDIX II

Wells Gray Park Time Chart

No one can claim to understand Wells Gray who doesn't also understand something of the geologic history that has bequeathed the park's mountains, valleys and lava flows. The following time line situates the major geological events discussed in the pages of this book.

1,200,000,000 years ago:	Wells Gray's oldest rocks take form.
750,000,000 – 500,000,000 years ago:	Kaza Group rocks are laid down as ocean bottom sediments.
200,000,000 years ago:	The western edge of North America is gliding, colliding, accreting, folding, accordioning, and faulting. Meanwhile the Cariboo Mountains are upthrusting.
130,000,000 – 65,000,000 years ago:	The Cariboo Mountains are upthrusting for a second time.
65,000,000 years ago:	Goodbye to the dinosaurs.
45,000,000 years ago:	The Chu Chua Formation is being laid down as streambed and swamp sediments. Meanwhile, the Cariboo Mountains are upthrusting for a third and final time.
2,000,000 – 11,000 years ago:	Numerous Ice Ages come and go.
1,400,000 years ago:	The Flatiron lavas are erupted.
600,000 years ago:	Whitehorse Bluff erupts from beneath an immense lake occupying the lower Clearwater Valley.
500,000 – 200,000 years ago:	Volcanoes erupt to form Murtle Plateau. As glaciers come and go, the park's tuyas erupt beneath them.
300,000 years ago:	While 1000 m of glacial ice fills the Clearwater Valley, volcanoes erupt on Trophy Mountain.
25,000 years ago:	The Cordilleran Ice Sheet engulfs the Clearwater Valley.
15,000 years ago:	The Cordilleran Ice Sheet is now so deep that only the tallest peaks poke through.
12,000 – 11,000 years ago:	The Cordilleran Ice Sheet wastes away, leaving behind hummocks on Murtle Plateau, recessional moraines at Battle Creek, and glacial outwash plains at Philip Creek. Meanwhile, Pyramid Mountain erupts explosively under stagnant ice.
11,000 years ago:	Silt-laden glacial meltwaters carve Helmcken and Spahats canyons.
7,600 years ago:	Dragon Cone erupts, extending a tongue of lava all the way to Clearwater River at the south end of Clearwater Lake.
7,000 – 6,000 years ago:	The Clearwater Valley has never been hotter.
5,000 – 2,400 years ago:	Mountain glaciers come and go.
2,000 – 500 years ago:	Kostal Cone erupts.
300 – 150 years ago:	The Little Ice Age comes and goes.
1939:	The Clearwater Valley is set aside as Wells Gray Provincial Park.

INDEX

Page numbers in **bold** refer to main entries, whereas page numbers in *italics* refer to illustrations. Be sure to check the following headings: ALGAE, AMPHIBIANS, BIRDS, FISH, FLOWERS, GEOLOGY, INSECTS, LICHENS, MAMMALS, MOSSES, MUSHROOMS, REPTILES, SHRUBS, TRAILS, TREES.